Sound in the Land

Essays on Mennonites and Music

Sound in the Land
Essays on Mennonites and Music

Edited by Maureen Epp
and Carol Ann Weaver

published by
Pandora Press

Library and Archives Canada Cataloguing in Publication

Sound in the land : essays on Mennonites and music / Maureen Epp, Carol Ann Weaver, editors.

Includes bibliographical references and index.
ISBN 1-894710-59-2

1. Church music—Mennonite Church. 2. Mennonites—Canada. 3. Mennonites—United States. I. Epp, Maureen II. Weaver, Carol Ann

ML3169.S724 2006   782.32'287   C2005-907058-7

SOUND IN THE LAND: ESSAYS ON MENNONITES AND MUSIC

Copyright © 2005 by Pandora Press
33 Kent Avenue
Kitchener, Ontario N2G 3R2
All rights reserved.
ISBN 1-894710-59-2

Book design by Nathan Stark

The art on the front cover is by Jo-Anne Harder, entitled "Ties That Bind." The original work is mounted in the Atrium at Conrad Grebel University College, Waterloo, Ontario. It is used here by permission.

All Pandora Press books are printed on Eco-Logo certified paper.

12 11 10 09 08 07 06 05   12 11 10 9 8 7 6 5 4 3 2 1

Table of Contents

Preface
    Carol Ann Weaver   7

Introduction
    Maureen Epp   9

Hymnals and Identity, Past and Present
Singing at Orangefield Mennonite Church
    Cheryl Denise   19
The Sound in the Land
    Mary K. Oyer   21
New Readings of Text and Music in the *Ausbund*
    Maureen Epp   34
Reviving Songs of Peace from the Vistula Delta
    Mark Jantzen   50
Identity and the Hymnal: Can Music Make a Person Mennonite?
    Katie J. Graber   64

Voices at the Edges
Tangle, Waking Early (two poems from *Awakenings*)
    Di Brandt   81
Benjamin Horch as an Insider-Outsider Musical-Theological Visionary
    Doreen H. Klassen   83
A Non-Mennonite Writes a Mennonite Piano Concerto
    Victor Davies   95
"Dear Nobe ... Ever Affectionately, Art": The Kreider-Farwell Correspondence
    E. Douglas Bomberger   100

Rebel with a Cause: Innovation and Grace
in the Music of a Reinfeld Boy
   Judith Klassen   112
Mennofolk Manitoba: Cultural, Artistic, and
Generational Perspectives in a
Music Festival Setting
   Allison Fairbairn   125

Voices of Performers, Composers, and Singer-Songwriters

Fraser Valley String Orchestra
   Leonard N. Neufeldt   141
(On) Being Mennonite, Being a Composer,
and Composing "Mennonite Music"
   Anna Janecek   143
Encountering (Mennonite) Singer-Songwriters:
J. D. Martin and Cate Friesen
   Jonathan Dueck   159

Experiences of Singing Today

The Music of What Happened
   Jeff Gundy   179
What are U.S. Mennonites Singing in Sunday
Morning Worship?
   Stephen Jacoby   181
"Gutierrez is Also a Mennonite Name":
Issues of Identity and Hymnody in Contemporary
Southern Ontario Mennonite Churches
   Anna Janecek   189
A Few Ways to be a Mennonite: Contemporary
Christian Music in a Community of Hymns
   Stephanie J. Krehbiel   201
"Pleasure Enough": Four-part A Cappella Singing
as a Survival Strategy for a Mennonite-in-Exile
   Laura H. Weaver   210

Contributors   217

Preface
Out of the Cave—Finding Mennonite Sounds in Our Lands

The May 2004 Sound in the Land festival and conference brought together traditions and innovations, possibly charting new paths for Mennonite music. Held at Conrad Grebel University College at the University of Waterloo, this event marked the first time that Mennonites, in their 300-plus years of being in North America, gathered together for the express purpose of discovering, hearing, studying, and celebrating collective Mennonite voices in music. With lingering memories of singing furtively in Swiss caves and consequently being described as "quiet in the land," Mennonites are finally wanting to take stock of our sounds in the land. For this we converged—composers, songwriters, performing musicians, scholars, creative writers, listeners—for three days of live music, scholarly papers, readings, and discussions about the sounds and meanings of our various musics, tossing the genre "Mennonite music" out into the world. But what is it?

    Mennonite music, we discovered, contains a plethora of styles and expressions, all of which were granted equal status and credibility at Sound in the Land. Live musical performances ranged from classical to avant garde, chamber to choral, four-part congregational to praise band, hiphop to jazz, soundscape to alternative, MC (rap) to bluegrass, pop, rock, fusion, folk, world, and alternative music. Within concerts and workshops the festival featured performances of commissioned pieces, new and old compositions, collaborations, workshops, and improvisations. In a world of increasing specialization, festivals of such stylistic inclusivity are rare and almost forbidden, as if too many open doors and too much cross-fertilization could be dangerous. However, when the umbrella of a festival is ethnic, cultural, and spiritual rather than merely stylistic, new hybrids can develop that recognize convergences as *part* of the continuity of a people. And as such, the blending of otherwise disparate styles can create essential, almost expected new fusions within such a community.

In order to explore Mennonite music from an even broader context, Sound in the Land invited scholars and writers dealing with historical, theoretical, poetic, ethnomusicological, cultural, and confessional aspects of Mennonite music. Presentation topics ranged vividly from hymn singing to orchestral playing, from Russian Mennonite *Kernlieder* to contemporary folk music, from sixteenth-century *Ausbund* hymns to "off-the-wall" praise songs, from soundtrack construction to concerto composition, from chatty radio to children's opera, from Pennsylvania zither to Khortiza *Ziffern*, all in the interest of discovering more about the roots, reasons, and sounds of Mennonite voices then, now, and maybe tomorrow. Poets spoke, scholars sketched, bards sang, bands formed, sopranos performed, violins soared, pipes roared, choirs and keys, winds and reeds, drums and gongs, mallets and songs . . . And in the end, what do we know?

It has been said that when singing was no longer practiced in certain monasteries and convents, those institutions ceased to exist. But Mennonites are *still* singing and making music, and as long as there's singing and music-making, there's life. However, just like life, singing and all forms of music-making change continually or cease to exist. We can no sooner prescribe an unchanging, orthodox Mennonite song than we can a static belief system. Nor can we run back into the caves that sheltered us in previous times of danger but no longer can hold us, though at times we may seek their security and protection. Out in the land and in our daylight, we can discover, document, and dance with the many sounds of Mennonite music today, celebrating its ever-widening scope, embracing its multiple styles, and recognizing all of it spinning together into a richer sonic fabric than yet imagined.

Future "Sounds" may find new "Lands," leaving this 2004 Swiss-Russian Mennonite festival in the dust. Next time around there may be Menno reggae from Jamaica, hot Mennobeat from Kenya, swarms of Mennopop groups from India, East Asia, Latin America, and First Nations. How can we travel enough land, and how can we best prepare for a more global sound within this composite song?

Carol Ann Weaver
April 13, 2005

Introduction

Maureen Epp

Sound in the Land: Essays on Mennonites and Music is an outgrowth of the festival and conference hosted by Conrad Grebel University College at the University of Waterloo in the spring of 2004. The event gathered participants from Canada and the United States for performances, workshops, poetry readings, and formal papers, all of which reflected in some way the intersections between Mennonite culture and music. This book makes available many of the formal papers that were presented, with the addition of several essays that were commissioned later on topics that had been planned for festival sessions but did not materialize at that time. Although a book cannot fully recapture the multi-faceted nature of an event like Sound in the Land, the editors decided to also include selections of poetry from the readings that were similarly interspersed throughout the festival weekend.[1]

To say that music is an important element of Mennonite cultural and religious identity is merely to state the obvious. However, the essays presented here enlarge upon what has often been understood by that familiar statement in two ways. First, as Carol Ann Weaver notes in her preface, "music" as practiced by Mennonites has been granted as broad and inclusive a definition as possible. The types of music examined are not restricted to hymn-singing or choral music (although these are given due consideration), but also include folk, pop, and alternative music idioms, non-western musics, and music rooted in the western European art tradition.

Second, the discourse about music and music-making in these essays comes from a similarly broadened perspective. Writing about music for devotional or worship purposes is a familiar point of view in Mennonite-related publications, well-represented by informative hymnal commentaries or by more celebratory writing such as the recent *Singing: A Mennonite*

Voice (cited by several authors in this volume).[2] This type of writing is important, and the authors included in this book also have things to say about the use of music in church settings and its ability to touch individuals on a personal level. At the same time, however, the primary aim of the *Sound in the Land* essays is to offer descriptive rather than prescriptive accounts of Mennonite-rooted music, either as practiced in the past or experienced in the present. Many of the authors present findings based on recent scholarly research, with the aim of making their findings relevant to non-specialist readers. In particular, disciplinary approaches such as ethnomusicology, popular music studies, and cultural theory—approaches that are still relatively new within music scholarship as a whole—are well-represented here. These newer research methodologies open up topics for inquiry that in the past might not have been considered central to advancing an understanding of Mennonite culture and music, and as such are one reason for the diversity of subjects and musical styles covered by this volume.[3]

The contents of *Sound in the Land: Essays on Mennonites and Music* have been topically arranged in four sections. The first section, "Hymnals and Identity, Past and Present," begins with what has traditionally been at the nexus of Mennonite identity and music-making: hymns. What do hymns and hymnals tell us about how Mennonites have defined themselves, both historically and recently? Mary Oyer's essay (adapted from her keynote address at the Sound in the Land festival) surveys hymnals used by North American Mennonites from the early nineteenth century to the present day. Oyer demonstrates how seemingly mundane decisions, such as how a table of contents is organized or which of the ten or more original verses of a hymn have been chosen for inclusion, can reveal significant changes in denominational theology and worship practices. A particular highlight of Oyer's address at the Sound in the Land festival was the inclusion of many sung hymn examples. References for these hymns, the majority of which are in either the *Mennonite Hymnal* (1969) or the more recent *Hymnal: A Worship Book* (1992), have been retained so that readers can easily locate these same examples.

The two essays that follow reach further back into history. My own paper draws on recent research into Lutheran Reformation song as a basis for examining several hymns from one of the earliest surviving Anabaptist hymnbooks. Because most of the hymn tunes named in the sixteenth-century *Ausbund* originated from other sources such as folksong, Catholic plainchant, or Reformation song, it is natural to downplay their expressive value and instead concentrate largely on the hymn texts. Yet in some cases, earlier

Introduction

functions and meanings associated with the borrowed tunes contribute additional layers of meaning to the new hymn texts, enlarging our understanding of key Anabaptist issues such as baptism and communion. Mark Jantzen writes about the historical and political context for Mennonites living in the Vistula Delta (Prussia) during the 1860s and describes a new hymnal issued during this period. In light of an increasingly nationalistic government and a new military draft that no longer exempted Mennonites, the decision to include three hymns under the heading "Love of Enemies" constituted not only a theological response but a political statement as well, Jantzen suggests. The final essay in this section turns from historically-situated inquiry to the present day and offers a theoretical model to address the question, "Can music make a person Mennonite?" Referring to surveys conducted in her home congregation as well as recent literature on music and expression of ethnic identity, Katie Graber proposes that actions (singing), social discourse (talking about singing), and a collective acknowledgement of the hymnal's importance are all factors that interact to generate a definition of Mennonite-ness.

The essays in the first section all have a familiar starting point—hymnals and hymn-singing—yet each of them also touches on aspects of Mennonite hymnody that have been influenced by or borrowed from other faith traditions and social movements. The essays in the second section, "Voices at the Edges," address this phenomenon more directly, each profiling an individual who stands at some distance from the centre of Mennonite church and community life. In her portrait of Benjamin Horch, Doreen Klassen suggests that it was in part Horch's Lutheran roots that nourished his belief in the value of music as artistic expression and not only as a conveyor of religious texts. This belief was not always welcomed by other Mennonite Brethren church leaders and educators with whom Horch worked. Horch's visionary outlook also included the conviction that Mennonites—along with other ethnic minority groups—should find ways to share their cultural heritage with the wider world. The following essay by Victor Davies provides a direct example of how this conviction bore fruit in the *Mennonite Piano Concerto*, a work Klassen refers to as the "apex" of Horch's innovative efforts. Davies, a Canadian composer, describes being approached by Horch to write a piano concerto based on Mennonite hymn tunes and reflects on why Horch felt that he—a non-Mennonite—was well-suited for this project. As Davies quickly recognized, many of the hymns he was given to work with were not exclusively "Mennonite," since he himself remembered singing them as a child, with English rather than German words.

An individual such as Horch may have sometimes been considered an outsider by traditionalist Mennonites, yet ultimately his voice was heard. Others, despite their professional or family connections to the Mennonite community, remained on the fringes where, as Douglas Bomberger observes, "the sense of isolation could be particularly intense." Such was the case for Noble Kreider, a little-known American composer and pianist who taught at Goshen College during the early decades of the twentieth century. Kreider experienced a deeper sense of kinship with friend Arthur Farwell, a fellow composer and advocate of American music, than with the Mennonite community in which he was situated. Surviving correspondence between the two men reveals their shared (and sometimes unconventional) beliefs on spiritual and musical matters.

Another individual who established connections outside his immediate community was A.M. Friesen, a dynamic evangelist and musician from southern Manitoba who grew up in the Old Colony Mennonite church. Friesen left his conservative roots to embrace the possibilities offered by music recording technologies, and radio and television broadcasting. In evaluating Friesen's impact, Judith Klassen moves beyond the simple duality of insider-outsider dynamics to consider the "locality" of Friesen's music on the one hand versus the far-reaching potential of modern communications media on the other. This section ends with Allison Fairbairn's examination of Mennofolk Manitoba, a yearly music and art festival that consciously positions itself as a forum for voices at the edge. Fairbairn explains what Mennofolk offers to young adults who may not completely identify with the established church and its institutions and yet still wish to retain a Mennonite identity, singling out the performance of one participant as an instructive example.

The two essays in "Voices of Performers, Composers, and Singer-Songwriters" present an opportunity to hear from a cross-section of contemporary creators and performers of music. Anna Janecek shares highlights from interviews conducted with five classically-trained composers, surveying their respective backgrounds, musical training, and compositional output before turning to questions about Mennonite music. Is music by Mennonite composers necessarily "Mennonite"? And to what degree do these composers feel that their cultural-religious heritage influences the music they create? All five composers are unanimous in acknowledging the importance of their respective Mennonite upbringings, yet are also wary of the label "Mennonite composer." Questions about the relationship between Mennonite origins and musical expression are raised again in Jonathan Dueck's in-depth profile of singer-songwriters J. D.

Martin and Cate Friesen. Although the two have traveled different professional paths—Friesen along the independent folk-singer route and Martin on the commercial recording-label route—their careers also have elements in common. Perhaps even more than the composers surveyed by Janecek, Martin and Friesen hesitate to identify themselves as "Mennonite musicians," yet both find much of value in their religious and cultural roots.

The final set of essays in *Sound in the Land: Essays on Mennonites and Music* returns to the focus on hymns and worship music with which the book began, but with an emphasis on "Experiences of Singing Today." The first two essays feature statistically based analyses of congregational singing in the United States and Canada. Stephen Jacoby surveys a large cross-section of Mennonite Church congregations in 2003 to determine the range of hymns, hymnbooks, and musical styles typically used in worship services, while Anna Janecek examines a more selective sample of churches in southern Ontario between 1990 and 2003 to measure how successfully "international" or non-western hymns have been integrated into Sunday morning singing. Although the investigative parameters used by Jacoby and Janecek differ, their findings provide complementary snapshots of congregational singing in North American Mennonite churches at the turn of the new millennium. The data shared here will surely form a useful benchmark for future studies of a similar nature.

Stephanie Krehbiel's essay addresses an issue that many church denominations (not just Mennonites) consider particularly relevant to the experience of singing today: the ongoing debate (sometimes described as "the worship wars") between those who want to maintain a traditional hymnody and those who urge the adoption of worship music that reflects a more current, popular music style. Krehbiel talked to the pastors and participants of two Mennonite congregations in South Dakota, listening carefully to their respective positions on the question. For some, hymns may represent the impersonal and patriarchal limitations of the Mennonite ethnic heritage, while for others, contemporary Christian music is uncomfortably linked with the individualism and consumerism of mainstream North American society. This section—and with it, the book—concludes with Laura Weaver's personal reflections on her need for traditional a cappella hymn-singing, which she compares to other fundamental needs for food, drink, and human companionship. A self-described "Mennonite-in-exile," Weaver reminds us of the power music has to help us maintain a sense of rootedness throughout the changing circumstances of life.

The organization of this volume's contents into the four sections just described is, of course, only one possible arrangement; readers will notice that many of the essays could just as easily have been placed in a different group than the one to which they were assigned. Running through the variety of subject matter and writing contained in *Sound in the Land* are several recurring and related themes. The first of these themes is the diversity of music-making that can be called "Mennonite." Although "four-part a cappella singing" functions as a valid definition of Mennonite music for many people, it clearly does not account for the whole of Mennonite musical practices, either in the past or the present. An awareness of musical diversity is particularly relevant now, as Mennonites in the western hemisphere are being encouraged to redefine themselves in relation to the broader context of Mennonites worldwide. Embracing a growing wealth of musical styles and practices as "Mennonite music," several *Sound in the Land* authors suggest, is one way to express a more globally-informed identity.

An appreciation for non-western musics not only reflects the growth of a worldwide Mennonite fellowship, but also mirrors the current popularity of "world music" with North American audiences and musicians alike. This points to a second theme recurring throughout the *Sound in the Land* essays, that of the ongoing incorporation of contemporary music, both secular and sacred, into Mennonite music practices. This may be perceived as a recent phenomenon, clearly exemplified in discussions about new styles of worship music derived from popular and folk-based idioms. Yet as the historically based essays show, Mennonite adoption of mainstream and popular music extends back through the mid-twentieth-century inclusion of Gospel songs in hymnals to the sixteenth-century Anabaptist hymns modeled on popular folk songs. The possibility that valuable elements of Anabaptist-Mennonite heritage—such as hymns of German origin—may be lost through their replacement with popular music genres is a matter for serious discussion, but to question contemporary worship music on grounds of historical precedence is to overlook what has actually occurred throughout the history of Mennonite music-making.

A third theme, one closely tied to notions of diversity and inclusivity, is the significance of individuals, genres, and styles perceived—by Mennonites or by others—to be "outside" the centre of religious or historical Mennonite traditions. While this idea is in the foreground of the book's second section, "Voices at the Edges," examples are also documented throughout the rest of the book. The range of these examples suggests that such outside voices play a critical role in keeping Mennonite musical expression active and strong; perhaps these voices deserve to be listened to more attentively than has sometimes been the case.

The themes that repeat throughout the *Sound in the Land* essays do not prompt a simple response to the question, "How are Mennonite identity and music related?" If anything, they suggest the necessity of remaining open to a plurality of answers. As with other collective expressions of religious and cultural identity, music has the potential not only to unite groups of people, but also to exclude. A single answer to the question of what constitutes "Mennonite music" would only serve to perpetuate divisions between those of different artistic tastes, different generations, and different ethnic or national origins. The diverse forms, purposes, and contexts of musical activity presented by the writers in this volume encourage us to think beyond such divisions. In another collection of essays on Mennonite identity, Walter Klaassen comments that "as long as folkways and ethnic traditions continue to throw up barriers to people, those traditions remain unredeemed and unliberated. Wherever they are celebrated as the human cultural coat of many colors and serve to unify people from diverse traditions, they serve their proper function."[4] It is my hope that readers will find in *Sounds in the Land: Essays on Mennonites and Music* a composite account of Mennonite music that is both celebratory and liberating.

Acknowledgements

I would like to thank the original organizers of the Sound in the Land festival and conference for entrusting me with the task of editing this book, an experience that proved valuable and rewarding in every way. Particular thanks are due to Marlene Epp, Laura Gray, Doreen Klassen, Leonard Enns, and Hildi Froese Tiessen, who generously shared their time and wisdom as editorial advisors at various stages in the assembly of this book. Carol Ann Weaver gave the same and a great deal more—my heartfelt gratitude to Carol for her continued engagement with this project, long after the initial vision for the Sound in the Land festival was realized. Thanks also to Jo-Anne Harder for graciously allowing us to reproduce her artwork on the front cover, and to Nathan Stark and Arnold Snyder at Pandora Press for guiding the book through the final stages of publication.

Financial support from the following institutions, organizations, and individuals, for both the Sound in the Land festival and this volume, is gratefully acknowledged:

AMI Business Solutions
City of Waterloo
Conrad Grebel University College Marpeck Fund

Maria Meyer
Mennonite Foundation of Canada
Mennonite Savings and Credit Union
Peter Letkemann
Robert and Mary Gosselink
Social Sciences and Humanities Research Council of Canada
University of Waterloo Dean of Arts
Waterloo Regional Arts Council

Notes

[1] Several of the Sound in the Land performance events are available as CD recordings through the Conrad Grebel University College Music Department: *Sound in the Land,* Friday, May 28, 2004 — Classical Concert; *Sound in the Land,* Friday, May 28, 2004 — Bluegrass Concert; *Sound in the Land,* Sunday Afternoon, May 30, 2004 — Chamber Music Concert; *Sound in the Land,* Sunday Evening, May 30, 2004 — Choral Concert with DaCapo Chamber Choir (all CDs produced by Conrad Grebel University College; recorded and engineered by Chestnut Hall Music, http:www.chestnuthallmusic.com).

[2] Marlene Kropf and Ken Nafziger, *Singing: A Mennonite Voice* (Scottdale, PA: Herald Press, 2001).

[3] I do not wish to imply that scholarship on historical and contemporary aspects of Mennonite-related music has been lacking in the past. Articles on musical topics regularly appear in periodicals such as the *Mennonite Quarterly Review* and *Journal of Mennonite Studies,* for instance; research into Mennonite music traditions has also been published in mainline venues for music scholarship. For a more detailed overview of recent trends and publications, see Jonathan Dueck, "Worship Wars, World Music, and Menno-Nots: Recent Studies in Mennonite Music," *Journal of Mennonite Studies* 23 (2005): 123-136.

[4] Walter Klaassen, "Fig Leaves and Anabaptists," in *Why I am a Mennonite: Essays on Mennonite Identity*, ed. Harry Loewen (Kitchener, ON; Scottdale, PA: Herald Press, 1988), 150.

Hymnals and Identity
Past and Present

Singing at Orangefield Mennonite Church

Cheryl Denise

Our four-part harmony,
and the reading of shape notes
is the closest we ever get to ecstasy.
Voices add their own harmonies
become soft and loud
but nothing else moves.
Our men can't dance.
When we sing a Negro Spiritual
from the Hymnal
they're afraid to come loose,
squashing the easy sway of bodies,
the natural dance of preschoolers.
They timidly slap their thighs
awkwardly laugh.

The words in the old hymns,
the ones taught by grandparents
say we'll spend eternity singing.
They sound so certain.
Will the guys be standing stiff-legged in pews,
the women separate from the men,
God wildly waving his baton?
What if a woman sways
gets a tambourine
plays it on her hips?

Sound in the Land

I want to stay here
and be born Catholic next time,
for the dances
after midnight mass,
the ones at weddings
with loud families swinging hands,
singing on or off key,
dancing, like we were made to.

The Sound in the Land

Mary K. Oyer

Where have Mennonites been and where are we going in music? Fifty years ago, a conference such as Sound in the Land would have been inconceivable. The subjects for papers then might have been limited to topics like "In Defense of the Christian Professional Musician," "Can There Be Meaning in a Hymn Beyond the Text?" or "Can One Be Both a Cellist and a Christian?" We can tell from the scope of papers presented at Sound in the Land and included in this volume that today, the subject is very broad. I am going to focus my remarks on hymnody, in part because it has been the primary area of my work during the last few decades. But it is also a field that touches so many aspects of life that it provides an opportunity to gain perspective on who we are, what we believe, and how our culture is changing. Our hymns tell us, for example, how ecumenical we are and have been, though we talk of being separate from the "world" around us. Hymns reveal our changing theological emphases over the years as well as our evolving patterns of worship. They touch on every aspect of our corporate life — its sociological, political, scientific, aesthetic, and religious dimensions.

I plan to look at North American Mennonite hymnals of the last 200 years for what they reveal of our past. But I need to begin with the most important South German-Swiss Anabaptist hymnal — the 1564 *Ausbund* — whose core of fifty-one hymns was written by Anabaptist prisoners in the dungeons of Passau on the Danube River. These texts spoke of martyrs for the faith and offered praise to God. By the early seventeenth century the number of hymns in the *Ausbund* had been expanded to 140, which the Amish still use, basically unchanged.

The *Ausbund* had texts only, but the compilers gave a tune name for each. The work of scholars such as Rosella Reimer Duerksen and Rupert Hohmann has shown that the tunes were borrowed from many sources:[1]

some were folk songs; a few were Catholic chants (*HWB* 256) and many were German Lutheran melodies, whose AAB form Luther borrowed from the German *Meistersinger* guilds (*HWB* 133, 329).[2] Occasional tunes came from Calvin's settings of the Psalms. Calvin had also borrowed from secular sources and from the French Academy's quantitative approach to poetic meter, resulting in alternating long and short syllables rather than accented and non-accented syllables, as can be seen in the setting of Psalm 42 (*HWB* 500). The Anabaptists chose one of the tunes used to sing Luther's text on Psalm 130 ("Aus tiefer Not," *MH* 234); this tune is still sung by the Amish every time they meet, to the words "O Gott Vater, wir loben dich." Calvin had borrowed the same tune for his text on Psalm 113. And so these three reforming groups—Lutherans, Calvinists, and Anabaptists—shared hymn tunes. They were enemies on theological grounds, even killing each other, but they valued each other's music.

In 1803, the Franconia Conference in eastern Pennsylvania published a hymnbook in German, *Zions Harfe*, and the next year Lancaster Conference issued *Ein Unpartheyisches Gesangbuch*.[3] Both hymnals opened with a number of Psalms from Calvin's *Genevan Psalter* (1551) translated into German; the main body of both books consisted of hymns from German sources. The Franconia hymnal included three *Ausbund* hymns, but the Lancaster book contained sixty-three out of the *Ausbund's* 140 hymns, thus maintaining continuity with the Anabaptist past.

The first Mennonite hymnal in English was an 1847 collection called *A Selection of Psalms, Hymns, and Spiritual Songs . . . by a Committee of Mennonites*.[4] A note in the front indicated that the tune named for each hymn came from Joseph Funk's *Genuine Church Music* (1832).[5] This Mennonite tune book was one of the many singing-school books of the southern and eastern United States published to teach people to read music with shape notes. Both the 1847 hymnbook and Funk's *Genuine Church Music* represented a striking change in words and music for Mennonites who had moved to America and adopted English for worship. There were no *Ausbund* texts, and probably because of this change in language, the Germanic musical background was almost lost. Words now came from English authors: Isaac Watts, Charles Wesley, John Newton, and William Cowper. Watts was especially popular in America in general, and with Mennonites in particular. In the later 1927 *Church Hymnal*, he was represented by fifty-seven texts, in contrast to thirty-two by Wesley. I remember how often we sang hymns by Watts in my childhood, and I realize now how much they shaped my piety. Watts always saw God as ruler of the whole universe; the human being was humble and powerless (*HWB* 82). In contrast, Wesley's hymns tended to express a more intimate relationship between Christ and the soul (*HWB* 618).

The American folk influence was strong in the shape-note tune books, with melodies that were distinctive and memorable (*HWB* 143, 567). These books also contained American "classical tunes" by Lowell Mason and Psalm tunes from both Great Britain and New England. Initially, the melody was sung by the tenor, the middle of three voices. Four-part harmony came to the singing schools in the middle of the nineteenth century, when the title of Funk's *Genuine Church Music* was changed to *Harmonia Sacra* (1851).[6] Surely this movement must have helped develop American Mennonite interest in a cappella part-singing.

Not until over forty years later did the Mennonites produce another hymnal. Its title, *Hymns and Tunes* (1890), was accurately descriptive: hymns and tunes were now joined in one volume.[7] If the compilers could not find a hymn they needed for Mennonite worship, they wrote one. Around thirty authors have German Mennonite names, and seventeen of the tunes were written "By Com." (by committee). One we sang rather often in my childhood was "Follow the path of Jesus," a text that carried Anabaptist themes. Another we still sing is "I owe the Lord a morning song"(*HWB* 651). To me, this hymn seems very Mennonite in its straightforward statements, without poetic images or metaphors. Yet it has worn well. The Methodist composer Austin Lovelace developed it into an anthem, altering its Mennonite character somewhat in changing the words "I owe" to "I sing."

General Conference (GC) Mennonites emerged in the middle of the nineteenth century, joined by those of Russian background who were then settling in North America. They produced a German hymnal parallel in character to *Hymns and Tunes* and gave it the same name in German: *Gesangbuch mit Noten* (1890).[8] Many of its hymns were German translations of nineteenth-century American hymns. Only four years later, the GCs published their first book in English. They chose the best hymnbook they could find on the American market, *A Blending of Many Voices*, removed the two hymns about infant baptism, and gave it the title *Mennonite Hymnal: a Blending of Many Voices* (1894).[9] The contents represented a wide range of texts and tunes that might be called the "classics" of hymnody: hymns that had passed the test of time.

In 1902, the Mennonite Church (MC) published *The Church and Sunday School Hymnal*, a book that is still in print.[10] Its section on missions helps us see how the church has moved toward quite a different understanding of missions in the last 100 years, as shown by the following mid-nineteenth-century text:

> Over the ocean wave, far, far away,
> There the poor heathen live, waiting for day;
> Groping in ignorance, dark as the night,
> No blessed Bibles to give them the light.
>
> *refrain* Pity them, pity them, Christians at home,
> Haste with the bread of life, hasten and come.
>
> Here in this happy land we have the light
> Shining from God's own word, free, pure and bright
> Shall we not send to them Bibles to read,
> Teachers and preachers, and all that they need?
>
> *refrain* Pity them, pity them ... [11]

This hymn did not last. But another one, "From Greenland's Icy Mountains," appeared in later hymnals:

> Can we, whose souls are lighted with wisdom from on high
> Can we to men benighted, the lamp of life deny?[12]

I am afraid that it was only in the 1960s that I began to realize the arrogance embedded here. The idea that we might sing hymns by Christians from those countries to which we had sent missionaries gave a completely new perspective to those of us who worked on the 1969 *Mennonite Hymnal*.

In the 1911 Supplement to the *Church and Sunday School Hymnal*,[13] editors F. S. Coffman and J. D. Brunk collaborated on a hymn quite different from those Mennonite examples in the *Hymns and Tunes* of 1890:

> In thy holy place we bow
> Perfumes sweet to heaven rise,
> While our golden censors glow
> With the fires of sacrifice.
> Saints low bending, prayers ascending ... [14]

In this case there is much more poetic imagery—so much, in fact, that when the GC members of the joint hymnal committee saw it in the 1960s, they asked us MC members all kinds of questions: "Do you have holy places? Do you remember the saints? Do you use censors? Incense?"[15] What were Coffman and Brunk longing for in worship that they were not finding? Were they opening up to the mystery of liturgical worship, in which more than didactic speech is needed?

In 1927, both churches produced hymnals: the *Church Hymnal* for the MCs and *Mennonite Hymn Book* for the GCs.[16] Both books were limited, and perhaps for the same reason: their respective compilers did not quite anticipate what congregations needed. Both included many English Victorian hymns and American hymns in European style, but very little German content. Although Gospel songs of the Moody-Sankey type (*HWB* 102, 332) had been around for fifty years, few of them appeared in either book. Just before the *Church Hymnal* was to be published, a group of MC leaders appointed themselves examiners of the proposed contents. They judged it lacking in songs with refrains (i.e., Gospel songs) and asked the editors (S. F. Coffman and J. D. Brunk, who had not been invited to the meeting) to add 150 such songs. For some reason the editors carried out the demand even though they were severely disappointed. This move weakened the hymnal by narrowing its scope and unfortunately, the book was not replaced for over forty years.

The GC *Mennonite Hymn Book* lasted for only thirteen years. In the new *Mennonite Hymnary* (1940), editor Lester Hostetler skillfully combined German chorales, Gospel songs, hymns for children, and Psalms into a fine collection of "books" within the hymnal that acknowledged the people's heritage and changing styles of hymnody.[17]

In the 1960s, the General Conference and Mennonite Churches decided to work together on *The Mennonite Hymnal* (1969).[18] It was a surprising move because members of the hymnal committee had to cross cultures dramatically to do it: historically, the MCs had been primarily concerned with function and simplicity in worship, whereas the GCs had leaned towards artistic quality. Yet each group valued unique qualities the other possessed. The GCs brought their rich German chorale background to the MCs, who had lost that part of their own heritage when they moved to using English. The MCs brought folk tunes from their singing school heritage, which the GCs found attractive. It was also fortunate that we had an excellent committee chair, Vernon Neufeld, who led by consensus.

The social and religious upheavals of the 1960s created a lively atmosphere. Language was changing through various translations of scripture undertaken in the 1950s. Unaware of gender issues then, the hymnal committee's most challenging language problem was "Can one use the word 'you' in addressing God?" Space travel entered our thoughts. Civil rights activities pointed toward justice hymns. Cross-cultural hymns were beginning to appear in a few American hymnals—we chose six from Asia. Vatican II (1962-65) encouraged Catholics to use the vernacular rather than Latin for worship, so large numbers of folk-like songs were published. New musical styles emerged in the popular music realm and crossed over to the sacred. The use of the guitar for accompaniment involved amateurs more fully than did the organ, and also seemed to encourage the use of everyday language.

But the timing was not right for including the new folk styles in the 1969 hymnal, or perhaps the committee just lacked courage. We knew Sydney Carter's "Lord of the dance," for example, but could not imagine Mennonites using it. Shortly after the hymnal was published, however, the song spread throughout the church, used sometimes as a protest song.

The area most surprising to me during the 1960s came through research into the origins of texts and music. Hymnal editors of the mid-twentieth century were beginning to pay attention to the original text and music, and to document sources carefully. When constructing previous hymnals, Mennonite editors had simply cut out the material they wanted from an existing hymnal and pasted it into a dummy. If the chosen hymn had markings for dynamics or featured an "Amen" at the end, these were included in the Mennonite book. It seemed that there was rarely an overall editorial plan, apart from the use of "Amen" for every hymn in the 1927 and 1940 GC hymnbooks.[19]

I had the opportunity to spend my 1963-64 sabbatical year studying in Scotland with Erik Routley, leading hymnologist at the time. He directed me to the original forms of hymn texts in the excellent libraries of Edinburgh. I soon discovered that many had been altered over time: most hymns initially had a large number of stanzas, and the choice of stanzas could change the character of the hymn considerably. "There's a wideness in God's mercy," by the Catholic Frederick Faber, is a good example (*HWB* 145). Its thirteen stanzas began with:

> Souls of men why will ye scatter
> Like a crowd of frightened sheep?
> Foolish hearts! Why will ye wander
> From a love so true and deep?[20]

Our first stanza is number four of the original. The seventh stanza reads:

> There is grace enough for thousands
> Of new worlds as great as this.

That was a remarkable discovery in a decade when a man first walked in space, so the stanza was included in the 1969 hymnal, although the 1992 committee took it out. We also liked the stanza that said:

> But we make his love too narrow
> By false limits of our own;
> And we magnify his strictness
> With a zeal he will not own.

The final, thirteenth stanza was too sweet for the 1960s, so we omitted it:

> If our love were but more simple
> We should take him at his word;
> And our lives would be all sunshine
> In the sweetness of our Lord.[21]

One more example comes from "For the beauty of the earth," a communion hymn with eight stanzas (*HWB* 89). Mennonites learned four or five stanzas, omitting those that may not have sounded Mennonite. But one of these stanzas is important to people in the arts:

> For the joy of ear and eye
> For the heart and mind's delight
> For the mystic harmony
> Linking sense to sound and sight.[22]

A young Russian woman who attended Elkhart Seminary in the early 1990s was brought up under Communism but had discovered Russian icons, which eventually drew her to become a Christian. When she was asked to lead a chapel service, she searched our hymnbook in vain for a hymn that acknowledged the importance of the senses in conveying the Christian message until she finally found this stanza. Perhaps this is what Coffman was hoping for when he wrote about our bowing in the holy place, with incense around us and censors "glowing with the fire of sacrifice."

Early in the 1980s, the Mennonites (both MCs and GCs) decided to join with the Church of the Brethren in making a new hymnal. Because the cooperation between two church groups had worked well for the *Mennonite Hymnal*, this decision seemed promising. Times had changed, however. A cumbersome organization of committees made consensus unfeasible, and voting, which is much more divisive, became a necessity. In addition, we soon realized that Mennonites and Brethren had different views on the use of music in worship. The most important hymns in each group show a striking difference in piety: compare the reflective character of "Move in our midst"(*HWB* 418) to the more exuberant "Praise God from whom" (*MH* 606; *HWB* 118).

The most difficult issue for me was inclusive language. It was new territory with no neutral guide, such as an original text, against which to resolve differences. It seems to me a miracle that the hymnal actually came into being, and that both Brethren and Mennonite churches consider the book their own. Fortunately, the Holy Spirit was at work, and Rebecca Slough had the vision and administrative skill to see it through to the end.

The 1992 *Hymnal: A Worship Book* contains a great variety of musical styles. Although the four-part character of previous books predominates, unison songs also appear, especially in the many cross-cultural hymns that would lose their uniqueness if Western harmonies were added. Instruments are needed or desirable on some hymns, and an accompaniment book supplies arrangements and suggestions for ways to vary the singing. The number of Mennonite texts and tunes, translations, and musical arrangements increased significantly.[23]

It is interesting to compare the tables of contents of our hymnbooks, because they tell something about the priorities of the people who made and used them. For example, the organization of the 1992 *Hymnal* shows a focus on corporate worship for more than half of its contents, followed by more personal, intimate sections, such as "Worship in Our Faith Journey." This approach was fresh and new to Mennonite hymnbooks. The table of contents most unlike the 1992 *Hymnal* was that of the 1890 *Hymns and Tunes*. There, twenty-six categories were arranged in alphabetical order rather than in some theological or descriptive grouping: Activity, Atonement, Baptism, Christmas, Consolation, Conversion, Crucifixion, Death, Evening, Heaven, Invitation, and so on.

The section of communion hymns lets us compare the growth and change in the concept of communion in Mennonite hymnbooks. The 1927 *Church Hymnal*, for example, had six hymns in that category. These emphasized remembrance of Christ's suffering and death. One hymn ended each stanza with the words "I will / We will remember thee;" another with "Until he comes."[24] Thankfulness and love each enter in only one hymn. The music tended to be inward and reflective, and almost like a lament in "According to thy gracious Word" (*MH* 400).

In contrast, the 1992 *Hymnal: A Worship Book* has a section of twenty-eight communion hymns. Remembrance is certainly one of the themes, but the hymnal's Worship Committee also found Biblical bases for linking communion to the Exodus, to Passover and Liberation, as well as to the Messianic banquet—the Feast of the Lamb described in Revelation. The risen, living Christ who had supper with the Pilgrims of Emmaus offers another perspective, as does the image of the church as a fellowship of love and unity. These themes all appear among the twenty-eight hymns, often several in one hymn. And the melodies cover a wide range of emotions, many of which would have seemed unsuitable for the solemn remembrance of Christ's suffering typical of my childhood. Some open up and express outward energy: "I come with joy to meet my Lord" (*HWB* 459). The reflective type is there, too: "Eat this bread" (*HWB* 471). A few offer the sense of mystery one often finds in more liturgical services (*HWB* 462, 463).

Where are we going? From my perspective, I see two trends that have profound implications for our future music-making: our growing ethnic diversity, and the expansion of musical styles used in worship.

Although Mennonites originated in northern Europe, the group's original ethnic identity has since been considerably broadened, first by migrations to North America and then through missionary activity in Asia, Africa and South America. Since the middle of the twentieth century, missionaries have increasingly moved away from a colonial model of establishing churches towards encouraging local expressions of the Gospel. The traditional model and the new have proceeded simultaneously. While in Tanzania in the 1970s, I sang hymns gathered from American and British hymnals, including the *Church and Sunday School Hymnal* (1902), the *Church*

Hymnal (1927), and Sankey's *Sacred Songs and Solos*.[25] But at the same time Don Jacobs, missionary anthropologist, was talking with Tanzanians about their own culture, their traditional concept of God and of creation. Yet hymns seem to change more slowly than ideas about faith, perhaps because they involve emotions as well as thought.

At this point in history there are more Mennonites south of the equator than north, and a Mennonite World Conference meeting in India or Africa makes clear that orally-based cultures predominate. We have the opportunity to meet these cultures on their terms. The four-part harmonies so important to western Mennonites are quite foreign to newer Mennonites, and they do not constitute a global Mennonite meeting. On the one hand, I feel keenly the loss of a rich inheritance; on the other hand, I see value in expanding the expressive possibilities of our hymn-singing. Asian hymns can offer us a far more reflective and meditative style of worship than we usually know, and their ornamental melodies extend our range of expression ("Sarennam").[26] African hymns bring energy and a complexity of rhythm and dance to our music, prompting us to rethink our ideas about the meaning of the body and of its place in Christian worship (*HWB* 10, 64). Understanding songs from other cultures is especially timely now, when an atmosphere of suspicion and fear dominates. I hope passionately that every ethnic group can both maintain its own heritage and value the music of others.

The second trend is the explosion of new music styles in Western worship. For a long time I have been aware of the fact that music can unify a congregation, but can also tear it apart. I think that the destructive aspects usually have to do with tensions over differing styles of music. For the first forty years of my life it was the clash between German Lutheran chorales and Gospel songs. But when Mennonites began to adopt the folk styles and instruments in the 1960s, the clash took on new opponents. Chorales and Gospel songs were pretty much in the same camp, pitted against the new secular style that used popular instruments. The two sides could also be described as traditional and folk, or as classical and popular styles. Formal and informal approaches to worship might be still another description.

Since the 1960s, the rift has been widening. I believe that in recent decades the break lies between people who use the book, and those who sing by ear and read words projected on a screen—book people and oral people. As we work for better understanding, I think we might try to reason through the values and limitations of the book and the ear, though reason is only one approach. The emotions are also deeply involved in this question.

People who read hymns have a natural entry into the rich history of hymnody and thus of the development of the church in many dimensions. Those in North America who read music do much to perpetuate the four-part singing tradition. They make possible our ability to sing any hymn in a modern hymnal. They value Western harmonies with their tensions and resolutions, but much of the world prefers a melodic or rhythmic emphasis. At its worst, singing from music notation seems elitist to people who cannot afford hymn books or the cost of learning to read music. Some people would argue that four-part singing keeps strangers from coming to a church with that practice, but on the other hand, there are people who come because of that particular approach to music.

People accustomed to oral traditions of music-making are often very quick to learn music, even on one hearing. There is no written notation that stands in the way of their catching the music. The notation in hymnbooks does not tell us what the tempo is, how to attack a note, how long to sustain it, or what kind of tone is appropriate. All quarter notes in a hymnal look alike on the page. (Incidentally, this seems to me one reason why some people long for more life in hymn singing.) People who sing by ear can simply imitate a good leader and have a chance of making a good sound immediately.

Music from orally-based traditions often repeats words and melodic patterns over and over again. In many parts of the world there are no hymn books; a leader can supply the changing words while the group repeats refrain-like material, as in many African-American spirituals ("I couldn't hear nobody pray") and in songs from the Taizé community (*HWB* 152). As non-liturgical Christians, Mennonites have tried to avoid repetition—"vain repetition," it was called in my youth. We expect a constant change of words to keep us focused on ideas and overlook the special gifts of repetition—gifts that appeal to the memory and the artistic sense.

I am afraid that too often our church culture resembles the political world around us in the polarization that keeps us from discussing controversial issues. But I believe that we must continue talking, especially on a congregational level. I suggest that the congregation, or small but diverse groups within it, discuss questions of this sort:

- Are hymn books on the way out? If so, what do we lose? What do we gain with contemporary Christian songs? What would be the value of using both styles?
- What do we learn from each of the generations in our congregation? Do we know their favorite songs? Is there such a thing as a youth hymn?

- Can we try to discern the implications of what we are singing at the present time? Can we search for hymns that reinforce the Mennonite position of distinct separation of church and state, hymns that specifically reject triumphalism in text and music and instead praise Christ, the Servant-King of an upside-down kingdom? Do we have the resources, either written or oral, with which to lament the present world situation?
- How can we judge what is a good hymn? A hymnal has the advantage of new editions that weed out hymns that are no longer effective. With new songs we have not had time to see whether they will wear well over the years. Popular styles have a short life; they are valuable for their freshness but should be discarded when they become dull. But dull to whom? Who decides?

Long ago I thought a well-trained musician should make the decisions, but I soon abandoned that idea. I do not believe this is just the minister's job, either (I recall the minister who chose all the hymns for his congregation for thirty years). I now think this is a matter for the congregation to grapple with. What do they find nourishing? What do they want their children to hold in their memories when they are adults?

I am stimulated by one model of how cultural change takes place in congregations, as described by Thomas Troeger (poet) and Carol Doran (composer) in their book *Trouble at the Table*.[27] Troeger and Doran, who have several hymns in *Hymnal: A Worship Book*, see the hymns of a congregation rotating in three concentric circles around an axis. The central circle, which they call structural, consists of those hymns that by widespread agreement are essential to the congregation's life. The outer circle, called ephemeral, contains all the new songs that enter our consciousness. Songs pass through the central, conjunctural section for trial and judgement either on their way in toward the center, or out to the edge and perhaps off the scene altogether. This process goes on with traditional hymns in a hymnal, but for a church to be alive, the movement of new songs into the repertory of the congregation is also necessary.

This model does not place styles against each other as enemies but rather sees their complementary function. I believe that it would be valuable for a congregation to discuss what are the essential, structural hymns in its worship life and try to explain why, then move to discuss what songs are in the conjunctural and ephemeral circles. It might be a more productive and less threatening approach than to focus on what we like and dislike.

I hope that we can keep communication open among us so that diversity appears to us as a gift that enriches our group life.

Notes

[1] Rosella Reimer Duerksen, "Anabaptist Hymnody in the Sixteenth Century," PhD diss., Union Seminary, 1956; Rupert K. Hohmann, "The Church Music of the Old Order Amish of the United States," PhD diss., Northwestern University, 1959. The significance of borrowed hymn tunes in the *Ausbund* is explored further in Maureen Epp, "New Readings of Text and Music in the *Aubund*," in this volume.

[2] Citations for hymns throughout this paper use the following abbreviations: *MH* = *The Mennonite Hymnal* (Newton, KS: Faith and Life Press; Scottdale, PA: Herald Press, 1969); *HWB* = *Hymnal: A Worship Book* (Elgin, IL: Brethren Press; Newton, KS: Faith and Life Press; Scottdale, PA: Mennonite Publishing House, 1992).

[3] *Die Kleine Geistliche Harfe der Kinder Zions . . .* (Germantown: Michael Billmeyer, 1803); *Ein Unpartheyisches Gesangbuch, enthaltend Gestreiche Lieder und Psalmen. . . .* (Lancaster: Johann Albrecht, 1804).

[4] *A Selection of Psalms, Hymns and Spiritual Songs, from the most approved authors . . . By a Committee of Mennonites* (Harrisonburg, VA: J.H. Wartmann & Bros., 1847).

[5] *A Compilation of Genuine Church Music, comprising a variety of meters, all harmonized for three voices . . . by Joseph Funk* (Winchester: J.W. Hollis, 1832).

[6] *Harmonia Sacra* (Singers's Glen, VA: Joseph Funk, 1851. This was the fifth edition of Funk's *Genuine Church Music*.

[7] *Hymns and Tunes for Public and Private Worship, and Sunday Schools. Compiled by a Committee* (Elkhart, IN: Mennonite Publishing Company, 1890).

[8] *Gesangbuch mit Noten* (Allgemeinen Conferenz der Mennoniten von Nord-Amerika, 1890).

[9] *Mennonite Hymnal: A Blending of Many Voices* (Berne, IN: Mennonite Book Concern, 1894).

[10] *Church and Sunday School Hymnal. A Collection of Hymns and Sacred Songs*, J. D. Brunk, musical editor (Elkhart, IN: Mennonite Publishing Co. and Freeport, IL: J.S. Shoemaker, 1902).

[11] *Church and Sunday School Hymnal*, no.35.

[12] *Church Hymnal* (1927), no. 509 and *The Mennonite Hymnary* (1940), no. 333. [See notes 16 and 17, below, for full citations.]

[13] *Church and Sunday School Hymnal Supplement . . .* Compiled by Committee: C. Z.Yoder, J. D. Brunk, S. F. Coffman, J. B.Smith, S. S.Yoder (Scottdale PA: Mennonite Publishing House), 1911.

[14] *Church and Sunday School Hymnal*, no. 434.

[15] The hymn was left out of the 1969 *Mennonite Hymnal*, but it came back in 1992 (*HWB* 2).

[16] *Church Hymnal – Mennonite. A Collection of Hymns and Sacred Songs Suitable for Use in Public Worship, Worship in the Home, and all General Occasions* (Scottdale, PA: Mennonite Publishing House, 1927); *Mennonite Hymn Book* (Berne, IN: Mennonite Book Concern, 1927).

[17] *Mennonite Hymnary*, ed. Walter H. Hohmann and Lester Hostetler (Berne, IN: Mennonite Book Concern; Newton, KS: Mennonite Publication Office, 1940). Hostetler also wrote a handbook of essays and comments on each of the 623 hymns: *Handbook to The Mennonite Hymnary* (Newton, KS: General Conference of

the Mennonite Church of North America, 1949).

[18] The Mennonite Brethren also joined in the first few years of work on this hymnbook.

[19] In the 1969 *Mennonite Hymnal,* the "Amens" appeared only for prayer and praise; in the 1992 *Hymnal: A Worship Book,* all were removed.

[20] Maurice Frost, *Historical Companion to Hymns Ancient and Modern* (London: William Clowes and Sons, 1962), no. 364 has eight of the original thirteen stanzas by Faber.

[21] In the 1992 hymnal, the stanza was brought back, but with the last two lines changed as follows: "And our lives will be illumined / In the presence of the Lord." See *HWB* 145.

[22] Stanza no. 3 in *HWB* 89; in *MH* 58 this stanza was not included.

[23] For another perspective on the proportion of "Anabaptist" content in *HWB,* see Katie Graber, "Identity and the Hymnal: Can Music Make a Person Mennonite?" in this volume.

[24] *Church Hymnal,* nos. 318 and 313.

[25] Ira D.Sankey, *Sacred Songs and Solos* (London: Marshall, Morgan, and Scott, 189?).

[26] *Sound the Bamboo: CCA Hymnal 2000* (Hong Kong: Christian Conference of Asia, 2000), no.47.

[27] Carol Doran and Thomas H. Troeger, *Trouble at the Table: Gathering the Tribes for Worship* (Nashville, TN: Abingdon Press, 1992), 119-123. Troeger and Doran credit the Dutch theologican Schillebeeckx as a source for their ideas presented here.

New Readings of Text and Music in the *Ausbund*

Maureen Epp

In the early autumn of 1535, several groups of Anabaptists were captured near Passau, a city located on the Danube River close to the Austrian-Bavarian border. They were travelling from Moravia, which until that year had been a region of religious tolerance and a haven for Anabaptists fleeing persecution. That autumn, however, Moravian authorities had become hostile toward the Anabaptist communities in their jurisdiction, and a kind of reverse migration took place as Anabaptists attempted to move back into the south German territories from which they had originally come, looking for another safe place to settle. For the four groups—some fifty-five people altogether—apprehended near Passau, this was not to be: after being interrogated by authorities, the prisoners were locked in a dungeon for two years in the hopes that they would eventually break down and recant.[1]

During their imprisonment, the captured Anabaptists wrote hymns and presumably sang them together. Not surprisingly, many of the hymn texts speak about the path of suffering that comes with choosing to follow the way of Christ. In 1564, a small compilation of these hymns was printed under the title *Etliche schöne christliche Geseng wie sie in der Gefengkniss zu Passaw im Schloss von den Schwitzer Bruüdern durch Gottes Gnad geticht und gesungen worden* (Some Beautiful Christian Songs as they were composed and sung in the castle prison at Passau by the Swiss Brethren, through the grace of God). An expanded volume with some seventy additional hymns was published in 1583 as *Ausbund: Etliche schöne christenliche Geseng...* (Ausbund: Some Beautiful Christian Songs . . .), the form by which it is known today.[2] Martyr songs also make up a significant proportion of the expanded *Ausbund*, although this is not the sole topic: there are songs of praise and thanksgiving, and songs that expound on key points of doctrine. Thus the *Ausbund* is not only a profound witness to the persecutions and difficult way of life experienced by early members of the radical reformation, it is also a valuable record of the movement's emerging theology (or perhaps more accurately, "theologies"), as Anabaptists sought to articulate their beliefs in contradistinction to both the Catholic church and the various reform movements that surrounded them.

In this essay, I want to consider how words and music worked together in several *Ausbund* hymns, in their original sixteenth-century context. Recently published studies of the *Ausbund* have focused primarily on the hymn texts, making them more accessible to modern North American readers by translating the words into English and explicating their many theological and scriptural references.[3] A similar kind of translation and explication is also necessary for us to understand the significance of the melodies used to sing the *Ausbund* hymns, many of which carried with them particular historical and cultural references. These references would have been evident to most sixteenth-century ears, at least in German-speaking lands, but are not obvious to us today. Unearthing the associations that were linked with these melodies can give us some idea of how the combined impact of words and music in the hymns of the *Ausbund* would have struck the ears of its earliest users.

An important basis for investigating the music of the *Ausbund* is the fact that the majority of its contents are *contrafacta*: songs created by fitting new words to pre-existing melodies. This procedure is immediately obvious when one looks at a copy of the *Ausbund,* for unlike the hymnals we use today, the *Ausbund* contains no notated music. Above each hymn text is a heading that typically begins with a succinct characterization of the hymn's contents (*"Ein ander Marter-Lied . . . "*; i.e., "Another martyr song . . . "); this may be followed by the author's name or initials, after which is given the name of a tune (the *Ton* or *Weise*) to which the text should be sung. The tunes would have been familiar to users of the *Ausbund*, and many can still be located today.[4] In some instances, two or three tune names are provided for a given hymn. Sometimes these are simply alternative names for the same melody while at other times the multiple citations refer to several different melodies, each of which would fit the words of the hymn. In this way, if users of the *Ausbund* did not recognize the first melody they could choose another, equally suitable one.

The tunes named in the *Ausbund* were drawn from many sources, including Roman Catholic plainchant, Reformation hymnody, courtly song, Meistersinger tradition, and secular folk song.[5] In other words, the tunes are representative of the various song genres that were part of the broader culture surrounding the early Anabaptists. The notion of singing religious texts to well-known secular melodies may be somewhat surprising or even distasteful to us today, yet the practice was fairly common across Western Europe during the late Middle Ages and Renaissance-Reformation period, not limited to reform movements or to German-speaking territories.[6] The inevitable conclusion is that a clear distinction between categories of "secular" and "sacred" was not as important to people of the sixteenth century as it is to us today. Indeed, Luther is famously reported to have said, "Why should the devil have all the good tunes?" Nor was the practice of creating contrafacta limited to converting secular songs by supplying them with new, sacred words: like Luther, the early Anabaptists freely borrowed songs from other religious groups, replacing the original words with their own.

Regardless of whether a song's original identity was sacred or secular, the strategic advantages of combining familiar tunes with new words are particularly significant when we recall that during this period much of the population was either non-literate or only semi-literate.[7] Contrafacta songs do not require the ability to read music, only the ability to recall a familiar melody, and printed collections of such songs could avoid the considerable expense of including notated music. Even though the words of the *Ausbund* hymns were subjected to a literate process by being written down, collected, and printed as a book, many of the hymns still could have been readily transmitted by word-of-mouth, since remembering a new set of verses is not too difficult if they have been paired with an easy and familiar tune. And the tunes most frequently borrowed for contrafacta were pleasingly simple, featuring repetitive elements and limited melodic ranges, with few melismas or other "soloistic" flourishes.[8] Luther and his followers took full advantage of the familiarity and simplicity of popular folk melodies in their efforts to communicate with the less-educated sectors of the population.[9] By the same token, contrafacta songs were an ideal kind of music for the early Anabaptists, most of whom were trades- and craftspeople without high levels of formal education.

On the one hand, then, the practice of making contrafacta was so familiar and widespread that it scarcely requires comment. The multiple tune suggestions supplied for many of the *Ausbund* hymns would seem to indicate an approach to hymn-singing that was both pragmatic and casual: if you don't know or don't like one melody, simply choose another that fits. Yet on the other hand, there existed the potential to use contrafacta technique in a more purposeful manner. In her book *Music as Propaganda in the German Reformation*, Rebecca Wagner Oettinger examines a body of songs with strong polemical content that grew out of the Lutheran reformation. The texts of these songs speak to the intense and sometimes violent discourse that took place between Catholic authorities and Lutheran leaders. Many of Luther's chorales, it could be said, had the intent of religious propaganda. However, these other songs were not heard during church services but in the more informal context of the street, tavern, and marketplace. The tunes for these polemical songs were taken from the same large pool of well-known songs as were the hymns of the *Ausbund*.[10] Many are Lutheran chorale melodies whose original words were replaced with more blatantly political texts, and Oettinger argues that the relationship between recycled melody and new words could actually generate another level of meaning. Since a contrafactum could be successfully spread only if its melody was already widely known, listeners and singers of the new text would also have been inevitably reminded of the melody's other words:

> The new texts provide only a part of the meaning of those songs as they would have been understood by a listener of the day.... Upon the first hearing of a contrafactum, the "original" words are remembered and compared to the new text, providing a commentary and a filter through which the new text is understood.[11]

This interplay of old and new texts (in other words, intertextuality) is triggered through the use of a common and familiar melody.

A striking instance of how this worked is the song "Nun treiben wir den Babst hinaus" ("Now we drive out the Pope"), first published in 1546 and at one time thought to be by Luther himself.[12] Promoted as a song for children and widely reproduced, the inflammatory text called for the expulsion of the Pope, identifying him as the "whore of Babylon" and the "Antichrist," a false idol who had usurped the true High Priest Jesus Christ (see Example 1.1). Additional layers of meaning—the intertextuality—come from the designated tune, the medieval folksong "Nun treiben wir den Winter aus" ("Now drive we out the winter") (Example 1.2). This song was traditionally sung mid-way through the period of Lent as part of a symbolic ritual to banish the winter and welcome spring. As Oettinger points out, the obvious parallels between the wording of the old and new texts would have immediately called forth a series of associations. The Pope is equated with spiritual winter and darkness, and must be expelled in order that spring, or spiritual renewal, can take place. The word *ausstreiben* also means "to exorcize," and since the melody was already associated with Lent, a time of fasting and purification, the use of *ausstreiben* in this context implies that the pope is like an evil demon who must be exorcized if the church is to become pure again.[13]

Example 1.1

Nun treiben wir den Bapst hinaus (Johann Mathesisus, Wittenberg, 1545)

1. Nun treiben wir den Babst hinaus
   Aus Christus Kirch und Gottes haus
   Da[rin er m]ordlich hat Regirt
   Unzelich viel Seelen verfürt.

2. Nun trol dich du verdampter Son
   Der Rote braut von Babilon.
   Du bist der grewel und Antichrist
   Vol lügen mords und arger list.

1. Now we drive out the pope
   from Christ's church and God's house.
   Therein he has reigned in a deadly fashion
   And has seduced uncountably many souls.

2. Now move along, you damned son,
   You Whore of Babylon.
   You are the abomination and Antichrist,
   Full of lies, death and cunning.

7 stanzas altogether. Text and translation from Oettinger, Music as Propaganda, 324-326.

Is it possible that a similar process was at work in the combination of texts and melodies in the *Ausbund*? It must be acknowledged that the hymns of the *Ausbund* did not have quite the same purpose as the polemical songs analyzed by Oettinger. Largely meant to encourage Anabaptist followers to hold to their faith in difficult times, the *Ausbund* hymns recount inspiring martyr stories and remind readers of the true rewards awaiting them in heaven. One might describe them as defensive in character, mostly looking inwards, whereas the Lutheran propaganda songs are offensive, directly taking on their Catholic opponents. Yet not only do the songs of the *Ausbund* use the same contrafacta technique as do the Lutheran propaganda songs, they also draw on many of the same tunes. If these familiar melodies carried deep-seated associations for the broad public that Luther and his followers wished to reach, they must have carried the same associations for the early Anabaptists who lived in the same cultural milieu. What kinds of meanings would Lutheran chorales have held for the Anabaptists, who were both a part of the larger Reformation movement but also very consciously distinct

Example 1.2

Nun treiben wir den Winter aus (traditional folk song)

| Nun | trei - | ben | wir | den | Win - | ter | aus, | durch |
| Now | drive | we | out | the | win - | ter, | out |

| die - | se | Stadt | zum | Tor | hin - aus. | Wir | treib'n | ihm | ue - | ber |
| through | the | ci - | ty | and | the gate. | We | drive | it | o - | ver |

| Berg | und | Thal, | das | er | nich | wie - | der | kom - | men | sol. |
| hill | and | vale | that | it | will | ne - | ver | come | a - | gain. |

Melody with German text from Oettinger, Music as Propaganda; English translation mine.

from it? And what factors might have prompted them to pair a Catholic plainchant melody with new words of their own?

Ausbund hymns nos. 54 and 55 are examples of how the interplay of associations between an original song and its contrafacta version can reveal something of the Anabaptists' own response to their religious surroundings. The heading to hymn no. 54, "Merckt auf ein Sach," describes it as a song about child baptism (Example 2.1). In fact, the text is a strongly-worded argument *against* child baptism, one of the few *Ausbund* hymns that is overtly polemical. The Anabaptist rejection of infant baptism was a departure from both Catholic and Lutheran practice, and it is the Lutheran authorities who are singled out in "Merckt auf ein Sach." The first stanza sets the tone by referring to the strife caused in the present times by the *Schriftgelehrten*, or learned ones, a veiled reference to Luther and his highly educated colleagues. Stanzas 2 - 8 review scriptural teachings that "we" have found out for ourselves concerning conversion and baptism. But, as the beginning of stanza 9 declares, "... die Welt all's verkehrt": the world is upside-down and things are not right, because uninstructed young children are still being baptized. With this reference to an upside-down or inside-out (*verkehrte*) world, the writer of the hymn invokes a metaphor that was pervasive throughout late-medieval culture, used in both visual and literary imagery to signify the foolishness and moral corruption of the age. The *verkehrte Welt* metaphor was enthusiastically adopted by Reformation propagandists to underscore their message that the Catholic church's version of

Christianity was not merely incorrect, it was — on some points, at least — the opposite of what it should be. On broadsheets used to spread the Reformation message, woodcut illustrations depicted established religious and social hierarchies in reverse: the Pope is portrayed as the devil or Antichrist and often surrounded by scatological elements; a peasant celebrates Mass at the altar instead of the priest, who now ploughs the fields outside.[14] Thus with the phrase "die Welt all's verkehrt," the *Ausbund* hymn conjures up this familiar complex of images and associations and adds to it the inherent wrongness of child baptism.

In the stanzas that follow, child baptism is further denounced as idolatry (*Abgötterey*, stanza 10), and readers are warned to guard against the false teachers who promote the practice of child baptism. Near the end of the hymn (stanza 22), Luther is identified by name. The negative references to Luther and his associates (the *Schriftgelehrten*) at both beginning and end of the hymn function as a kind of frame, setting off the middle stanzas that articulate a "true" biblical understanding of conversion and baptism.

Example 2.1

Ausbund *no. 54 Merckt auf ein Sach und die ist wahr*

Ein ander Lied vom Kinder-Tauff, Im Thon, Erhalt uns Herr bey deinem Wort. Oder, Wohl dem der in Gottes etc.

1. Merckt auf ein Sach und die ist wahr,
   Bezeugen will ichs hell und klar,
   Wiewol darum g'schicht mancher streit,
   Von Schrifftgelehrten dieser Zeit.
2. Anfang und End in Christo b'staht,
   Der uns verkünd des Vatters Rath,
   Derwegen wir den Kinder-Tauff
   Durch G'schrifft ersuchen in dem Lauff.
9. Aber die Welt all's verkehrt,
   Taufft junge Kind, noch ungelehrt,
   Dem unwissenden jungen Kind
   Im Tauff abwächset die Erbsünd.
10. Das dieses sey Abgötterey,
    Thu ich hiemit beweisen frey,
    Weil solch'g'schicht ohn Gottes Rath,
    Durch fremde thür in schafstall gaht.

22. Luther spricht, alls was Gott wöll hon,
    Das hab er auch gebotten schon:
    Nun frag ich all G'lehrten frey
    Wo Kinder-Tauff gebotten sey?

1. Here is something that is true,
   That I will prove and make clear as day.
   Although there are many struggles about this
   Among the learned ones of this time.
2. Beginning and end are in Christ,
   He who proclaims to us the Father's will.
   Therefore we look for child baptism
   in His life, as shown by Scripture.
9. But the world is all reversed,
   Baptizing young children, still unknowing.
   From the innocent young child
   Original sin is washed away through baptism.
10. That this is idolatry
    I have just freely proven
    Because such a practice
    Creeps into the sheep stall without God's will.
22. Luther says, all that God wants
    He has already commanded.
    Now I freely ask all you learned ones
    Where is child baptism commanded?

(24 stanzas altogether; my thanks to Erika Friesen for her assistance in translating this text.)

The Anabaptist opposition to Lutheran teaching expressed in the text of "Merckt auf ein Sach" is further reinforced by the designated tune, which is from one of Luther's very own hymns: "Erhalt uns Herr bey deinem Wort" (1541). A strongly worded prayer for protection from religious enemies, Luther's text begins with specific references to the Pope and the Turks (Example 2.2). Just like "Nun treiben wir den Papst hinaus," "Erhalt uns Herr" was conceived as a hymn for children and achieved quick popularity.[15] It too became the basis of numerous contrafacta versions, many of which echoed the sentiments of the original in requesting God's protection from the papacy and other threats. A 1555 version includes prayers for secular rulers who hold to the "right faith" and identifies by name other rulers who are godless enemies.[16] The choice of this tune for "Merckt auf ein Sach" is quite striking because it takes one of Luther's most successful propaganda

Example 2.2

Martin Luther, "Erhalt uns Herr" (1541)

Melody with German text based on Markus Jenny, ed., Luthers Geistliche Lieder und Kirchengesänge *(Köln: Böhlau Verlag, 1985), 304; English transl. from Luther's Works: Vol. 53, Liturgy and Hymns, ed. Ulrich S. Leupold (Philadelphia: Fortress Press, 1965), 305.*

attempts and turns it on its head, using the same melody to criticize Luther himself for continuing the practice of child baptism — a musical expression of the *verkehrte Welt* motif of reversal or inversion.

"Merckt auf ein Sach" also subverts the original message of Luther's hymn and its related versions, that of a plea to God for protection from enemies. The Anabaptist position on infant baptism was a key reason for their ongoing persecution by religious and secular authorities. By combining the tune of Luther's "Erhalt uns Herr" with an anti-Lutheran text, the *Ausbund* hymn "Merckt auf ein Sach" implies that Luther too was an enemy, on par with the Pope and the Turks when it came to needing God's protection.

The hymn immediately following "Merckt auf ein Sach" also concerns a central issue of faith identity and practice, that of the Lord's Supper. The heading to "O Gott Vatter ins Himmels Throne" (no. 55) first states that it can be sung to any tune appropriate to Christian use, but then specifies "Pange lingua" (Example 3.1). "Pange lingua" is one of two Gregorian chant melodies that are cited in the *Ausbund* and again, it is a significant choice.

Using a traditional Catholic melody for a hymn with such important doctrinal content immediately provokes a comparison between the two faiths, implicitly reminding readers and singers that the taking of communion was a key area of difference between Catholic and Anabaptist faiths. Not only did the Anabaptists reject the Catholic church's theology of transubstantiation, but also its practices around communion. Although every Mass included communion, in the late Middle Ages it was usually only the priest-celebrant who partook of both the communion wafer and wine. Ordinary people were encouraged to receive the wafer at least once a year, usually at Easter, but their participation was not considered necessary. In contrast to this priestly ritual, the taking of both elements by all members of a congregation was central to both Anabaptist and Reformation theologies of communion.[17] The marked simplicity of an Anabaptist celebration of the Lord's Supper — members sitting around a table reading Scriptures, then sharing bread and wine amongst themselves — was so far removed from ceremonial Catholic practice that it constituted an "anticlerical" action, an implicit criticism of the priests and their rituals.[18]

Example 3.1

Ausbund *no. 55 O Gott Vatter ins Himmels Throne*

Ein ander Lied vom Brodbrechen, oder Abendmahl, mit was Weiss die Christen das gebrauchen sollen. Schmidt, Hans. Im Thon, Pangelingua.

1. O Gott Vatter ins Himmels Throne,
   Der du uns hast bereit ein' Krone,
   So wir in deinem Sohn beleiben,
   Mit ihm hie dulden Kreutz und Leiden,
   In diesem leben, uns ihm ergeben,
   Nach sein'r G'meinschafft allzeit streben.

2. In deinem Sohn thust du uns sagen,
   So wir Gemeinschafft mit ihm haben,
   Und sein Fusspfade nachfolgen,
   Thust uns mit deinem Geist versorgen,
   Der hilfft uns streiten, zu allen Zeiten,
   Wann der Weltfürst an uns thut reiten.

3. Zu einem Haupt hast du uns geben
   Dein lieben Sohn das reine Leben,
   Der hat uns vergebahnt die Strassen,
   Dass wir sein gemeinschaft nit verlassen
   Alle so ihn erkennen, sich Christen nennen,
   Sollen sich seiner Gestalt nicht schämen.

4. Darum O Christen-Häuslein kleine!
   Lasst uns betrachten allgemeine,

Wie er uns vorging hie auf Erden,
Dass wir ihm auch gleichförmig werden
In lieb und leiden, in sein'm Bund bleiben,
Seins Fleischs und Bluts hie nit vermeiden.

5. Also muss man die Speiss verhehmen,
Der Geist lehrt uns die gmeinschafft kennen
Von seinem Fleisch und Blut hie essen,
Der alte Mensch muss gar verwesen,
Mit seinen wercken, das soll man mercken,
Der geist Christi muss in uns würcken.

1. O God Father on Heaven's throne,
You who have prepared for us a crown,
If we abide in Your Son,
Here with Him bear patiently cross and suffering,
In this life yielding ourselves to Him,
Striving for His fellowship at all times.

2. In Your Son You testify to us.
If we have fellowship with Him,
And follow after His footsteps,
You provide us with Your Spirit,
Who helps us contend at all times,
When the prince of this world seeks to overcome us.

3. As Head You have given us
Your beloved Son, the pure life,
He has prepared the way before us,
That we do not forsake His fellowship.
All who know Him, calling themselves Christians,
Shall not be ashamed of Him.

4. Therefore, O Christian flock so small!
Let us all consider
How He went before us here on earth,
That we also become like Him,
In joy and grief abiding in His covenant,
Not shunning here His flesh and blood.

5. Thus one must perceive this nourishment,
The Spirit teaches us to understand the communion
Of partaking His flesh and blood,
The old man must completely perish

With his works, this we shall perceive,
The Spirit of Christ must work in us.

(27 stanzas altogether; English translation from Songs of the Ausbund, Vol.1 [Ohio Amish Library], no. 55).

Example 3.2

Thomas Aquinas, Pange lingua (1263)

1. Pange lingua, gloriosi
   Corporis mysterium
   Sanguinisque pretiosi,
   Quem in mundi pretium
   Fructus ventris generosi
   Rex effudit gentium.

1. Now, my tongue, the mystery telling
   Of the glorious Body sing.
   And the Blood, all price excelling,
   Which the Gentiles' Lord and King,
   In a Virgin's womb once dwelling,
   Shed for this world's ransoming.

(6 stanzas altogether; from Maurice Frost, ed., Historical Companion to Hymns Ancient and Modern [London: William Clowes & Sons, Ltd., 1962], no. 383).

The text of the hymn "O Gott Vatter" further articulates an Anabaptist understanding of the Lord's Supper, one that is linked directly to experiences of suffering and martyrdom. The opening stanzas contain a series of admonishments to endure hardship and remain faithful to Christ's example here on earth. Only after the true meaning of being in fellowship with Christ has been established is the topic of communion introduced in stanza 5. Subsequent stanzas reiterate the connection between experiencing suffering and taking communion ("The Lamb is eaten with distress/With bitter seasoning patiently..."; stanza 17) along with another touchstone of Anabaptist theology, that of renouncing the ways of the world.

Although the combination of a plainchant melody with an Anabaptist text on the Lord's Supper implies a criticism of Catholic doctrine and practice, other, more positive associations must have also governed the particular choice of the "Pange lingua" tune. "Pange lingua" was an old and widely known plainchant hymn that existed in two versions, both of which were associated with important events in the church calendar. The earliest set of words are attributed to Fortunatus (d. ca. AD 600); this version was associated with Passion week liturgies and often used as a processional hymn. A second hymn text beginning with the words "Pange lingua," attributed to Thomas Aquinas (1226-74), was sung at the Feast of Corpus Christi (Example 3.2).[19] Falling shortly after Pentecost, the Feast of Corpus Christi was established in 1264 by Pope Urban IV to promote the Veneration of the Host (i.e., the communion wafer representing Christ's body). The addition of this feast to the church calendar marked a growing interest in ritual activities devoted to the Host and by the late Middle Ages, Corpus Christi had become one of the highlights of the church year. Its celebration usually involved a procession through town or city streets that included local civic authorities, guild members, and even children, as well as clerical personnel.[20] "Pange lingua" was one of several hymns used to accompany the procession, and its customary use during such an important community event would have ensured that it was familiar to most people.

By the early sixteenth century, there were also several versions of the "Pange lingua" text in the German vernacular, further evidence of the hymn's common currency.[21] In this light, the Anabaptist appropriation of the "Pange lingua" tune is hardly surprising.[22] And although "O Gott Vatter" is the only hymn in the *Ausbund* to name "Pange lingua" as its tune, the same plainchant is specified for four hymns in other Anabaptist sources, one of which is also a communion hymn while the other two are about the Passion of Christ.[23] Clearly, the connection between "Pange lingua" and the liturgical traditions of Catholicism was not a barrier to the Anabaptists who chose to use it for their own hymns. Instead, its long history, the tune's familiarity, and its association with liturgical events devoted to Christ's Passion and the veneration of his body made it an ideal vehicle for the Anabaptists to express their own theology of the Lord's Supper.

In her study of Anabaptist hymnody, Rosella Reimer Duerkson observes the freedom with which the Anabaptists borrowed melodies from many sources for their hymns, and concludes that

> although theologically not in agreement with many of the doctrines of the major reformers, the Anabaptists seem to have harboured no prejudice against using melodic material which transcended the realm of their differences. To them, a tune was not to be associated with a specific group or a specific doctrine, but the common property of all.[24]

However, I would argue that the examples of the hymns "Merckt auf ein Sach'" and "O Gott Vatter" show that sometimes a tune was more than just a tune, more than a neutral vehicle for conveying a set of words. In these two *Ausbund* hymns, the borrowed melodies do not "transcend the realm" of differences between the Anabaptists, Lutherans and Catholics so much as carry with them residues of earlier meanings, against which we can reread the Anabaptist texts for greater depth and nuance.

It is unlikely that all 120-plus hymns in the *Ausbund* will reveal the same layers of meaning as the two I have described here. Nevertheless, I believe that these two examples illustrate the potential value of exploring other tune-and-text combinations in the *Ausbund*. In reading the *Ausbund* hymn texts, we clearly see how Anabaptists were working to define their own theological and social identity, and in so doing separate themselves from the world around them. Through the melodies that they chose to sing these texts, we are reminded that the Anabaptists were also a part of the culture that surrounded them, borrowing from it and responding to it just as we do today.

Notes

[1] A fuller account of the circumstances surrounding the capture and imprisonment of the "Philippite" Anabaptists, as they were sometimes called, can be found in Robert A. Riall, *The Earliest Hymns of the* Ausbund, ed. Galen A. Peters (Kitchener, ON: Pandora Press, 2003), 14-20.

[2] Some of the hymns in the expanded 1583 *Ausbund* date from the mid-1520s and therefore predate the "Passau" group. Minor changes and additions were made with subsequent *Ausbund* editions; however, its core content has remained essentially unchanged. For bibliographic descriptions of various editions and printings of the *Ausbund*, see Nelson P. Springer, "The Editions of the Ausbund," in Paul M. Yoder, Elizabeth Bender, Harvey Graber and Nelson P. Springer, *Four Hundred Years With the Ausbund* (Scottdale, PA.: Herald Press, 1964), 31- 40. In researching this paper, I have used a facsimile of the 1742 Germantown, Pennsylvania edition of the *Ausbund* originally printed by Chrisotpher Saur, reprinted under the *Mennonite Songbooks American Series*, vol. 1, gen. ed. Irvin B. Horst (Amsterdam: Frits Knuf, n.d.).

[3] *Songs of the Ausbund*, vol.1 (Millersburg, Ohio: Ohio Amish Library, 1998) contains complete translations of the hymns that continue to be sung in some Amish communities today. Riall and Peters, *The Earliest Hymns of the* Ausbund (Kitchener, ON: Pandora Press, 2003) is a translation and commentary on the "Passau" hymns only. More specialized studies also exist, notably on the *Ausbund's* many martyr songs. See Ursula Lieseberg, *Studien zum Märtyrlied der Täufer im 16. Jahrhundert* (Frankfurt am Main: Peter Lang, 1991); and Victor Doerksen, "The Anabaptist Martyr Ballad," *Mennonite Quarterly Review* 51 (1977): 5-21.

[4] Ernst Sommer, "Die Melodien der alten deutschen Täufer-Lieder," *Jahrbuch für Liturgik und Hymnologie* 17 (1972): 100-164 is the most recent and thorough overview of the music of the *Ausbund*, and provides extensive references to anthologies of sacred and secular song wherein the tunes can be located. Sommer's survey also includes the major hymn collections of sixteenth-century Hutterite and North-German Anabaptists, which share many tunes and texts with the *Ausbund*. Somewhat older but still useful surveys are Rosella Reimer Duerksen, "Anabaptist Hymnody of the 16th Century" (PhD diss., Union Theological Sem-

inary, New York, 1956); and Rudolf Wolkan, *Die Lieder der Wiedertäufer* (Berlin: B. Behr, 1903; repr. Nieuwkoop, B. de Graaf, 1965).

[5] For a detailed breakdown of *Ausbund* tunes according to origin, see Sommer, 152-158.

[6] For example, pre-Reformation Italian *laude* ("praise" songs) often borrowed well-known secular melodies of the time, as did French *noëls*. The printed collection *Souterliedekins* (Antwerp, 1530) contains metrical translations of the Psalms into Dutch, set to folk songs.

[7] Estimates for sixteenth-century literacy rates in Germany range from 5% to 30%. See Rebecca Wagner Oettinger, *Music as Propaganda in the German Reformation* (Aldershot: Ashgate, 2001), 23-30; and Arnold Snyder, "Orality, Literacy, and the Study of Anabaptism," *Mennonite Quarterly Review* 65 (1991): 372-73. As Snyder observes (388), the *Ausbund* is a valuable source for studying Anabaptism from the perspective of oral culture; a topic which deserves a much fuller treatment than the scope of this paper allows.

[8] Oettinger, *Music as Propaganda*, 94-99.

[9] The literature on Luther and music is quite extensive. For a useful introduction, see the opening chapters of Friedrich Blume's *Protestant Church Music: A History*, trans. F. Ellsworth Peterson (London: Victor Gollancz Ltd., 1975). A more specialized study that relates Lutheran music practices to theological and cultural issues is Helga Robinson-Hammerstein, "The Lutheran Reformation and its Music," in *The Transmission of Ideas in the Lutheran Reformation*, ed. Helga Robinson-Hammerstein (Irish Academic Press, 1989), 141-171.

[10] Of the tunes cited in the *Ausbund*, 26 were also used as a basis for the Lutheran propaganda songs surveyed in Oettinger's book.

[11] Oettinger, Music as Propaganda, 102.

[12] Ibid., 192-195.

[13] Ibid., 192-201.

[14] See R.W. Scribner, *For the Sake of Simple Folk: Popular Propaganda for the German Reformation* (Cambridge: Cambridge University Press, 1981), 164-69.

[15] Oettinger, *Music as Propaganda*, 191.

[16] Ibid., 167, 264 (song no. 66). The tune "Erhalt uns Herr" is still used today and can be found in both Lutheran and Mennonite hymnals, although naturally with revised words. See *Hymnal: A Worship Book* (Newton, KS: Faith and Life Press, 1992) nos. 217 and 225. *Lutheran Book of Worship* (Minneapolis: Augsburg Publishing House, 1978), no. 230, has a modified version of Luther's text.

[17] There were other distinctions in communion theology between the Anabaptists and other Protestant groups. See *Encyclopedia of Protestantism*, ed. Hans J. Hillerbrand (New York, London: Routledge, 2004), s.v. "Lord's Supper" by B. A. Gerrish.

[18] Hans-Jürgen Goertz, *The Anabaptists*, trans. Trevor Johnson (London and New York: Routledge, 1988), 113.

[19] See *Hymnal: A Worship Book*, no. 256 for the "Pange lingua" melody and an English version of the text by Fortunatus.

[20] David Hiley, *Western Plainchant* (Oxford: Clarendon Press, 1993), 24-25, 144-46. For a discussion of the social importance Corpus Christi processions, see Miri Rubin, *Corpus Christi: The Eucharist in Late Medieval Culture* (Cambridge: Cambridge University Press, 1991), 243-71.

[21] Wilhelm Bäumker, *Das Katholische Deutsche Kirchenlied in seinen Singweisen*

(Hildesheim: Georg Olm, 1962), vol. 1, no. 371, lists several German versions of "Mein Zung Erkling," dating from the early sixteenth century to 1628.

[22] Although the poetic meter of the *Ausbund* hymn "O Gott Vatter" does not perfectly match the "Pange lingua" melody as it is printed in *Hymnal: A Worship-Book*, no. 256, it is reasonable to assume that minor changes were made to the melody in order to accomodate the *Ausbund* text, as commonly happens in vernacular song traditions. Note the variations in the "Pange lingua" melody when paired with other vernacular texts in Bäumker, no. 371.

[23] Duerksen, "Anabaptist Hymnody," 83.

[24] Ibid., 116.

Reviving Songs of Peace from the Vistula Delta[1]

Mark Jantzen

The 1860s were a traumatic decade for the Mennonites of the Vistula Delta. In 1864 their country, Prussia, fought and won a war with Denmark and won a second war two years later against the Austrian Empire. Volatile relations with neighboring France led to a third war in 1870, which Prussia again won. All three of these wars were fought to create a unified German nation-state, a feat achieved finally in 1871. These wars were all accompanied, therefore, by fervid expressions of German nationalism which led, for example, to the final revocation of Mennonites' exemption from the draft in 1867. Into this context, the rural congregations of the Vistula Delta (near modern-day Gdansk, Poland) released a new hymnal in 1869 entitled *Gesangbuch für Mennoniten-Gemeinden in Kirche und Haus* (Hymnal for Mennonite Congregations at Church and at Home).[2]

One striking rubric in the table of contents was "Love of Enemies." In a decade when political events forced Prussian Mennonites to think about "enemies" in immediate and practical terms, the selection and inclusion of three hymns under such a provocative heading constituted a theological response expressed in hymnody to the intense pressure on Mennonites to join the Prussian army and to find their primary identity in the German nation instead of the Mennonite church. In a setting that glorified wars of national unification and the leaders who orchestrated them, the inclusion of "Love of Enemies" in a new hymnal went beyond being a theological and musical pronouncement. This act was also a political statement. Because none of these songs have previously been translated into English, an important hymnological voice in a dramatic debate has been lost to most North American Mennonites.

Vistula Delta Mennonites

The Vistula Delta was one of very few havens for sixteenth-century Anabaptists that remained relatively tolerant all the way through to the nineteenth century. Anabaptists fled here from waves of persecution in the Low Countries in the 1530s and 1560s, and a few came from Switzerland and South Germany as well. By the late eighteenth century about a dozen congregations with a total population of well over 10,000 had emerged.[3] The transition to German from Dutch was completed at different speeds in different congregations. By 1767, however, the rural majority of Mennonites was ready for a German-language hymnal, *Geistreiches Gesangbuch*, because, as the foreword noted, the congregations were already teaching their youth and preaching in German.[4]

A political transition with far-reaching repercussions occurred only five years later in 1772, when most of the area was taken by Prussia from Poland in the First Partition of Poland. The Third Partition in 1795 brought the rest of the Mennonites in the Vistula Delta under Prussian rule. The new rulers were more able to impose their will directly on their subjects than the Polish kings had been. The Hohenzollern who ruled Prussia, as it turned out, were particularly interested in increasing state revenues and the size of their army. As a result, Mennonites were soon forced to pay higher and more regular fees to avoid military service and found themselves barred from buying additional real estate for farming or business or even from buying a house from non-Mennonites unless they were willing to allow their sons to serve in the Prussian military. Thus beginning in 1788, a series of emigrations from the Vistula Delta to modern-day Ukraine ensued.[5]

Those Mennonites who remained in Prussia worked out a stable understanding with the Prussian government that released all Mennonites from military duty in exchange for an annual communal Mennonite tax and a moratorium on purchasing real estate. This equilibrium was shattered by the wars Prussia waged in the 1860s.

At the outset of the decade, Prussia was locked in a constitutional crisis. Revolutionaries had won the concession of a very limited constitution from the king in 1848. Liberals were forced to accept the king's absolute authority over the Prussian military in exchange for gaining the authority to approve all new taxes. When, however, the king and his minister of war, Albrecht von Roon, asked for additional money and a new military service law in 1860 in order to increase the size of the army, the parliament would not accept the royal proposal unless they were allowed to control important aspects of military service. This King William I refused as an affront to his royal authority. By 1862, all cooperation between king and parliament had ceased. Revolution was in the air and William thought of abdicating.[6]

The day was saved for the Prussian monarchy when Otto von Bismarck, who had been posted to Paris as Prussia's ambassador, agreed to serve William as Prime Minister. Bismarck pledged to uphold the king's royal prerogatives and not the constitution. He immediately intensified press censorship and prorogued the parliament, hoping to gain a more conservative body after new elections. He only succeeded in this goal after maneuvering Prussia into the two wars of the 1860s. After the 1866 war, Bismarck annexed to Prussia some of the north German states that had sided with Austria and forced the remaining countries north of the Main River to join a new North German Confederation. After the third war of German unification against France in 1870, the remaining independent German states were added to this Confederation, which now became the German Empire. The military victories of 1864 and 1866 so delighted nationalist sentiment in Prussia that Bismarck no longer needed to elect new parliamentarians to gain a majority in the Prussian parliament. Numerous former opponents now changed sides and formed a new party, the National Liberals, who together with conservatives backed Bismarck's policies. In 1867 the parliament retroactively legalized all of Bismarck's unconstitutional political activities, leaving little public alternative to the nationalistic acclamations of a united Germany's glory.[7]

Bismarck wrote a new constitution for the North German Confederation, which established a parliament to administer the new state. One of their first items of business was to debate an inaugural law on military service. Only three exemptions to the draft were proposed: the sons of the Prussian royal family who would, of course, have served as important government leaders in any case; the sons of the defeated ruling families of the minor German states; and the sons of Mennonite families of the Vistula Delta. After considerable debate, the first two exemptions were approved while the third one was struck down. King William I signed this draft law into effect on November 8, 1867.[8]

Prussian Mennonite Debates about the Draft

The Mennonite leadership was shocked by this turn of events and quickly worked out a lobbying strategy to persuade the government to preserve their military exemption. A delegation of five elders or leaders of congregations went to Berlin in October 1867 and again in February 1868. They met with King William I, his son the Crown Prince Frederick, representatives of both the House of Representatives and the House of Lords, and the majority of the Prussian cabinet ministers. This lobbying by Mennonite farmers of Prussia's top leaders resulted on several occasions in curious exchanges. At one point the War Minister, Albrecht von Roon, grabbed an elder's lapel and demanded to know if Mennonites believed that he as a soldier could get into heaven. The crown prince, when informed by the Mennonites that they would emigrate to Russia if their exemption was revoked, suggested they should go elsewhere, as the draft would be introduced there soon as well. In an unusual display of Mennonite generosity, one of the elders suggested to the king that they would gladly pay much higher taxes in exchange for maintaining the status quo. The result of all of this activity was that on March 3, 1868, the king signed a decree allowing Mennonites to serve in the army as noncombatants.[9]

This offer of compromise created a deep schism in the Mennonite community. Some advocated accepting military service outright or as noncombatants and using that service as leverage to end the special taxes and legal discrimination that Mennonites faced. A petition to parliament demanding full civil rights in exchange for accepting military service garnered signatures of almost 800 Mennonite males in 1868 and almost 1,300 in 1869. At the same time, over 1,800 Mennonites signed a counter-petition suggesting that they be stripped of their voting rights in exchange for permission to retain their exemption from military service. In the Heubuden congregation the issue finally led to an angry confrontation on Sunday, June 7, 1874, when Elder Gerhard Penner denied communion to church member Bernhard Fieguth, a freshly minted Prussian Mennonite soldier. In a case that went all the way to Prussia's High Court in Berlin, Penner's denial of communion to Fieguth was declared illegal, and Penner was forced to pay a substantial fine.[10] Thus the wars Prussia fought sparked bitter squabbling among Prussia's Mennonites, raising new questions about where one's enemies were to be found. The 1869 *Gesangbuch* was thus produced in a setting of incipient church schism.

The Three Songs concerning "Love of Enemies"

The desire for a new hymnal had been growing for a number of years. Already the foreword to the tenth and last Prussian edition of *Geistreiches Gesangbuch* noted the print run was being kept small since a new hymnal was being planned. This was in 1864, at the height of the constitutional crisis in Prussia and the same year as the war with Denmark.[11] An official decision was taken in 1865 by the conference of Mennonite congregations in West Prussia to elect a commission that was charged with producing a new hymnal.[12]

The rural congregations who sponsored this hymnal obviously rejected the simpler solution of adopting outright one of the two existing German Mennonite hymnals. South Germans had produced their first modern hymnal in 1832, *Christliches Gesangbuch zunächst für den Gebrauch der Evangelischen Mennoniten-Gemeinen in der Pfalz* (Christian Hymnal to be

Used by the Protestant Mennonite Congregations of the Palatinate). Already in 1856 they had released a third hymnal entitled *Gesangbuch zum Gottesdienstlichen und häuslichen Gebrauch in Evangelischen Mennoniten Gemeinden* (Hymnal for Church and Home Use in Protestant Mennonite Congregations).[13] The latter introduced a selection of three hymns entitled "Love of Enemies." Thus the rubric that appeared in the new 1869 *Gesangbuch* appears to have been borrowed from here.

A more immediate option, it seems, would have been to use the hymnal produced in 1854 by the local urban Danzig Mennonite church, *Gesangbuch zur kirchlichen und häuslichen Erbauung für Mennoniten-Gemeinden* (Hymnal for Spiritual Edification in Church and Home among Mennonite Congregations). Scholars have characterized the Danzig hymnal as more rationalistic and liturgical than that of the rural congregations.[14] In addition, it was also more patriotic, as it included sections on Christian government and the Fatherland. Lyrics included a prayer for God "to bless us by preserving our king on his throne."[15] Members of the Danzig Mennonite church were among those who had provided the intellectual arguments for accepting military service, so it is no surprise to find the tensions between more acculturated Mennonite soldiers and more traditional non-resistant Mennonites also reflected in the hymnals they produced.[16]

The rural Mennonites of the Vistula Delta in 1869 ultimately opted for selective borrowing from other sources instead of a wholesale adoption of another group's hymnal. While the rubric "Love of Enemies" had been borrowed from the south Germans, the constellation of songs compiled under it was new and unique to this hymnal.

The first song of the trio was also borrowed from the south Germans' 1856 *Gesangbuch*.[17] The lyrics of "Only where love is" ("Nur wo Lieb ist")[18] directly addressed the theological problem of hating one's enemies: "If you hate your enemy, know that thereby the kingdom of darkness has bound your spirit." Because both the author of these lyrics as well as the 1869 hymnal committee remain anonymous, there is no way to know for certain how or why this song was included in this hymnal. In adopting the hymn, the Prussians changed its tune. The south Germans sang it to the melody of "O wie selig sind die Seelen," a melody known also up north, since Prussians sang four hymns in their 1767 *Geistreiches Gesangbuch* to this tune. Yet they chose to set the text in their new hymnal to "Alles ist an Gottes Segen," a melody that was new to them but familiar to the Lutheran hymnody of their neighbors. The hymn "Only where love is" ("Nur wo Lieb ist") with its original tune crossed the Atlantic when the 1856 south German hymnal was reprinted in the United States in 1873 as the first official hymnal of the newly formed General Conference Mennonite Church. It appeared for the last time in a new hymnal in the General Conference's 1890 *Gesangbuch mit Noten*.[19]

1. Nur wo Lieb ist, da ist Wahrheit;
   ohne sie giebt's keine Klarheit,
   finster sind wir ohne sie.
   Heuchelnd wirst vor Gott du treten,
   wenn du nicht bedenkst beim Beten,
   daß er dich zum Bruder zieh'.

2. Denke nicht, der Herzensprüfer
   schau von deinem Wort nicht tiefer
   auf des Herzens Sinn und Rath.
   Hassest du den Feind, so wisse,
   daß das Reich der Finsternisse
   deinen Geist gebunden hat.

3. Nur die Sünde sollst du hassen,
   aber Sünder mild umfassen;
   sie zu richten, ziemt dem Herrn.
   Freut's dich, daß sie sind gebunden?
   Spottest du ob ihren Wunden?
   Komm, und hilf sie heilen gern!

9. Willst mit göttlichen Gefühlen
   du in leeren Worten spielen,
   und doch Christi Jünger sein?
   Geh zu ihm und lerne leben,
   lern im Leben das Vergeben,
   im Vergeben selig sein!

1. Only where love is can there be truth;
   without love we cannot see clearly,
   we are in darkness without it.
   You will appear before God as a hypocrite,
   if you forget when praying that
   God draws you near to your brother.

2. Do not think the one who tests your heart
   cannot see past your words
   and into the inclinations of your heart.
   If you hate your enemy,
   know that thereby the kingdom of darkness
   has bound your spirit.

3. The sin alone you should hate,
but the sinner embrace tenderly;
to judge them is for the Lord alone.
Do you rejoice that they are bound?
Do you laugh at their wounds?
Come and gladly help them heal!

9. Do you wish to feel divine,
yet play with empty words
and then still claim to follow Christ?
Go to Him and learn to live,
learn to forgive in life,
in forgiveness find blessing!

The second song in this section, "Jesus, since your blood has bought me" ("Jesu! Da du mich bekehret"), was a completely new hymn for Mennonite hymnody. The text was by Johann Jacob Moser (1702-1785), whom historians still consider important for his work in founding the modern German legal system. He worked as a law professor at the University of Tübingen, as president of the University of Frankfurt an der Oder, and as legal counsel to the nobles of the south German state of Württemberg. In the latter capacity he resisted the absolutist demands of the Duke of Württemberg to illegally turn over money needed to finance Württemberg's participation in the Seven-Years' War (1756-63). The Duke had Moser imprisoned in 1759 without bringing charges or putting him on trial. After the war concluded, he was released in 1764, having won widespread acclaim as a political prisoner and as a defender of the rule of law.

While in prison, Moser penned over 1,200 hymns, including the one Prussian Mennonites included in their 1869 *Gesangbuch*. Conservative Protestants known as Pietists celebrated the steadfast faith his hymns articulated.[20] Vistula Delta Mennonites were steeped in nineteenth-century Pietist literature and presumably picked up "Jesus, since your blood has bought me" ("Jesu! Da du mich bekehret") from there.[21] The tune, "Schmücke dich, O liebe Seele," was by Johann Crüger and is better known as the tune to "Soul, adorn thyself with gladness."[22] The hymn was also included in the General Conference's 1890 *Gesangbuch mit Noten* and disappeared from Mennonite hymnody after that. Perhaps the fact that Moser penned the final line of this hymn as a political prisoner made the text seem practical and appealing to the embattled Mennonites of the 1860s: "Oh, when will my enemies become God's friends and also mine?"

1. Jesu! da du mich bekehret,
   hast du mich auch dies gelehret,
   meinen Feinden zu vergeben,
   für ihr geist- und leiblich Leben
   und ihr übrig's Wohlergehen,
   inniglich zu dir zu flehen,
   auch mich immer mehr zu üben,
   sie von Herzensgrund zu lieben.

2. Es ist deine Gnadengabe,
   die ich von Natur nicht habe:
   und wenn ich nicht fleißig wache,
   regt sich leicht Zorn und Rache;
   wenigstens muß ich oft klagen,
   daß ich nicht von Lieb kann sagen;
   ja, ich könnt's geschehen lassen,
   wenn was träfe, die mich hassen.

3. Nun, laß auch in diesen Dingen
   deinen Geist mich weiter bringen;
   meine Schuld muß mich erwecken,
   ihre Schulden zuzudecken.
   Ja du wollest ihrer schonen,
   ihnen nicht nach Werken lohnen,
   und auch dort in jenen Welten
   meinetwegen nichts vergelten!

4. Sondern noch in diesem Leben
   Gnade zur Bekehrung geben,
   daß sie deinen Geist empfangen
   und Barmherzigkeit erlangen.
   Dies wird Haß in Freundschaft wandeln
   und sie lehren liebreich handeln.
   O, wann werden meine Feinde,
   Gottes und auch meine Freunde?

1. Jesus, since your blood has bought me,
   you have also kindly taught me
   how to forgive my enemies;
   to beseech you on bended knees,
   to bless their souls and bodies here
   and everything that they hold dear,

    and to instruct me for my part
    to love them dear with all my heart.
2. It is your gift of mercy
    that is not part of human nature,
    and if I do not watch with diligence,
    anger and vengeance arise easily.
    I must admit most often
    that I cannot speak of love;
    yes, I would gladly let it happen,
    let something smite those who hate me.
3. So in these things allow
    your spirit now to teach me;
    my own debts must alert me
    that their debts too have been paid.
    Yes, you want to release them,
    not judge them by their deeds,
    and in the world to come as well there
    should be no retribution on my account!
4. Better far in this life here
    to grant them the grace of conversion
    that they may receive your spirit
    and be taken up in your mercy.
    Transform thus hatred into friendship
    and teach them to do good.
    Oh, when will my enemies become
    God's friends and also mine?

The final hymn of this trio is the only one penned by a Mennonite. David Rothen (1805-1852) was born in Switzerland and moved to the Palatinate where he was baptized into the Mennonite congregation of Friedelsheim in 1830. He taught school nearby until he immigrated together with his wife Barbara in 1832 to the United States. In 1834 the couple settled near Bluffton, Ohio, where he continued to teach school until his death from typhoid at age 47.[23] His text "Transfigured bless'd Savior" ("Verklärter Erlöser") first appeared in the 1832 south German Mennonite *Gesangbuch*. It was set to the tune "Es glänzet der Christen" from 1825 by J. H. Tscherlitzky. Rothen's hymn enjoyed wide circulation, appearing in the 1856 south German hymnal and in the 1869 Prussian *Gesangbuch*, from whence it was taken up by the Russian Mennonites in their 1892 *Gesangbuch*.[24] In the United States, the song was included in the first General Conference hymnal, the 1890 *Gesangbuch mit Noten*, and in the last German-language hymnal of the Mennonite Church, *Deutsches Lieder- und Melodienbuch mit einem Anhang englischer Lieder* (German Song and Melody Book with an Appendix of English Songs).[25] "Transfigured bless'd Savior" was published in the General Conference's 1965 *Gesangbuch der Mennoniten*, used mostly in Canada and Latin America by German-speaking congregations.[26] It has also appeared in every hymnal of the south German Mennonites from 1832 to 1978, only to be dropped from the 2004 German Mennonite *Gesangbuch*.[27] This hymn thus enjoyed the most longevity of the three. The translation provided here is in meter and rhyme and can be sung to the tune available as hymn 598 in *Gesangbuch der Mennoniten* (1965) or as hymn 419 in *Gesangbuch* (1978). Echoes of the dramatic 1860s encounter of the Prussian Mennonites with German nationalism can be heard again if this hymn finds new singers in a new land.

The importance of these hymns for the Mennonite congregations of the Vistula Delta as they faced conscription in the 1860s cannot be determined precisely because we lack the records of the hymnal committee of the 1869 *Gesangbuch* and data on the frequency with which these three songs were sung. Out of 700 hymns in the 1869 *Gesangbuch*, only these three songs dealt explicitly with love of enemies. Clearly this aspect of theology was not as central to those Mennonite congregations as baptism or communion, represented by ten and thirty-five songs respectively. Nonetheless, the addition of songs on "Love of Enemies" in a Mennonite hymnal published in 1869 in a setting of growing nationalism and militarism is significant. A century earlier, conscription had not been an issue for Mennonites or indeed for most Europeans. The spread of universal conscription in the nineteenth century provoked opposition among Mennonites that in this case is illustrated by this innovation in their hymnody. This example is but one of many that demonstrate how opposition to conscription and military service came to shape Mennonite theology and practice in the second half of the nineteenth and first half of the twentieth centuries.

1. Verklärter Erlöser, sei freudig gepriesen
   von allen, die du bis zum Tode geliebt!
   Du hast dich als ewige Liebe bewiesen,
   Erbarmen und Gnade an Feinden geübt.
   Drum sollen die Deinen
   auch liebend erscheinen,
   als Kinder des Friedens,
   voll Sanftmuth und Milde,
   nach deinem erhabenen, göttlichen Bilde.

2. Nicht Freunden nur sollen wir Gutes erzeigen,
auch Feinden und Hassern mit Liebe und Huld,
ihr Schmähen erwiedern mit Segnen und Schweigen,
ihr Unrecht mit Wohlthun und Lammesgeduld.
Wir dürfen dem Triebe
der selbstischen Liebe
nicht folgen; wir müssen
den Fleischessinn brechen,
und nie uns gelüsten, uns selber zu rächen.

4. Was thaten denn vormals die gläubigen Zeugen?
Sie duldeten Güter-Raub, Marter und Pein,
Gefängniß und Folter mit flehendem Schweigen;
sie gingen durch Trübsal zur Herrlichkeit ein.
Sie litten mit Freuden
die bittersten Leiden.
Nichts konnte die Helden
zur Gegenwehr zwingen;
sie wollten die Krone des Lebens erringen.

5. O Heiland, auch uns gieb die göttlichen Triebe
der Sanftmuth und Güte zum Dulden in's Herz!
Auch gegen die Feinde erfüll' uns mit Liebe,
damit wir uns niemals bedienen des Schwerts!
Entreiß uns der Erden,
daß himmlisch wir werden,
und wie du mit Wohlthun,
mit Lieben und Segnen
dem Unrecht, dem Haß und dem Zorne begegnen.

1. Transfigured bless'd Savior, we lift praise eternal.
Your love cannot be by death from us riven.
You have revealed yourself to be love fraternal,
to enemies pity and mercy given.
Let those whom you draw near
As love's heralds appear,
as children of your peace,
with kindness filled and mild.
We follow the footsteps of God's worthy, pure child.

2. Not alone to our friends ought we do what is good.
No, also with love and respect enemies'
ill-treatment with mute blessings repay as we should,
injustice with charity greet on our knees.
Impulses dark and wild?
Self-centered love now riled?
No, our path is diff'rent,
From lusts earthly we break
so never to covet our own vengeance to take.

4. What did then the faithful, true witnesses of old?
They suffered through martyrdom, torment, and theft.
They met prison's torture with silence deep and bold.
No trials would leave them of glory bereft.
Suff'ring counted as gain,
joy then replaced great pain.
To violent self-defense
no force could bring them round
for they strove to hold fast to eternal life's crown.

5. O Savior, sincere longing in our hearts please give
with meekness and goodness suff'ring to endure!
With love for our enemies fill us so we live
without raising swords, Jesus, keep our hearts pure!
Lift us up from the earth,
bestow heaven's new birth,
so that we may, like you,
through our actions engage
with love's blessing deeds of injustice, hate and rage.

Notes

[1] My thanks to student assistants Victoria Eastes and Sam Schrag for locating musical and biographical information used in this article and to Professor William Eash, Anne Buller, Miranda Crile, Margaret Penner, Scott Janzen, Chris Janzen, Amber Celestin, Kara Stucky Janzen, and Aaron Linscheid for bringing these hymns back to life in performances in Beatrice, Nebraska; Waterloo, Ontario, and North Newton, Kansas.

[2] Danzig: Im Selbst-Verlage der Mennoniten-Gemeinden Westpreußens, 1869. This hymnal went through four editions to 1901. See *Mennonite Encyclopedia*, s.v. "Hymnology of the Mennonites of West and East Prussia, Danzig, and Russia," by Cornelius Krahn.

[3] For overviews of Mennonites in the Vistula Delta see Wilhelm Mannhardt, *Die Wehrfreiheit der Altpreußischen Mennoniten* (Marienburg: Selbstverlag der alt-

preußischen Mennonitengemeinden, 1863); H. G. Mannhardt, *Die Danziger Mennonitengemeinde: Ihre Entstehung und ihre Geschichte von 1569 - 1919* (Danzig: Selbstverlag der Danziger Mennonitengemeinde, 1919); and Horst Penner, *Die Ost- und Westpreußischen Mennoniten*, 2 vols. (Weierhof: Mennonitischer Geschichtsverein, 1978 and Kirchheimbolanden: Selbstverlag, 1987). English-language introductions are available in Peter J. Klassen, *A Homeland for Strangers: An Introduction to Mennonites in Poland and Prussia* (Fresno, CA: Center for Mennonite Brethren Studies, 1989) and *Mennonite Encyclopedia*, s.v. "West Prussia," by Horst Penner.

[4] *Gesangbuch in welchem eine Sammlung geistreicher Lieder befindlich*, 10th ed. (Danzig: Edwin Groening, 1864), iv. The first edition was printed in Königsberg in 1767. On the influential history of this hymnal, see Peter Letkemann, "The Hymnody and Choral Music of Mennonites in Russia, 1789-1915" (PhD diss., University of Toronto, 1985), 75-112 and "A Tale of Two *Gesangbücher*," in *Preservings* 18 (June 2001): 120-30 as well as Walter Jost, "The Hymn Tune Tradition of the General Conference Mennonite Church" (PhD diss., University of Southern California, 1966), 96-9, 115-29, 158-164.

[5] Penner, *Mennoniten*, 2:19-36; Mannhardt, *Wehrfreiheit*, 120-50; Mark Jantzen, "At Home in Germany? The Mennonites of the Vistula Delta and the Construction of a German National Identity, 1772-1880" (PhD diss., University of Notre Dame, 2002), 35-110.

[6] The centrality of the 1860s to German history is indicated in the structure of several influential surveys that break the history of nineteenth-century Germany at this date. See, for example, Thomas Nipperdey, *Germany from Napoleon to Bismarck, 1800-1866* (Dublin: Gill Macmillan Ltd, 1996) and the Oxford History of Modern Europe series: James Sheehan, *German History, 1770-1866* (Oxford: Clarendon Press, 1989) and Gordon Craig, *German History, 1866-1945* (New York: Oxford University Press, 1989, 1978). Hagen Schulze ends with 1867 in *The Course of German Nationalism: From Frederick the Great to Bismarck, 1763-1867* (New York: Cambridge University Press, 1991). On the political aspects of military service in the 1860s, see Gordon Craig, *The Politics of the Prussian Army, 1640-1945* (New York: Oxford University Press, 1955), 136-79; and Gerhard Ritter, *The Sword and the Scepter: the Problem of Militarism in Germany*, 4 vols. (Coral Gables: University of Miami Press, 1969-1973), 1:123-58.

[7] Craig, *German History*, 1-22.

[8] Otto Pflanze, *Bismarck and the Development of Germany*, 3 vols., 2nd ed. (Princeton: Princeton University Press, 1990), 1:341-61; Jantzen, "At Home in Germany?" 319-24.

[9] Peter Bartel, "Beschreibung der persönliche Bemühung der fünf Aeltesten bei den Hohen und Allerhöchsten Staatsmännern in Berlin um Wiederheraushelfung aus dem Reichsgesetz, worin der Reichstag uns Mennoniten am 9. November 1867 versetzt hat," *Christlicher Gemeinde-Kalender* 29 (1920): 70-79; Penner, *Mennoniten*, 2:69-79. A copy of the 1868 decree is reprinted in Penner, *Mennoniten*, 2:260.

[10] Jantzen, "At Home in Germany?" 329-57.

[11] 1864 *Gesangbuch*, 10th ed., viii.

[12] Abraham Driedger, "Die Entwicklung des Gemeindegesanges unsern westpreußischen Gemeinden," in *Mennonitische Blätter* 78, no. 4 (April 1931): 32.

[13] Published in Worms, this was a very influential hymnal in southern Germany, appearing in a third edition in 1950. Jost, "Hymn Tune Tradition," 61-73;

Mennonite Encyclopedia, s.v. "Hymnology of the Swiss, French, and South German Mennonites," by Harold S. Bender.

[14] Letkemann, "Two *Gesangbücher*," 128-30; Jost, "Hymn Tune Tradition," 93-4.

[15] *Gesangbuch zur kirchlichen und häuslichen Erbauung für Mennoniten-Gemeinden* (Danzig, 1854), no. 588.

[16] Jantzen, "At Home in Germany?" 291-301, 329-57; John D. Thiesen, "First Duty of the Citizen: Mennonite Identity and Military Exemption in Prussia, 1848-1877," *Mennonite Quarterly Review* 72.2 (April 1998): 161-87.

[17] *Gesangbuch zum Gottesdienstlichen und häuslichen Gebrauch in Evangelischen Mennoniten Gemeinden* (Worms, 1856), no. 434.

[18] The translations of hymn texts and titles are my own.

[19] Walter Hohmann, *Outlines in Hymnology with Emphasis on Mennonite Hymnology* (North Newton, KS: Self-published, 1941), 53, 63; Jost, "Hymn Tune Tradition," 148-58, 164-77.

[20] Reinhard Rürup, *Johann Jacob Moser: Pietismus und Reform* (Wiesbaden: Franz Steiner Verlag, 1965), 1-12; Andreas Gestrich, "Johann Jacob Moser als Politischer Gefangener," in *Johann Jacob Moser: Politiker, Pietest, Publizist*, ed. Andreas Gestrich and Rainer Lächele (Karlsruhe: G. Braun Buchverlag, 2002), 43-55.

[21] Jantzen, "At Home in Germany?" 216-25.

[22] This text and tune are no. 473 in *Hymnal: A Worship Book* (Newton, KS: Faith and Life Press, 1992).

[23] P. B. Amstutz, *Historical Events of the Mennonite Settlement in Allen and Putnam Counties, Ohio*, trans. Anne Konrad Dyck (Bluffton, OH: Swiss Community Historical Society, 1978), 42; *Mennonitische Lexikon*, s.v. "David Rothen," by Christian Neff and Ernst Crous.

[24] See Hohmann, *Hymnology*, 53, 66. The mislabeled "fifth edition" of this hymnal was published in 1929 in Canada for the 1920s immigrants; see *Mennonite Encyclopedia*, s.v. "Hymnology of the American Mennonites," by Harold S. Bender.

[25] Hohmann, *Hymnology*, 53, 66; Martin E. Ressler, *An Annotated Bibliography of Mennonite Hymnals and Songbooks 1742-1986* (Gordonville, PA, 1987), 35. *Deutsches Lieder- und Melodienbuch mit einem Anhang englischer Lieder* (Elkhart, IN: Mennonitische Verlagshandlung, 1895).

[26] *Gesangbuch der Mennoniten* (Newton, KS: Faith and Life Press, 1965), no. 598, under the rubric of "Anabaptist songs" (*"Täuferlieder"*).

[27] *Gesangbuch*, 2nd ed. (Ludwigshafen: Konferenz der Süddeutschen Mennonitengemeinden e. V., 1978), no. 419, under the heading of "Peace Witness" (*"Friedenszeugnis"*). Its omission from the new German Mennonite hymnal used by the south Germans was reported in an August 4, 2004 e-mail to the author from Torsten Seefeldt, vice-president of the Berlin Mennonite Church's board.

Identity and the Hymnal: Can Music Make a Person Mennonite?

Katie J. Graber

When people at Madison Mennonite Church sing during a Sunday worship service, they stand and hold their hymnals, facing the front in semicircular rows. With the help of the notation and words on the page, as well as their familiarity with many of the songs, they produce what they consider to be Mennonite music. At Madison Mennonite, this tends to be a cappella four-part harmony, with only occasional accompaniment from piano, acoustic guitar, or other instruments. Though most people in the congregation would agree that their singing is Mennonite music, dubious areas lie between that designation and other sounds and identities. What of the times the congregation sings a song from another hymnal or tradition? What if a group of non-Mennonites performs songs from a Mennonite hymnal? David Rempel Smucker tells the story of a Mennonite woman who left her home community to attend college and joined a choir led by another Mennonite. Though the rest of the choir was not Mennonite, the group frequently sang a song from the Mennonite hymnal that the woman associated with her home congregation.[1] This curious ability to transplant a memory or conception of Mennonite-ness into a (nearly) non-Mennonite setting shows the ability of discursive constructions to be flexible to the point of losing meaning. If I can perform my conception of Mennonite music with non-Mennonites, then where are the boundaries?

These flexible boundaries are enacted at Madison Mennonite Church, the church I currently attend, and the congregation with which I conducted surveys and interviews about music between summer 2003 and spring 2004.[2] Madison Mennonite is a congregation made up of people who consider themselves Mennonite because of "hundreds of years of Mennonite ancestors," as well as people who consider themselves "converted" or "non-ethnic" Mennonites. There is even at least one person who considers herself "of Mennonite heritage but not necessarily raised as a Mennonite."[3] The "ethnicity" and "heritage" these people refer to is largely Swiss-German or Russian. Madison Mennonite Church is the only Mennonite church in Madison, Wisconsin, a town of about 200,000 people. The church has a phone list (the closest it comes to having a membership record) of about 140 people, and the average weekly attendance is around 100. The majority of adults are between twenty-five and fifty years old, and over forty of the regular participants are under eighteen years old. Many people in the church are affiliated with the university in town, including professors and current and former graduate students. Several members hold graduate degrees from other institutions, including seminaries.

The level of musical education in the group ranges from private lessons to graduate study. In addition to the congregation's participation in singing during Sunday worship services, at least twenty different people are regularly involved in leading or providing music for services—this comes in the form of playing or singing a prelude, leading singing, or accompanying congregational singing. Several Madison Mennonite members make up a folk music group called Piecework, which has participated in the Mennofolk festival at Camp Friedenswald in Cassopolis, Michigan.[4] The group has played for church services, and the woman who writes many of their songs has also written hymns that the congregation sings on occasion.

Although this description seems straightforward, the definition of a Mennonite church—or of a Mennonite, for that matter—is not as simple as it may seem. Too often people conceive of definitions and identities as fixed entities, which leads to easy statements such as "Mennonite music is four-part a cappella singing." I will return to such statements, which I repeatedly heard in surveys and interviews, but I will situate them in a more flexible framework in order to discuss Mennonites, music, and the construction of meaning. The flexibility comes from understanding identity as grounded in the material interaction of language and social action. Madison Mennonite's church handbook demonstrates this approach when it states that "individuals who attend the worship and other church activities regularly may consider themselves members and will come to be acknowledged as members by others."[5] The act of attending church activities is connected to the linguistic label of membership; thus, people can call themselves members (or Mennonites) when their words and actions align with one another. These conceptions of identity combine actions and definitions of actions, working together to create a meaningful designation of identity.

Music affects this complex of identity formation when people attribute particular meanings to the act of singing and the sounds they produce.

Singing, the hymnal, and identity are three elements that encounter or collide with one another as people continually talk about and produce what they call Mennonite music. The process is dynamic, as each encounter has the potential to change and redefine the people and their ideas. Singing creates contexts in which Mennonites can perform their identity, while the hymnal physically and metaphorically ties together the concept of Mennonite music. The identity that singers produce or perform is just one of many aspects of the Mennonite musical tradition located outside of the hymnal, yet still closely related to it. Though Mennonite identity and Mennonite music cannot be found in one particular place, singing from the hymnal and suspending this action in a network of linguistic definitions helps pin down or produce a sense of their reality.

Singing: Performance and Condensation

In discussions of music at Madison Mennonite Church, people have collectively agreed to name four-part singing "Mennonite." Nearly every respondent to my first survey (Survey I) defined Mennonite music as "four-part," "a cappella," or "four-part a cappella" singing. At the same time, many people acknowledged that this was not the extent of the definition of Mennonite music. Several respondents included a disclaimer of some sort, such as one person who wrote that perhaps "this definition is somewhat narrow."[6] There is nothing inherently Mennonite in a cappella four-part singing: not all Mennonites sing in this style, and Mennonites are not the only people who sing this way. The question is, then, how can people continue to use this definition despite the divergence even within the North American Mennonite church? The continual process of defining Mennonite music as Madison Mennonite members do comes from singing a cappella, naming that action "Mennonite," and then experiencing a cappella singing as Mennonite. These steps do not actually fall in such discrete order, but rather always overlap with one another: each time we call singing "Mennonite" we are able to experience it as such, and each time we experience singing as Mennonite we are able to label it accordingly.

The alignment of designations and actions results in—or perhaps is caused by—the performance of identity. When people sing in a way they have designated Mennonite, they are performing their Mennonite-ness. Performance is a problematic concept in some Mennonite circles, since it connotes a sort of self-glorification that is contrary to Mennonite values of community and humility. Mennonite worshipers value participation over performance; participation is meant to generate a unified community that worships God rather than one that focuses on itself, or especially on any one particular member. In a unified community, no one should feel self-conscious or uncomfortably aware of his or her actions. This ideal is expressed in one woman's account of hymn singing in Marlene Kropf and Kenneth Nafziger's *Singing: A Mennonite Voice*: "I forgot about the people watching on the balcony. I forgot about the people seated around me. All I can remember is ... entering into the most perfect praise I knew how to do."[7] A member of Madison Mennonite articulated nearly the same idea when she wrote that "good singing experiences can occur when I am not self-conscious when I am singing. It's important for me to just enjoy the experience of participating in song without worrying that others will think I sound bad."[8] Rather than focusing on themselves or the actions they are involved in, these people value the music that allows them to forget themselves.

However, we can also value singing as performance when we understand performance in terms of our (worshipful) Mennonite identity. Everything we do and say is performative of some aspect of our identity. This conception of performing identity goes beyond the traditional idea of performance as the opposite of participation, and beyond the idea that performance is defined by pieces of art, works of music, performers and audiences. Performance of identity at Madison Mennonite church includes participating in music. In singing hymns together, people perform their identities as singers, as a congregation, and as Mennonites.

In order to describe the relationships between different kinds of performance—musical performance and identity performance—I turn to Paul Gilroy's work that questions the correlation between music and authentic ethnic or racial identity. Gilroy describes how identity formation or enactment can happen in the material performance of music:

> [Identity] is lived as a coherent (if not always stable) experiential sense of self. Though this identity is often felt to be natural and spontaneous, it remains the outcome of practical activity: language, gesture, bodily significations, desires. These significations are condensed in musical performance, although it does not, of course, monopolize them. In this context, they produce the imaginary effect of an internal racial core or essence by acting on the body through the specific mechanisms of identification and recognition that are produced in the intimate interaction of performer and crowd.[9]

Gilroy's discussion of racial identity can be applied to Mennonites, who often identify themselves by ethnicity as well as by religious belief, both in their community and in congregational music-making. Instead of "performer and crowd," we can think of the interactions between an individual singer and congregation. The moments of condensation Gilroy describes are those in which a Mennonite feels that everything makes sense, when discourse and definitions align with experiences. It is the particular interaction of music and language, situated in a community that continually negotiates its own definitions, that allows this process of identity formation.

The Hymnal: Physical Presence, Flexibility, and Continuity

The way Mennonites have held together a linguistic definition of Mennonite music is in large part through the physical presence of the hymnal. In my surveys, one person even defined Mennonite music as "a body of music encapsulated in the Mennonite hymnal."[10] Present-day Mennonites rely on the musical and textual notation in the hymnal more than do people in many other traditions and historical periods. When we sing hymns, we try to reproduce the song that is notated on the page, and even when we sing from memory, we are singing what we once learned from the book. Furthermore, we refer to songs by their placement within the hymnal; for example, people at Madison Mennonite Church (like other congregations, surely) easily match their favourite hymn titles to their numbers. Many Mennonites also collectively identify their hymnals by their physical appearance, calling them "the blue book" or "the red book."[11] Another respondent to my survey demonstrated the link some people make between sounds, actions, and the visual physical object when she defined Mennonite music as "singing hymns [and] songs out of the blue book and green book."[12] For her, Mennonite music is not just the written notation within the books, but also the act of making music from those notes. All of these definitions indicate that the Mennonite musical tradition depends on the physical existence of the hymnals, not only to aid the production of sound but also as one link between the elusive qualities we attribute to music, and the material experience of sound and self.

"The hymnal" is also a metaphorical concept that encompasses a wide variety of actual books. Within the Mennonite tradition, hymnals have changed radically throughout history. It is the conception of all of these books collapsed into a discrete object that allows so many Mennonites to claim the same musical heritage despite vast differences. Madison Mennonite participants were very aware of this configuration when they made the decision to purchase *Hymnal: A Worship Book* in 1992. Though some members suggested considering non-Mennonite hymnals, the discussion recorded in the minutes of a church meeting stated: "The desire to purchase the new hymnal to preserve and augment our ties to the wider Mennonite church was . . . strongly voiced."[13] Owning the same concrete object as other Mennonite churches would allow them to participate in a larger shared musical heritage. The notated hymns give substance to the immaterial sounds they hear and participate in making at other Mennonite churches, meetings, and conventions.

Although people tend to think of "the hymnal" as one object, even North American Mennonite hymnals have changed through the years in language, musical style, and specific content.[14] In 1803 and 1804, Mennonite groups in the United States published new hymnals that incorporated musical notation for the first time. Later hymnals abandoned unison singing in German for four-part harmony in English. In the twentieth century, Mennonite hymnals have included gospel songs, Taizé songs, and international hymns.[15] Changes and additions to each new hymnal were often controversial at the time of publication; however, despite differences in opinion about content, the songbooks were (and still are) considered Mennonite hymnals.

All of these changes reflect trends in other Protestant denominational hymnals as well—Mennonites follow wider society much more closely than we like to think. Many users of Mennonite hymnals are not aware of the book's history, nor of its close relationship to broader culture. I asked Madison Mennonite participants to guess the dates of hymns in *Hymnal: A Worship Book*, and the number of hymns written by Mennonites. Twelve of the sixteen respondents guessed a higher-than-actual percentage of Mennonite-written texts or music—the highest estimate was 92 percent, whereas the actual number of hymns in *Hymnal: A Worship Book* that are written, translated, arranged, or composed by Mennonites or Anabaptists is only about 8 percent.[16] The majority of respondents also believed that more texts and tunes were from the 1600s and fewer were from the 1900s than is actually the case. About 8 percent of the texts and 3 percent of the music in *Hymnal: A Worship Book* originated in the 1600s, and most people guessed at least 10 percent; about 29 percent of texts and 26 percent of music originated in the 1900s, and most people guessed 20 percent or less.[17] These figures show that Mennonites assume their hymnal to be more tied to Mennonite tradition than it actually is. More input from Mennonites and from the time of the earliest Mennonites would imply that the book is more distinctive and less connected to the inclinations of mainstream America's Protestant hymnals. Despite the changes to our hymnals and their reflections of broader society, these books have been consistently viewed, used, and talked about specifically as "Mennonite music" by the people of Madison Mennonite and many other Mennonite churches.

Although the contents of the current hymnal distinguish it from earlier Mennonite hymnals, the variety within it allows one single book to be used in a range of ways, and thus allows many different types of people and groups—who may have different beliefs and ethnicities—to claim the same Mennonite musical identity. Mennonites' relationships to the hymnal allow them a feeling of stability as they orient themselves as individuals and as communities around this conception of an unchanging physical object that is present in so many churches across North America. The concept of "the hymnal" (all of the historical books under one heading) allows flexibility as well, as it has taken on different meanings throughout the historical changes experienced by Mennonite groups, reflecting the continual redefinition of individual and group identity. The hymnal is additionally important because of its connection to identity and language. We call our hymnals Mennonite, and therefore the songs within them are Mennonite and the singing of those songs is a Mennonite act.

Identity: Materiality and the Ineffable

The power of Mennonite singing lies not in some mystical, unspeakable, disembodied realm but in the physical performance of community oriented around the hymnal. Jeff Todd Titon, in his study of an Appalachian Baptist group, argues that most language in religious services is functional, or "put simply, language in religious practice not only says something but also does something. A worshiper who prays not only says a prayer but performs the act of praying."[18] Titon includes singing in this conception of "language in religious practice," and he describes how these linguistic events are also acts of creation: "The very existence of a prayer," he explains, "depends on its performance. The prayer (sermon, testimony, etc.) is the utterance."[19] In the same way, the existence of a song is dependent on the act of singing— or as Nancy Rosenberger Faus explains, "music is not only an aid to worship but an act of worship itself."[20] These embodied situations, that is, the act of singing and talking about singing, effectively construct the entity from the inside. In other words, the act of singing creates Mennonite music, and thus helps create what "Mennonite" is.

Although I argue that the hymnal is central to the Mennonite musical tradition, I do not mean to imply that it is meaningful in itself or on its own. The people and situations around the hymnal help give it significance. Yet at the same time, aspects of Mennonite musical tradition that are not in the book are paradoxically related to it. Our songs and conversations about Mennonite music are dependent on the stability of a written tradition, but they are also given an ineffable feeling because of their relationship—of absence—to the hymnal. The sounds and the physical experiences of singing that cannot be notated seem transcendent because they are not contained in the hymnal. Feelings of belonging and connection to the past and to other Mennonites—all important aspects of identity formation—are not written into the hymnal. Neither are the physical sensations that respondents to my surveys repeatedly mentioned, those unexplainable effects of singing that sent shivers down their spines or raised the hair on their arms. People claimed that words could not explain these musical phenomena, implying that language, like the notated hymnal, relies on something beyond itself for its full meaning. Likewise, the "I just can't explain it" part of singing relies on the hymnal: if we did not have the physical object of the hymnal with its notation, then we would not have this excess. The notation seems mundane, and it is this contrast to the beyond-ness of singing that feels so sublime.

In the same way that the bodily act of singing is related to the ethereal sounds and feelings it can produce, the tradition of naming certain music and identities as Mennonite has both physical and extra-physical qualities that are linked and give one another stability and sublimity. The acts of singing and talking about singing take place in material spaces between physical people, but at the same time these acts point to something beyond the immediate context. Kropf and Nafziger comment on these kinds of interactions in a section titled "Crossing the boundaries of time" when they claim, "the physical act of singing together creates a bond not only in the present but with memories of the past."[21] These memories and expectations are constituted through language and can in this way be united in a musical present. Thus, the importance of music in any Mennonite church today draws its power from discursive constructions of individual and group history.

Even with this grounding in material language, defining Mennonite music and identity is slippery since there is no essence, no one thing (or even a stable group of characteristics, qualities, or activities) that we can call Mennonite. Rather, our identities and musical practices are continually defined and redefined through actions that we label Mennonite, and conversely, through practices labeled Mennonite that we act out. Because these understandings come about through linguistic representations and series of actions, our identity is never present in a full and united way. I cannot understand or articulate the entirety of my identity, but I can condense it for a moment into a word (for example, "Mennonite") or an action (such as singing). When Mennonites sing, then, we are both representing a single identity, which can never truly exist as a unified whole, and performing a fragmentary identity, which we represent as unified in order to understand and experience ourselves as stable. This process of performing and constructing identity can only happen through mutual belief in the meaning of symbolic practices held together by discourse. Networks of words and meanings determine the content and limit of "Mennonite," and the way people and practices relate to each other is constrained by these constructions.

The reason that language can be meaningfully attached to social actions such as singing is because of the materiality of both. We often think of language—like musical sounds—as ethereal, disembodied, and immaterial. In actual practice, though, both language and music rely on our physical bodies in social situations. At Madison Mennonite, singers see and hear other bodies when they stand as a group, hold their hymnals, and create their sounds. They attach those material resonances, the physical feeling of singing in four parts, to historically situated definitions—at this moment in Madison, the common definition maintains that "Mennonite music is a cappella four-part singing." This connection between the sounds, physical sensations, and definitions allows people at Madison Mennonite to define a cappella singing as more Mennonite than other sounds and physical sensations.

Conclusion: Exclusion and Identity

Performing or enacting community through singing is a participatory act; at the same time, any group of people implicitly defines itself by the exclusion of non-members. People at Madison Mennonite Church see their musical identity as different from that of other churches. One member wrote, "Mennonites feel that four-part a cappella singing is unique and we are proud that many members of a Mennonite church are comfortable singing in parts."[22] She uses singing to distinguish Mennonites from non-Mennonites, but Mennonites also use singing to distinguish themselves from other Mennonites. Madison Mennonite Church's use of four-part a cappella singing is often held in contrast to praise songs and accompanied singing. The group in Madison is able to feel like a community in part because of its separation from other groups. This necessity of defining oneself by exclusion is the structure of prejudice and conflict, and music contributes to this process when participants use music to perform their identity. Yet if people and groups can understand identity as something that is flexible and continually defined, they can be more accepting and tolerant of different viewpoints and musical tastes within the church. Understanding identity in terms of the interplay between language, social action, and physical sensations is one foundation for this kind of flexibility.

By continually singing and talking about singing, many Mennonites have collectively agreed that it is important to Mennonite identity. My answer to the question "Can music make a person Mennonite?" is yes, though not in any simple way that claims "I sing, therefore I am Mennonite," or "I'm Mennonite, therefore I sing." Rather, it is the complex interaction and layering of actions, objects, sounds, and words that construct what we together understand as Mennonite identity. We understand our identity through the use of the hymnal, as well as through those elusive moments when the ephemeral aspects of music and discourse line up with our physical experiences. If all of the divergent aspects of identity performance, the ineffable element of the experience of musical sounds, and the embodied social actions that present and represent identity can converge with our definitions of identity, we have allowed for the broadest possibilities for musical meaning.

Notes

[1] David Rempel Smucker, "Lifting the Joists: How German-Speaking Mennonites Became English Hymn Singers," *Christian Living* 48, no. 8 (2001): 24.

[2] Surveys were conducted by email or hard copy (Surveys I and II) and during adult Christian Education discussions (Christian Education Surveys A, B, and C). See Appendix for a complete copy of survey questions.

[3] Responses from Survey I.

[4] For further discussion on Mennofolk events in Ontario and Manitoba, see Allison Fairbairn's paper, "Mennofolk Manitoba:Artistic, Cultural, and Generational Mediation in a Music Festival Setting," in this volume.

[5] Madison Mennonite Church Handbook, 1.

[6] Anonymous respondent to Survey I.

[7] Marlene Kropf and Kenneth Nafziger, *Singing: A Mennonite Voice* (Scottdale, PA: Herald Press, 2001), 84.

[8] Emily Polanco, respondent to Survey II.

[9] Paul Gilroy, "Sounds Authentic: Black Music, Ethnicity, and the Challenge of the Changing Same," *Black Music Research Journal* 11, no. 2 (Fall 1991): 127.

[10] Anonymous respondent to Survey I.

[11] The "blue book" is *Hymnal: A Worship Book* (Elgin, IL: Brethren Press; Newton, KS: Faith and Life Press; Scottdale, PA: Mennonite Publishing House, 1992). The "red book" is *The Mennonite Hymnal* (Scottdale, PA: Herald Press and Newton, KS: Faith and Life Press, 1969). These two hymnals consist largely of hymns written in four parts, many of which also appear in other Protestant hymnals. Compared to earlier hymnals, *Hymnal: A Worship Book* includes more hymns from outside of North America and Europe, as well as more songs consisting of a sung melody with instrumental accompaniment.

[12] Caroline Brock, respondent to Survey I. The "green book" refers to *Sing and Rejoice! New Hymns for Congregations*, ed. Orlando Schmidt (Scottdale, PA: Herald Press, 1979), another songbook used at Madison Mennonite Church. This book includes more melodies with guitar or piano accompaniment than either *Hymnal:*

A Worship Book or *The Mennonite Hymnal.*

[13] "Madison Mennonite Church Congregational Meeting – Wednesday 11 September 1991: Minutes," p. 2 (held at Madison Mennonite Church archives). Thanks to Madison Mennonite Church archivist Leila Shenk for directing me to these sources.

[14] For a more detailed examination of Mennonite hymnals in North America, see Mary Oyer, "The Sound in the Land," in this volume.

[15] Taizé songs generally consist of a brief, four-part harmonic ostinato for the congregation with instrumental or solo vocal additions. See "Music of the Taizé Community," in *Hymnal: Accompaniment Handbook*, ed. Kenneth Nafziger and Rebecca Slough (Elgin, IL: Brethren Press; Newton, KS: Faith and Life Press; Scottdale, PA: Mennonite Publishing House, 1993), 307. One example of a Taizé song is *Hymnal: A Worship Book*, no. 247.

[16] Christian Education Survey A. I calculated these statistics from the list at "Anabaptist and Mennonite Hymns Index," Mennonite.net, http://hymns.mennonite.net/anabaptist_and_mennonite.shtml [Accessed 4 June, 2004].

[17] Christian Education Survey A.

[18] Jeff Todd Titon, *Powerhouse for God: Speech, Chant, and Song in an Appalachian Baptist Church* (Austin: University of Texas Press, 1988), 206.

[19] Ibid., 207.

[20] Nancy Rosenberger Faus, "Music in the Church of the Brethren," in *The Importance of Music in Worship*, edited by Nancy Rosenberger Faus (Scottdale, PA: Mennonite Publishing House, 1993), 22. Faus makes this statement about the Church of the Brethren, another Anabaptist group that participated in the creation of the *Hymnal: A Worship Book.*

[21] Kropf and Nafziger, *Singing: A Mennonite Voice*, 54.

[22] Kathy Nissley, respondent to Survey I.

Appendix

Surveys I and II were conducted through e-mail or hard copy, between summer 2003 and spring 2004. Not everyone answered every question, and people often gave more than one answer to a question. The complete results are held at Madison Mennonite Church Archives.

Survey I questions

    Name:

    Age:

    Occupation, hobbies, how you spend your time:

- How long have you attended Madison Mennonite Church (MMC)?
- In addition to attending, how are you involved at MMC? (setting up, reading scripture, attending potlucks and other MMC groups, etc.)
- What other churches or Christian institutions have you attended/been affiliated with and how? (schools, service organizations, etc.)

Identity and the Hymnal

- Describe any musical activities associated with those other organizations (choirs, singing for prayer or worship services).
- What does the phrase "Mennonite music" mean to you?
- What is your sense of how Mennonites as a group think and talk about Mennonite music? For example, how do we define "Mennonite music," and why and how is it meaningful in specific contexts or generally?
- Do you remember reading or being told these things, or how did you come to these conceptions?
- Do your own thoughts on these questions generally agree or disagree with these ideas?
- What is your musical background outside of a church setting?
- Can you read music?
- What part do you sing in four-part hymns?
- How did you learn to sing that part?
- Are you able to improvise harmony or a descant along with a melody line?
- What are some of your favorite hymns? least favorite? Can you articulate why you like or dislike them?
- Are the words or sound of a hymn most important to you?
- Please try to describe the sound of your favorite hymn, of Madison Mennonite singing, or of Mennonite music in general.
- Are there types of hymns that you like more or less than others?
- If you had to help compile the next Mennonite hymnal, what would you change? What would you preserve? What do you think would present difficulties?
- Do you ever disagree with the text of a hymn? How do you deal with that?
- If you could change something about Madison Mennonite music, what would it be?
- Is there anything else you'd like to say on the topic of Mennonite music?
- Would you be willing to be interviewed further? In person, by phone or by e-mail?
- May I use your name along with your answers in a paper or presentation?

Survey II questions

- What hymnal did you grow up with?
- What do you remember of your church's change to the *Hymnal: A Worship Book* (the blue hymnal)?
- And/or
- What were your first perceptions of the *Hymnal: A Worship Book*?
- Do you think the music at MMC has changed since you started attending?
- For example: use of instruments, songs commonly sung, other…
- What is your religious and ethnic background?
- How do you think this affects your experience as a Mennonite at MMC, if at all?
- Do you have any other comments about ethnicity in the Mennonite church?
- Do you see ethnicity affecting musical practices or traditions in the Mennonite church?
- Do you have any other comments on gender, class or any other related issues?
- What happens when you sing? How do you feel, what do you think about, etc.? How does this happen, what contributes to both good and bad experiences?

Christian Education Surveys

The following surveys I conducted in person, during my presentations on Mennonite music during Christian Education (Madison Mennonite Church's version of Sunday School). Christian Education attendance is lower than that of the regular worship service, and during these three weeks there was another option for people to attend. Thus, the number of respondents varied each week. I led discussions on the history of the hymnal, music and identity, and music at Madison Mennonite Church, and I began each session by asking attendees to write answers to the questions below. Because I conducted these surveys orally, the questions may not have been exactly as stated, and respondents could ask questions and clarifications as they answered. All of these were anonymous.

Christian Education Survey A (November 16, 2003)

- What percent of *Hymnal: A Worship Book* is written by Mennonites/Anabaptists?
- What time/era are most of the hymns from (guess percentages)?

- What do you mean by old-time/old-fashioned hymns? Who sang them, when were they regularly sung, when were they written?

Christian Education Survey B (November 23, 2003)
- Do you identify yourself as Mennonite?
- What does that mean to you? (Why or why not?)
- What are some other ways (words you use) you identify yourself?
- How is Mennonite music unique/different from other denominations?
- How is MMC music unique/different from other Mennonite churches?

Christian Education Survey C (November 30, 2003)
- What hymnal did you grow up with?
- Did your church have a choir?
- How often did it practice?
- How often did it perform? Only on Sundays, or other times as well?
- What kinds of instruments were used in your church? Solos or as accompaniment to singing?

Voices at the Edges

Tangle

Di Brandt

Tangle of wild tansy
in every crack

old rag and bone shop
left open
to rain

Clear high notes
piercing the sky

Like weeds, grandma said

The knife edge of pleasure

forced to dance
blitzed by love, oh

Underground rivers

Diamonds

leaf mould

Waking Early

    Transparencies

    Pink dawn

        above the trees

    Poetry of birds

      symphonic,

            country matters ....

      yawn

     slow   pleasuring

          the day

two poems from AWAKENINGS (after Dorothy Livesay)

Benjamin Horch as an Insider-Outsider Musical-Theological Visionary

Doreen H. Klassen

A visitor who knew "Uncle Ben," as many a musician affectionately called Benjamin Horch, might have been welcomed to his home in Winnipeg, Manitoba by a song, and often by the following quodlibet, while his beloved wife Esther chided him saying, "Oh Ben, give her a chance to sit down first":

> O wir warten auf den Heiland bis er kommt,
>   (O we're waiting for the Saviour 'til he comes)
> She'll be comin' 'round the mountain when she comes,
> O wir warten auf den Heiland,
> She'll be comin' 'round the mountain
> O wir warten auf den Heiland bis er kommt.

Although Horch would sing the song with a twinkle in his eye, the song nevertheless expressed some of the serious issues that concerned him throughout his life. It alternated a language that Mennonites had spoken historically (German) with one used in their contemporary Canadian cultural environment (English), and so indexed the cultural and musical changes they had experienced in their numerous geographic relocations. Furthermore, it demonstrated the accessible, folk-like nature of hymn tunes, yet seemed to suggest, almost irreverently, that conventional sacred-secular dichotomies are irrelevant. But what was the twinkle in his eye about? What motivated this man, this romantic dreamer who could visit his internist and come home with financial support for the writing of a new symphonic work, a Mennonite piano concerto no less?[1]

Born into a musical Lutheran family that was more likely to discuss the Bachs and the Mendelssohns than the Friesens and Penners at the dinner table, Horch was brought to Winnipeg from a village near Odessa (Ukraine) as a two-year-old in 1909. His parents, desirous of a more evangelical religious experience, left the Lutheran church for the North-End Mennonite Brethren (MB) Church where Horch's love for music was nurtured through choral and youth orchestra opportunities. Horch soon distinguished himself as a vocal soloist—in school musicals, in the Winnipeg Festival, and in Anglican and Mennonite circles alike. Already as a young man, he gained recognition as a conductor and won the affections of a prominent MB minister's daughter, Esther Hiebert, also a fine vocal soloist and later a hymnologist, radio program host, and social worker.

According to Horch's biographer, Peter Letkemann,[2] Horch never applied for a job, whether as itinerant choral workshop leader in Mennonite churches across Canada, founder of the music program at the Mennonite Brethren Bible College (MBBC) in Winnipeg in 1944, or program host at radio stations such as CFAM in southern Manitoba in the late 1950s and later at the Winnipeg studios of the Canadian Broadcasting Corporation (CBC). During retirement years and virtually until his death in 1992, Horch turned to synthesizing his ideas concerning church music and to promoting the commissioning of classical compositions such as the *Mennonite Piano Concerto*, works based on the folk musical idioms of ethnic minorities.[3] The piano concerto may have been the apex of a half-century of Horch's persistent efforts as a musical innovator within the Mennonite church, a role often criticized by those who failed to understand the historical, sociological, and theological bases for Horch's vision, yet lauded by those who drew inspiration from his passionate pursuit of musical integrity.

In conversation and informal writings, Horch identified several sets of seemingly oppositional concepts fundamental to ways in which he wanted to shape musical thinking and practice, particularly among Mennonites. Four of these issues addressed in this discussion include: 1) the interrelationship of text and music; 2) the role of performance versus composition in a church music education program; 3) the function of the chorale versus the gospel song tradition of the *Kernlied*;[4] and 4) the relationship between ethnic minority and dominant society musical traditions. These four issues bring us chronologically through Horch's life. The first two—the interrelationship of text and music, and the nature of musical education in the church— were concerns for Horch in his mid-century involvement with MB institutions and their modes of musical praxis. The third issue — the chorale versus the *Kernlied*—expressed Horch's on-going attempt to establish a balance between conventional church music and more contemporary, charismatic idioms. The last issue explores the role of music in establishing an ethnic minority voice within a dominant society, an issue he actively pursued in his later years.

With respect to the first issue—the interrelationship of text and music—Horch shared with other Mennonites in positions of musical leadership a commitment to foregrounding the text of a vocal or choral composition. Like other musicians, he strove to communicate the essence of the text, yet his methods often left him open to criticism by those who felt his approach favoured the musical aspects of hymns, anthems, and classical choral works over their textual components.

The conventional approach used by Horch's Mennonite critics in the early to mid-twentieth century was to focus on musical accuracy in a manner they claimed would highlight the text. Consequently, these conductors focused on pitch, note values, enunciation, and maintaining a strict tempo when they rehearsed with their church choirs. Horch's critics assumed that accuracy within these musical aspects would allow the words of the song to communicate with its listeners. For these conductors, the music was considered to be at the service of the lyrics, or "the message," as they called the text.

Horch, believing that it was the musical element that gave life to the lyrics, focused on painting the text with a musical brush, emphasizing contrasting dynamics and flexible tempi. Young people were inspired by Horch's passion. In fact, one of his former students recalled his experience at a *Saengerfest*,[5] the song festival which characteristically ended week-long regional Mennonite choral music workshops throughout Ontario and western Canada, saying:

> We were sitting in the balcony in the Herbert Church and the downstairs was loaded with music . . . it was a terribly wide church . . . one of those old ones. And Ben Horch was using the whole width of it—running to the piano with his hair all over the place, and his arms—like he needed the whole front, just as excited as he could be. And that for us, for me, was a beautiful experience . . . like music can be exciting stuff. . . . And then coming to college here, actually having him as a teacher was a highlight.[6]

Young people, like this young man, were enthralled, but the elders were shocked by Horch's antic—his "wild" ways, they called them—and particularly by the fact that he conducted with two hands. To his critics Horch would say that one would drive a tractor with both hands and besides, "why conduct with only one hand and have the other one just hanging like a sausage?" Conducting with only one hand, for Horch, was equivalent to acting as a metronome, and so because he felt the power of the music, he conducted with two hands, the one maintaining the *Takt*, as he called the metrical aspect of the music, and the other infusing the text with life by elasticizing the metre and drawing out contrasting dynamics. Young people who studied with Horch brought to their churches a positive response to the oft-asked question—*"Kann die Kunst zum Ehre des Herrn dienen?"* (Can art serve to honor God?)—because Horch had enabled them to discover and express the artfulness of a Brahms symphony within a gospel song.[7]

The second dichotomy, identified in this discussion as the role of performance versus composition in music education, brought to light contradictory notions of what constituted an adequate education for a church musician. Discussion on this issue included questions such as: Should all students in a Bible college be expected to study music or only those deemed "musical"? Should the repertoire of the church musician consist of the hymnal and the occasional choral anthem, or could it also include classical choral works? Should the instrumental accompaniment for hymns consist of the piano only as was common in many MB churches, an electric organ, or also the orchestral instruments that many young people were beginning to study? Additionally, should the focus for a church college music education be the performance of a prescribed repertoire, or should the church musician also be expected to compose or arrange music for the choir?

Although Horch subscribed strongly to an essentially lay musical tradition within the church, he nevertheless assumed that even the laity had to be trained to sing, whether through choral workshops or a college music program. That Horch's vision went beyond conventional understandings of participation is evident from the reluctance with which his theological colleagues welcomed him at church-related educational institutions. In fact, Horch reports that when he was first hired to begin the music program at MBBC, the president, A. H. Unruh, told him, "We really didn't want you, but Kroeker [who had paid for Horch's education at Biola College] insisted. But, now that you're in our midst, we hope you'll feel welcome."[8]

Why this guarded welcome? What did Horch's theological colleagues fear? Problems arose essentially from differing understandings of what constituted church music and consequently on what constituted an adequate education for those in positions of musical leadership within the church. For Horch, the curriculum was an expansion of the regional choral workshops held over the preceding decades in Russia and Canada, so it included the mass choir of the workshops which, in the college context, began to perform sacred oratorios—works sometimes considered too "artful" by his critics—and a smaller a cappella or unaccompanied choir, capable of performing more challenging classical repertoire. To enhance the performances of the oratorio choir, Horch also established the Mennonite Symphony Orchestra, a far cry from simply singing hymns with piano accompaniment as some of his theologian colleagues had envisioned. Horch regarded the orchestra as a means of involving a large group of young people in accompanying choral music, as well as a way of avoiding one of the essential weaknesses he saw in liturgical musical traditions, namely, the overpowering of the human voice by the pipe organ.[9] Inherent in training singers and orchestral players, as well, was the need for leaders with more sophisticated conducting skills.

But even more significant was Horch's vision that the curriculum would develop the composition skills of church musicians who would learn to create an indigenous Mennonite choral repertoire. This repertoire would include both new compositions and through-composed anthems,[10] or what Horch called "emergent Mennonite anthems," based on *Kernlieder* and other selectively-borrowed "Mennonite" hymns.[11] Thus, the curriculum would encourage music students to write choral and instrumental compositions rooted in their own musical and theological heritage. Just as theologians were taught to exegete and make memorable the scriptures, so, Horch thought, musicians were to extemporize and make memorable the rich hymnic heritage of the Mennonites.

The failure of MBBC administrators to understand Horch's vision resulted in the curtailment of the composition program. This left the college's Sacred Music Program with only its performance component. It was beholden to traditions outside of the church and open to the suspicion that its goal was to serve its own performance and artistic ideals, yet students returned to their churches and drew the youth through performances of oratorios, dynamic hymn singing, and by occasionally sneaking in one of their own compositions although modesty, and at times fear, prevented them from identifying them as their own work.[12]

The third dichotomy, the one I call the *Kernlied* versus the chorale, is addressed most fully in Horch's twenty-nine-page document, "The Mennonite Brethren Church: A History of its Musical Development, 1860-1984." This manuscript was primarily an extended letter to his former MBBC colleague, J. B. Toews, who in his later years admitted the short-sightedness of his earlier resistance to Horch's ideas and now invited Horch to rearticulate his vision for church music education. But Horch also wrote in response to former MBBC president A. H. Unruh's accusation that Horch had awakened *ein Sinn fuer die Musikbildung* (a mindset for music education) among the young people.

The "rough draft"[13] that Horch eventually sent to Toews in the mid-1980s had six sections, although only the first two were developed in depth. These placed non-conformist church music traditions, and particularly the MB musical tradition, within a historical continuum, and demonstrated the historic tension between the *Kernlied* and the chorale. The first section provided a historical background by identifying "Four streams of congregational song histories" culminating with "The sixteenth-century non-conformist Anabaptist era."[14] In the second section, "The awakening of *ein Sinn fuer die Musikbildung*" in the MB church, Horch referred to four distinctive musical awakenings: first, 1860—the beginning of the Mennonite Brethren Church in the southern Ukraine; second, the North End Chapel in Winnipeg, Manitoba where ministers provided musical leadership, often to reach out to the youth;[15] next, the *Dirigenten Kurse Leiter* (choral workshop leaders) of 1913-1944, a category in which Horch differentiated the rural workshops modeled on the Russian Mennonite tradition from the urban workshops, influenced by more sophisticated music education in the public schools and the impact of music festivals; and lastly, the founding of the Music Department at MBBC in 1944.

The other four sections of the paper were still to be developed, so consisted primarily of headings. The first two of these were "The classical awakening," as Horch called the impact of choral workshops and MBBC on the youth, and "The merging twentieth century worship pattern tradition," which encompassed the post-1960s blending of liturgical and non-conformist traditions. The final two sections—"The twentieth century MB composer" and "The Anabaptist Mennonite composer of the twenty-first century"— appeared only as headings in the paper but frequently crept into conversations. These were to some extent prophetic, as the range of "Mennonite" compositions at the 2004 Sound in the Land conference ably demonstrated.

For Horch, the most significant aspect of MB musical development was those junctures he identified as "musical awakenings," eras when a new musical genre became associated, particularly among the youth, with spiritual renewal. The bulk of his discussion is devoted to three awakenings he considered significant turning points within the MB church as a whole: "1860," as he called it, "the classical awakening," and the "Christian rock" era.[16] The first awakening, the 1860 separation of the Mennonite Brethren from the larger Mennonite church, was significant for Horch because of its strong musical component. The newly-formed church distinguished itself from the larger group both by singing *Kernlieder*, German translations of American gospel songs, or songs of hurt and hope as Horch often called them, rather than the traditional chorales, and also by using lay choirs rather than the conventional *Vorsaenger* to introduce this repertoire, thus affirming the congregational nature of this breakaway group.[17] The second musical awakening, Horch claimed, occurred in the mid-twentieth century when Canadian Mennonite young people developed *ein Sinn fuer die Musikbildung* both through the inspiration communicated by well-trained choral conductors as well as through exposure to classical works that combined musical sophistication with theological depth. The third musical awakening, the one Horch felt the church was involved in at the time of his writing, he called the Christian rock era, a time when young people were once again rejecting a musical idiom gone stagnant, in this case conventional hymnody, and replacing it with a dynamic alternative which spoke renewal to and for them.

But Horch often expressed the nature of renewal and its tension with tradition in more abstract terms. Although he spoke frequently of the *Kernlied* as the musical root of the Mennonite Brethren, as opposed to the chorale which typified other Mennonite groups, for Horch, the *Kernlied* and chorale were not only literal genres but also metaphors. Most often, the *Kernlied* represented for Horch the exuberance of spiritual awakening expressed musically in any genre, so from that standpoint, the historic *Kernlieder*, the classical anthems and oratorios of the mid-century, and also the 1970s-80s Christian rock explosion were each in turn a kind of *Kernlied*. At other times he decried the absence of the *Kernlied*, or in other words, historical musical continuity in the MB Church, particularly in the *Worship Hymnal* of 1971, a denominational hymnal which introduced a more formal English worship tradition to replace the balance of chorale and *Kernlied* that Horch and his colleagues had incorporated into the MB *Gesangbuch* of 1955.[18]

The chorale too had several layers of meaning for Horch. Sometimes he spoke of the chorale as simply perpetuating tradition, symbolic of musical and also spiritual stagnation, by comparison with the renewal found through *Kernlieder*. At other times, Horch admitted to finding a more artful musical language and greater theological depth in the chorale. At these times, he emphasized the chorale's potential as a vehicle for theological teaching and reflection by comparison with the more emotional message of the *Kernlied*. And so the "disciple" of Horch often had to listen carefully to discern what particular shades of meaning the *Kernlied* versus the chorale had for Horch in any given conversation.

A humble man of devout faith, Horch was not content to shroud the faith within his own denomination, nor to fight only those musical battles from which he could benefit personally. Instead, he constantly looked for ways of encouraging not only Mennonites but also other minority groups to express their musical identity within the arenas valued by the dominant society, the last of the four dichotomies in this discussion. Horch's sensitivity to minority group issues may have begun with the dissonance he felt between his Lutheran classical music background and the conservative hymn-based musical culture of the German-speaking Russian Mennonite immigrants who became the predominant group in his English-speaking North-End MB Church in Winnipeg in the mid-1920s. It could also have stemmed from his empathic Lutheran-Mennonite identification with a largely Jewish north-end high school population which had also historically experienced hurt and hope. His need and opportunity to take concrete action intensified during his years with Winnipeg's CBC where, he concluded, Canada's public broadcasting network was geared toward a dominant society with little, if any, place for officially sanctioned ethnic minority expression. Consequently, Horch lobbied for programming that could afford musicians like Miriam Brightman of Rosh Pina Synagogue in Winnipeg an opportunity to perform the music nearest to their own hearts.

Realizing the east-west disparity in programming, Horch also instituted a prairie choirs program to feature the rich choral heritage of ethnic groups on the Prairies. He also actively engaged in fostering the integration of ethnic folk musics into the mainstream classical arena. Although he had expressed these ideas in numerous other venues, Horch more formally articulated a three-fold goal in a circa-1983 informal communiqué to several members of the Manitoba Mennonite Historical Society: 1) to assist a minority-group need for upward mobility into the dominant Anglo-French Canadian musical culture of serious music; 2) to do this by commissioning Canadian composers of international stature; and 3) to do this primarily with melodic folksong material *unencumbered by language* (my emphasis).[19]

Horch's intention was to bring integrity to the voice of ethnic minorities by having their music recast within a musical form respected by the dominant society — that is, through the classical orchestral work. This proposal states, as Horch so often argued, that musical sound can communicate unencumbered by text. Horch contended that when restrictive ethnic markers such as minority language texts are removed, a musical work can not only speak for a small group to a surrounding multicultural society, but that it can in fact create a bridge between the groups. Horch felt that performing the *Mennonite Piano Concerto*, a classical composition which used the tunes but not the German texts of the *Kernlieder*, would give Mennonites that element of respectability within the larger society that would provide an opportunity for them to speak of their faith.

Horch's vision was to commission a classical work for "the whole multicultural mosaic" of some eighty Canadian ethnic minority groups identified by the Canadian League of Composers in the early 1980s. The works were to be unencumbered by words because he truly believed that *"wenn eine Volkspoesie vertont wird mit einer Melodie, dann ist die Melodie immer wichtiger denn der Text,"* translated by Horch as: "When a poem is framed by a melody, it [the melody] is thereafter always more important than the text."[20] As Horch argues in his proposal, not to create classical instrumental works based on these musical "frames" is "to continue to ghettoize ethno-Canadian folk music."[21] He points to the example of Winnipeg's annual *Folklorama*, a two-week multi-ethnic festival, often featuring ethnic food, music and dance, and material culture. Although *Folklorama* energizes many ethnic minority groups and boosts Winnipeg's tourism potential, its critics would use the late historian Frank Epp's phrase —"romantic pluralism"[22]—to describe an opportunity for ethnic minority visibility with no attendant opportunity for explicitly articulating beliefs or for improving the group's long-range socio-economic status. This awareness fuelled Horch's passion for commissioning classical works based on "folk music."

Horch's categories—text versus music, performance versus composition, *Kernlied* versus chorale, ethnic minority versus dominant society—appear to be binary oppositions, but Horch was not prone to seeing the world in either-or categories. Instead, he frequently referred not only to "synthesizing," but also to "embracing" when speaking of musical and cultural differences. For Horch, the oppositions were not essentially about irreconcilable differences but about discerning how to explore, and in fact, to enjoy the power of differences.

What was his secret, the source of his inspiration to pull things apart and then to delight in the possibilities for their reconfiguration? How did he, as he often sang to his guests, embrace the tension of "awaiting the second coming" while living with the realities of "coming 'round the mountain?"

I contend it was the blend of his Anabaptist-Lutheran theology with an inquiring mind that allowed him to make such an impact both as a dean of Mennonite music-making and as a crusader on behalf of all minority musics. Firstly, as a Lutheran Horch believed that all well-crafted music was sacred, and consequently, that all genres of music—whether hymns, classical compositions, or rock—could be used to foster and express spiritual renewal. The idiom chosen for renewal, he thought, had less to do with what the church considered to be sacred than with what the larger society saw as the music of social change within a given era. Additionally, as an Anabaptist Horch subscribed strongly to a lay, congregational emphasis in church music, reflective of an emphasis on the priesthood of all believers. Consequently, Horch's approaches to church music—the mass choir, the orchestra, and the writing of choral compositions accessible to the church choir—all focused on inclusiveness, rather than on developing a musical elite. As an MB, Horch also believed that the church ought to be an evangelical community and that music was not only the tool for evangelism par excellence, but also the tool to prevent "spiritual arrest." And lastly, as a keen inquirer concerning the relationship between music and its cultural context, Horch persistently tested his ideas against the scholarly literature, particularly against the works of ethnomusicologists like John Blacking, Maynard Solomon, and Christopher Small.[23]

Horch's impact came from his view that all music is a gift from God, that any musical idiom can speak God's truth, that the most powerful texts may be nonverbal, that minority groups can gain "musical acceptance" within a dominant society, and that "whatever is true... whatever is lovely, whatever is admirable... think about such things,"[24] or whistle them, with a twinkle in your eye.

Notes

[1] Funded by the Fast Foundation of Winnipeg, Manitoba-born composer Victor Davies was commissioned in 1975 to write the *Mennonite Piano Concerto* to commemorate the 450th anniversary of the founding of the Mennonites. Although the work is integral to this discussion, it will not be discussed in detail in this paper—see Victor Davies, "A Non-Mennonite Writes a Mennonite Piano Concerto," in this volume.

[2] Peter Letkemann, "Benjamin Horch (1907-1992)," *Journal of Mennonite Studies* 11 (1993): 326-43.

[3] This included works like George Fiala's Ukrainian Symphony; a composition on the *Kernlied* "Die Zeit ist kurz," written by Carol Ann Weaver and performed by David Falk (voice), Lyle Friesen (mandolin), Carol Ann Weaver (piano) at the Horch's Golden Wedding celebration; the *Kernlieder* Cycle by German composer Thomas Jahn premiered by bass soloist William Reimer; and plans for a symphonic tone poem on Japanese poems, to be written as a redress for the internment of Japanese fruit farmers from British Columbia's Fraser Valley in western Canadian WWII war camps while their farms were taken over by Mennonites (detailed in a 16 May 1985 letter to Victor Davies), as well as plans for a symphony based on the choral anthems Mennonites had brought with them from Russia.

[4] The *Kernlieder* were German translations of American gospel songs borrowed by Mennonites, and especially by the Mennonite Brethren in the Ukraine.

[5] See discussion of the *Saengerfest* tradition in Wesley Berg, *From Russia with Music: A Study of the Mennonite Choral Singing Tradition in Canada* (Winnipeg:

Hyperion Press, 1985).

⁶ John Regehr, interview with the author, Winnipeg, Manitoba, 29 May 1984, "Mennonite Music-making in Canada, 1920-1970," Centre for Mennonite Brethren Studies, Winnipeg, Manitoba, cassette tape MM-2-1-21.

⁷ Horch often hummed "*Wie lieblich ist's hienieden*" ("What blessedness, when brethren unite with one accord"), a hymn about communal unity based on a tune from Johannes Brahms' Academic Festival Overture, when illustrating the artfulness of hymn tunes. He also uses the expression "[to] match with Brahmsian insight" in a letter to Victor Davies dated May 16, 1985.

⁸ Ben Horch, "The Mennonite Brethren Church: History of its Musical Development, 1860 to 1984 (abstract) June 29, 1984," 4.

⁹ In conversation, Horch, who was unusually open to musical innovation within the church, nevertheless frequently expressed a strong dislike for the organ because its strength could overpower the human voice and, he felt, lead to the death of congregational hymn-singing.

¹⁰ In through-composed compositions, the melody and accompaniment used for successive verses of a song vary to better reflect the nature of the text.

¹¹ From a tape titled "On the Subject of Mennonite Musical Traditions" (March 1983), Horch's response to a letter from Peter Letkemann of 19 February 1983, in which Horch chides Peter for ignoring "a midway performance term between amateur and professional." In the same taped response, Horch uses the term "corporate selectivity" to describe how borrowed hymns "were synthesized into a rhythmic and harmonic idiom that Mennonites looked upon as indigenous."

¹² Discussed in greater detail in the author's "Musical Transitions among Canadian Mennonite Brethren," in *Bridging Troubled Waters: The Mennonite Brethren at Mid-Twentieth Century*, ed. Paul Toews, (Winnipeg: Kindred Press, 1995), 227-246, 284-291.

¹³ Horch was constantly revising this paper, and insisted that it be called a "draft" or an "abstract" and even printed the words "rough draft" on my personal copy in order to demonstrate its incompleteness, and that it was a work in progress.

¹⁴ The other eras were The New Testament Church, The 4th Century Church in Rome, The 16th Century Lutheran Church, and The 16th Century Non-Conformist Anabaptists.

¹⁵ These included William Bestvater, Rev. Erdman Nikkel, and Horch's father-in-law, Rev. C. N. Hiebert.

¹⁶ Whether he identified three musical awakenings or four (as listed above) often depended on the particular argument Horch was trying to forward.

¹⁷ The *Vorsaenger* was a male singer chosen to lead congregational singing with his voice. Within the larger or existing Mennonite Church (*Die Kirchengemeinde*) two, three, or even more *Vorsaenger* sat at the front of the church facing the congregation. They announced the number of a song, set the "pitch," and led the congregation vocally. By contrast, within the newly-formed MB church in Russia, ministers lined out songs texts, although volunteer choirs began to assume a leadership role in introducing new hymns.

¹⁸ *Gesangbuch der Mennoniten Bruedergemeinde* (Winnipeg: Christian Press, 1955).

¹⁹ From an undated (c. 1983) handwritten communiqué by Benjamin Horch to Ken Reddig, then Archivist at the Centre for Mennonite Brethren and Chair of the Manitoba Mennonite Historical Society, and Doreen Klassen, Chair of the

Manitoba Mennonite Historical Society's Arts Committee.

[20] Horch frequently used this comment in discussion of his theology and philosophy of music. According to Peter Letkemann (personal communication 16 October 2004), this comment is "found in a letter of 16 May 1984 to J. B. Toews (Fresno)—written when Ben sent J. B. his Draft of MB Musical Development... He cites Meyers, *Handbuch über die Musik* (Mannheim: Bibliographisches Institut, 1961) as his source—the actual source, however, reads: 'Die Melodie im Volkslied ist im allgemeinen wichtiger als der Text' (p. 205)."

[21] Horch often supported this assertion by pointing out that he had heard of Jewish listeners who felt that the Mennonite Piano Concerto, and particularly the second movement and the melancholic *Kernlied* on which it was based, expressed their own history of "hurt and hope."

[22] Frank H. Epp, "Problems of Mennonite Identity: An Historical Study," in *The Canadian Ethnic Mosaic: A Quest for Identity*, ed. Leo Driedger (Toronto: McClelland and Stewart, 1978).

[23] Horch was especially taken by Blacking's *How Musical is Man* (Seattle: University of Washington Press, 1973) with its perceptive chapter titles—"Humanly organized sound," "Music in society and culture," "Culture and society in music," and "Soundly organized humanity"—but also cited Maynard Solomon's writings on Ludwig van Beethoven, and Christopher Small's *Music, Society, Education* (London: Calder, 1977). In fact, it was common for "Uncle Ben," as I called my mentor, to read me a paragraph or so from these books, to launch into his interpretation, and then to ask for my perspective as an ethnomusicologist or for clarification on anything he might have misunderstood because, as he would say, "You know I'm not a trained ethnomusicologist," although his insights were as perceptive as or even beyond those of one formally trained in the discipline.

[24] From Philippians 4: 8, a New Testament verse Horch frequently quoted in our discussions.

A Non-Mennonite Writes a Mennonite Piano Concerto

Victor Davies

In 1973 Ben Horch, a well-known Mennonite choral conductor and radio producer for the Canadian Broadcasting Corporation (CBC), approached me about composing a "Bible Belt" (Horch's words) concerto for piano, based on traditional hymns. I was enthusiastic about the idea, and Horch applied for funding from the CBC but was turned down. Horch complained about this during a visit to his internist, Dr. Bernhard Fast, who suggested that the Fast Foundation might be able to help commission a Mennonite piano concerto. Thus was the work born.

Horch wanted the composition to be based on Mennonite hymns, and so the Mennonite Historical Society compiled a list of fifty hymns: twenty-five from the General Conference Mennonite Church, and twenty-five from the Mennonite Brethren Church. Horch indicated that I was free to use as many or as few of these hymns as I wanted in developing the piece, and that I could transform the material in any way I felt necessary.

I had no idea what Mennonite hymns were and knew little about Mennonites, but was excited to accept the challenge of turning hymns—songs of communal worship—into a secular, virtuoso piano concerto. When I received the list of hymns, I learned from Horch that these pieces were largely Victorian English hymns and American gospel songs that the Mennonites had appropriated and adapted with German lyrics during their travels. I knew nearly all of the hymns from my United Church background and realized in later years that engaging with these hymns during the composition of the concerto was a musical homecoming for me.

My first task was to plan how this vocal music of collective utterance, used for worship, could be transformed into a concerto form; that is, a dramatic dialogue between the individual and the group, and one that involves conflict. This dramatic construction is fundamentally different from the emotional unanimity generated by hymn singing.

The second movement was the first of the concerto's three movements to take shape. On examining the hymns repeatedly to see what kinds of thematic or melodic ideas might direct me to the solution of their transformation, I discovered "Wehrlos und verlassen" ("In the rifted rock I'm resting") and felt it was a tune of such depth that there would be ample material to create a set of variations. Thus the second movement was decided, and it was only a matter of working out the variations to unfold in ever-increasing complexity before returning to the simple beauty of the hymn.

For the first movement, I decided to use several hymns to create a sonata with two contrasting themes. The first theme is largely based on the hymn "O Jesu, wieviel Gutes" ("O Christ what bounteous kindness"), modified to provide both a theme and motives for development. The second theme uses "Welchen Jubel welche Freude" ("Shall we gather at the river," or "What jubilation, what joy") in its entirety because of the tune's familiarity and memorability.[1] Having determined the raw material for the movement, I then constructed a dialogue between the piano and orchestra. Beginning with the joyous content of the two themes, the dramatic path I took was that of an individual believer who falls into doubt. The appearance of doubt, the ensuing struggles and subsequent affirmation of belief became the framework for the musical development of the first movement.

I decided the third movement would be a rondo, a movement alternating between a recurring main theme and a series of contrasting themes. This structure provided an ideal opportunity to include a number of hymns. I chose "Wie süss tönt Sabbatglockenklang" ("How sweetly chime the Sabbath bells") as the main theme, not knowing that this hymn was usually performed quite slowly. Played at a brisk tempo, the tune suggested to me a cheerful, simple aspect, and indeed the sound of bells. It also suggested a fun-loving individual determined to carry on and be heard in the face of other, more staid themes that would interrupt it. The tune's brevity made it an ideal main theme, one that would lend itself to using different orchestral colours for each restatement.[2] At the end of the movement, I reprised the main themes of the first and second movements and concluded with a final flash of "How sweetly chime the Sabbath bells."

When Ben Horch first approached me about composing the concerto, he said pianist Irmgard Baerg would play and her husband, William Baerg, would conduct the premiere of the work. I had no idea who these two Mennonite musicians were, but when I met them, I was delighted to find two brilliantly talented individuals who had received advanced schooling in the United States, Canada, and Germany. I could not have wished for better collaborators in bringing the concerto to life.

The premiere of the concerto was to take place in 1974, but because I was working on a very large recording project it did not happen until a year later. I had done some work on the concerto in 1974, but as I became increasingly preoccupied with my recording project, I put all my sketches in a brown envelope. In the summer of 1975, nine months after putting the envelope away, Bill, Irmgard, and I were teaching at the Neepawa Holiday Festival of the Arts, and Irmgard asked me what the concerto she would be playing in three months was like. To the amazement of us all, I described the structure, thematic content, and many details of the finished piece in a fifteen-minute lecture. Two weeks later, I sat down to write the concerto again. As time was short, I developed a two-piano sketch: one piano part consisting of the piano solo and the second piano, the orchestral framework. As the writing proceeded, I would give Irmgard photocopies of these bits and she would paste them in a scrapbook — at the time it all seemed normal. Irmgard was a model of patience and forbearance, and somehow Bill learned the score. When the piano part was finished, I created the full orchestra part, which was completed on October 22, 1975.[3]

The concerto's premiere took place on October 27, 1975 at the Winnipeg Centennial Concert Hall. The event was a *Saengerfest* (song festival) to commemorate the founding of the Mennonite faith. The piano soloist was Irmgard Baerg, with the Winnipeg Symphony Orchestra conducted by William Baerg. Although the concerto received a standing ovation, reactions from the Mennonite community were mixed, ranging from an enthusiastic embrace by younger members of the community to hostility from one reviewer, who felt I had satirized Mennonite tradition. Generally, those who expressed reservations felt that I had not been respectful of the original material. However, over the years those reservations seem to have disappeared, and the work seems to have been accepted by the Mennonite community.[4]

Why did Ben Horch choose me, a non-Mennonite, to compose a Mennonite Piano Concerto?

Horch knew my music from having recorded several works of mine with the Winnipeg Symphony Orchestra. Although I was conversant with twentieth-century materials and techniques, Horch knew my strengths and interests lay with traditional form, melody, harmony, and rhythm. I think he felt such an approach would be useful in making the work more widely acceptable, and one of Horch's goals was to increase the profile of the Mennonite community and its traditions within broader society.

Furthermore, Horch hoped that Mennonites would look to their cultural roots for inspiration for future creative works. He wanted to affirm the artistic values inherent in the hymns as a foundation upon which to build, and I think he felt that if this affirmation came from someone outside the fold, it would have more impact than if it came from someone within the Mennonite tradition.[5] Because I approached this material with no preconceptions from a Mennonite perspective and only looked at what it could become musically, I was able to transform it without the emotion of tradition attached to it. When I wrote the concerto, I assumed that the hymns I had chosen were in current use in Mennonite churches. It was only much later that I learned this material was considered old-fashioned.

One theory that Horch wanted to illustrate was that hymns are not sacred in and of themselves, and only become so through their use in worship. The transformation of hymn material into a completely secular form such as a piano concerto would test his thesis. Of course, he did not tell me this when I was commissioned to write the piece! Only many years later did I learn this on one of our many visits, when we discussed musical aesthetics and every other musical topic in great depth. Horch seemed happy with the piano concerto, and he proposed a number of other pieces that we discussed at length but that never came about.[6]

From its modest beginnings, the *Mennonite Piano Concerto* has been heard around the world in live performances and radio broadcasts. The concerto also became the basis for the score to the feature-length documentary drama *And When They Shall Ask* (1979), produced by David Dueck. Dueck used the recording of the concerto (featuring Irmgard Baerg as piano soloist with Boris Brott conducting the London Symphony Orchestra) to help market the film.[7] The recording is a frequently requested work on Canadian Broadcasting Corporation (CBC) radio, and is also a regular favourite on classical music radio stations in the United Kingdom, Europe, Australia, and the United States.[8]

If the *Mennonite Piano Concerto* has had any impact on Mennonite composers old or young, I couldn't say. I was a willing and enthusiastic participant in Ben Horch's vision, and with the generous support of the Fast Foundation and family, his dream came to life.[9] It will be interesting to see in twenty years what further life the work has. History will be the judge of its continued success.

Notes

[1] Fragments of "Lobt Gott, ihr Christen alle gleich" ("Let all together praise our God") are also part of the first movement.

[2] Other hymn tunes used in the third movement are: "Ein reines Herz, Herr" ("A pure heart, Lord, create in me"), "Wirf Sorgen und Schmerz" ("In sorrow and pain"), "Wie soll ich Dich empfangen" ("O how shall I receive Thee"), "So nimm denn meine Hände" ("Take thou my hand, O Father"), and "Solang mein Jesus lebt" ("While my Redeemer's near").

[3] The concerto was dedicated to the father of Dr. Bernhard Fast. The dedication reads as follows: "Commissioned by the Fast Family, 'in memory of Bernard B. Fast (1896-1969) who served the Mennonite community with love and devotion as a teacher, Sunday School Superintendent, and Minister for many years. His affection for songs of the Mennonite faith were [sic] an inspiration and constant joy to him throughout his life.'"

[4] Horch said: "In his concern for preserving the feeling of a sincere musical tradition Victor Davies has brilliantly caught the essence of our spiritual history, and interpreted it in a new form—essentially re-creating Mennonite history in the *Mennonite Piano Concerto*." Each week I receive e-mails and letters from listeners around the world, requesting the music or sharing their reactions to the piece. Among my favourites is the letter that said the CD was the perfect Bar Mitzvah gift (!). The most moving letter was from a Mennonite pastor who wrote that upon hearing of his father's death, he drove all night from Winnipeg to Alberta, listening to the concerto all the way because it had given him such great comfort.

[5] A prominent Mennonite broadcaster told me that if the concerto was to succeed I would have to change the title. I of course declined. Although the work was originally titled "*A* Mennonite Piano Concerto," it seems now to have become "*The* Mennonite Piano Concerto."

[6] One such piece was a song cycle of poems about the Japanese internment during World War II. Another was a guitar concerto similar to the Mennonite Piano Concerto, based on *Kernlieder*. When I said that I didn't know many Mennonite guitarists and thought that a choral work might be more appropriate, he agreed. The work became my oratorio "Revelation," (1996) again a commission from the Fast family.

[7] Campion Records 1304; CD release in 1989 on Water Lily and Campion Labels.

[8] Radio stations include the United Kingdom's BBC3 and Classic FM (the largest broadcaster in the UK). In the United States the concerto has been syndicated on American Public Radio and National Public Radio; it was ranked in the "Classical Top 20" list of Radio Kansas and reached the top 100 all-time favourites on Seattle's KING FM station. In live concert performances, Irmgard Baerg (pianist), Karin Redekopp Edwards (pianist), and Howard Dyck (conductor) have been the most frequent performers of the work.

[9] Family members are Bernhard, Luise (Goossen), Cornelius, Cornelia (Dahl), and William Fast.

"Dear Nobe . . . Ever Affectionately, Art": The Kreider-Farwell Correspondence

E. Douglas Bomberger

The title of this collection of essays derives from the centuries-old description of Mennonites as "The Quiet in the Land." First out of necessity, and later out of habit, Mennonites have tended to keep to themselves, and their communities have often been insular. While much attention has been focused on the historical isolation of Mennonites from the outside world, comparatively little has been devoted to persons who were on the fringes of these communities. For such persons, who may have had family ties or professional connections to the community but were not in the inner circle of commitment to it, the sense of isolation could be particularly intense. Composer and pianist Noble Wickham Kreider, who lived in Goshen, Indiana, from 1874 to 1959 and taught at Goshen College, found relief from this isolation in a long friendship with the well-known composer and publisher Arthur Farwell. An extensive correspondence preserved in the Farwell Collection of the Sibley Music Library in Rochester, New York, and by Kreider's student Charles Burkhart provides evidence of their close contact over nearly half a century.[1]

Noble's father was William B. Kreider, a homeopathic physician who grew up in the Mennonite church. His mother, Nettie C. Wickham, was not a Mennonite, which may explain why the parents joined the Presbyterian church but does not fully explain why Noble professed to be an agnostic for much of his life. In one letter he confided to Farwell, "For some reason faith is very shadowy and a condition I am unable to accept."[2] Sometime before 1900 the family built a large house on the corner of South Sixth and Monroe Streets, where Noble and his parents spent the rest of their lives.

Kreider studied piano with Clarence Forsyth of Indianapolis, whom he accompanied on a European trip in the 1890s.[3] It is not clear whether Kreider studied in Germany, but by the first decade of the twentieth century, it is clear that he was a virtuoso pianist with a significant portfolio of his own compositions for the instrument. It was at this point that he began to seek outside contacts in the music world.

During the summer of 1906, he made a trip east, calling on Farwell at his home in Newton Center, Massachusetts. Farwell was best known at this time as the founder of the Wa-Wan Press, dedicated to publishing the works of American composers. Though the press was noted for works based on Native-American musical materials, it was not limited to folkloristic compositions. Farwell later described the encounter in a 1909 article in *Musical America*:

> The summer added still another to my circle of composer friends, in the person of Noble Kreider. He came from his home in Goshen, Indiana, bearing the inevitable portfolio of manuscripts—that wondrous and mysterious portfolio, which it may be will contain shining records of the most dazzling sun-flights of the imagination, and it may be, will not. This was one of the pleasant surprises, however, and in Kreider's compositions there were numerous evidences of the truly poetic nature, and of the unmistakable touch of the artist.[4]

Within a few months, Farwell had published the first of several piano pieces that would appear in the Wa-Wan Press and was introducing Kreider to other like-minded musicians. That Farwell and Kreider felt an immediate affinity is indicated both by Farwell's complimentary comments in letters to other musicians and also by the fact that they undertook a performing tour together that fall.[5] In their extensive correspondence they used the familiar shortened names favoured by midwestern families—"Art" for Arthur and "Nobe" for Noble. Over the years their friendship endured many trials, as both men enjoyed triumphs and suffered setbacks in their personal and professional lives.

Kreider taught piano in his home, at a conservatory in Chicago, and from 1930 at Goshen College. He taught his college students in his home, which was more convenient for him and allowed the students to make use of his fine Mason & Hamlin grand piano. As a part-time teacher, Noble did not participate in all aspects of college life, though he made a profound impression on many of his students. His cousin, Carl Kreider, served as dean of the college during part of his time there and may have been influential in keeping him on the faculty. Students interviewed for this paper recalled his commitment to technical facility and beautiful tone, as well as an annoying habit of humming while he played.[6]

Kreider enjoyed traveling, both within the United States and abroad. He visited Asia and the Caribbean on several occasions and filled his home with furniture and artworks from these trips. In 1913 he traveled to southern California, where he wrote the score for a silent film entitled *Samson*.[7] In 1915, when Farwell became ill from the stress of working on a Broadway play, Kreider took him on a trip to Bermuda to recuperate.

Even though he was not compelled to serve in World War I, Kreider volunteered for the hospital corps, serving in France as an ambulance driver. This experience was profoundly unsettling for the composer, and he never regained his prewar level of creativity. He seems to have been plagued by depression; in one letter he confessed to Farwell, "I feel I never will want to write music again. Things bob to the surface right along but [as] there seems so little real reason for putting them down, I don't."[8] During this period Farwell was a strong advocate. When Kreider was not included in John Tasker Howard's *Our American Music* of 1930, Farwell wrote to the author:

> I have not looked through the work with a view to what might be regarded as omissions, but I happened to notice that the name of Noble Kreider does not appear. He is one of the rarest souls that has composed in America, and his music is among the most beautiful that we have. But not much of his has been published, and that is mostly his earlier work. The war set him back—almost ended him—but now he is producing work of the rarest and most exquisite order.[9]

Farwell taught at Michigan State University in East Lansing from 1927 to 1939, allowing the two composers to see each other often. In one letter from 1935, for instance, Kreider asks, "I am wondering if you want me to come to you May 24th for my usual over the week-end visit?"[10] These years saw the deaths of both of Kreider's parents, as well as Farwell's divorce from his first wife. The letters from the 1930s demonstrate repeatedly that mutual support and practical advice were important elements of their friendship. In another undated letter, Kreider writes, "Dear Art, Thank Gertrude for her share in my last visit. You know as well as I what being with you means, as near happiness as I can have ici-bàs. Your love + sympathy do so much for me, filling me with high resolve and defining my ideals."[11]

In the 1940s, Farwell was in New York City, where his financial and artistic prospects were less than satisfactory. He was cheered by letters and visits from Kreider, who also sent him sugar from Indiana on at least one occasion shortly after the war. Farwell made an extended visit to Goshen during the summer of 1946, at which time he reviewed a concert by Kreider's student Burkhart for the *Goshen News*. Kreider and Burkhart visited New York in December 1946, treating Farwell to a performance of the Broadway production of *The Iceman Cometh*. Farwell's children recalled that when their father died in 1952, Kreider sent an unusually large flower arrangement that was placed on the grand piano.[12] Kreider died seven years later, in 1959.

This synopsis gives a brief overview of their friendship, but digging deeper into the letters provides clues to Kreider's life and music as well as the reasons why these two composers felt such a strong bond. First and foremost, the two composers agreed on many musical issues, sharing a high-minded, idealistic view of music for edification rather than entertainment. Farwell wrote to Arne Oldberg of Kreider's music shortly after their first meeting in 1906: "He is a truly poetic nature, and writes genuine piano music. He has fed on Chopin and Brahms, and will I feel sure, establish a true individuality of his own. We will issue his Ballad, op. 3, in a month or so."[13] This ballad, which is almost entirely chordal, gives a good sense of Kreider's Brahmsian early style. The Chopinesque elements in his compositional style are especially evident in the Impromptu, op. 5.

As the years went by, the two often shared their new works with each other, and Kreider found Farwell's advice to be important to his own creative process. In one letter from the 1930s, he wrote, "I celebrated Christmas by writing. It was funny I had not the slightest idea I would write and in the most incomprehensible way I began and wrote part of a piano Prelude which will be finished soon. I shall not be able to judge of it till you have heard it."[14] On another occasion he wrote, "Your visit was such a comfort. It inspired me to finish the Study, I think, the next day. Anyhow it is done and will stay so excepting a bit of polishing."[15]

The two composers were quite frank with each other, and they did not always agree on solutions to specific compositional problems. Kreider wrote in another letter, "The suggestions reached me and were examined with great interest. The second I could not consider, as it changed the melodic line but the first has helped and will undoubtedly be partly used. Thanks for it. As you know often a friend will feel the very thing we were searching."[16]

The letters contain numerous comments about other musicians as well, showing that the two shared many views. Reporting to Farwell on his progress with a transcription of a piece by Tchaikovsky, Kreider confided, "I only pray the wraith of the great Russian will not be angry at my attempts. I assure you and him and all concerned I am being as reverent as is in my power. I can't understand how Tschaikowsky [sic] allows himself to do the obvious, the common thing at times. Some of the chords are unbelievably common."[17] Farwell wrote in a letter of 1946, "I agree with you about Brahms (human being like ourselves) but think him only sprite-like and dancy in continuously even and straightforward rhythm without sentiment in *that particular* work. Sentiment and rubato ruin it for me."[18]

A second important reason why they seem to have felt an affinity was their respective positions as outsiders. As a non-Mennonite in a Mennonite town, Kreider often felt alienated; as a concert pianist teaching for a college that had only one piano and was primarily concerned with a cappella singing, he felt underappreciated. In one letter he confided, "I am so alone here, not a soul to whom I can show my works! . . . How often when I am writing I long to go to you for advice!"[19] Regarding his playing, he wrote on another occasion, "I am supposed to play at the college tonight. I feel all in. I wonder how I can feeling as I do and knowing what I will have to play upon. 'Guess I will play the larghetto from the Chopin F Minor Concerto."[20]

Farwell was a much more famous musician, but he also spent much of his career feeling isolated. Having spent his first eighteen years in the Midwest, he never felt completely comfortable in Massachusetts. This led to a certain personal and professional distance from the musicians around him in Boston.[21] His major contribution to American music, the Wa-Wan Press, was founded because of a conviction that he and other American composers were not receiving adequate recognition and publication opportunities. This press, which operated from 1901 to 1911, published the works of thirty-seven different American composers, including Kreider and other non-Indianist composers. He later wrote about his motivation for founding this press, "I was just plain mad, and I vowed I would change the United States in this respect. I was not willing to live in a country that would not accept my calling."[22] His idealistic venture brought attention to a significant group of previously neglected composers and earned him a reputation as an innovator, but even his most fervent admirers would not have said that he was able to "change the United States."[23] In his later years, Farwell grew increasingly bitter about the lack of interest in his own works. The last surviving letter, written May 26, 1948, from New York, is particularly poignant:

> Meanwhile, I am the "forgotten man" about here. None of the current generation of artists ever heard of me, especially as the leading orchestra conductors will no longer play anything of my generation. And now Schirmer is going to destroy the plates of the bulk of my songs which they published unless I will buy them from them (which I can't do) and the few remaining copies. You see I haven't got around to going after singers to sing them, so they just lie on Schirmer's shelves. Yet I feel that they represent a lot of my finest work, and in the long run would prove a real contribution to American song literature. It's rather tragic, to me, and I am pondering how I can turn defeat, in this respect, into victory.[24]

For most of their careers, the two were able to take consolation in their mutual feelings of neglect and isolation. In a letter of May 21, 1946, Farwell remarked with tongue in cheek: "Now that Booth Tarkington is gone, that leaves you the noblest Roman of them all—as living protagonist of Indiana genius—does it not?"[25]

A third, and perhaps most important, area of commonality was their mutual interest in spirituality. Kreider's self-professed agnosticism did not mean that he had no interest in spiritual life—quite the contrary. The subject of religion comes up often in his correspondence, often in a flippant way, as in this comment on his recent reading: "Just had a bit, quite a bit of Thomas Aquinas and am more than ever convinced I prefer to continue in my Pagan ways. Doubtless I could do just as much as a Catholic, but not so privately."[26] Burkhart reports that after the deaths of his parents, Kreider believed that unexplained sounds and other supernatural phenomena took place in his home. He participated in séances to communicate with the spirit world. Burkhart summed up Kreider's spiritual side by saying that he had a "religious awe in the face of the universe," despite his lack of participation in organized religion.[27]

These beliefs coincided with Farwell's unconventional religious beliefs. He was introduced by his mother to astrology and Eastern mysticism, and he later dabbled for a time in Theosophy.[28] His high regard for Christ found expression in his composition of music for *The Pilgrimage Play* (1921) and other works on sacred topics rather than in conventional Christian observance.

Farwell's most extensive spiritual writings were those that explored the notion of intuition. He believed that this crucial but little understood aspect of the creative process had strong spiritual overtones, and his own experiences led him to codify his conclusions in a lecture, "The Science of Intuition," and an unpublished book, "Intuition in the World-Making." His initial acquaintance with the spiritual power of intuition came about because of extreme demands on his time, as he later recalled:

> In 1913, I received commissions for the compositions of music for a series of pageant dramas. I knew that to do this extensive work against a time schedule I should have to operate in a very different way from my usual one, which at that time, was not free from the occasional necessity of waiting about, or straining for musical ideas. . . . In thinking about the task before me I conceived, in a half-fanciful way, that the universe must contain somewhere or somehow all the musical ideas which had never yet been thought of or written down. I believed that if I could find the right means of access to this universal store, I could put my hand at once on any musical themes I needed. To attempt

this I thought of a "place of music," where the universe concentrated all these ideas, and where they could be had on application. I imagined a great assemblage of all possible means of producing music, a universal orchestra, including all instruments, and a chorus. Thus I gave the "universe" the chance to produce and play for me any theme I needed, on any instrument or instruments. Then I set this musical mass equipment, in my mind, in a semi-distant, misty dream-spot, far enough away to be free of any interference from myself. As definitely as possible, I then thought of a particular kind of theme I needed for a certain scene in the drama on which I was working—a Roman march, a pastoral motive, or whatever it might be. I watched the musical equipment of the universal store I had created, intently out of a dreamy state of my own, with closed eyes, keeping out of my mind every thought except the one on which I had concentrated. It required only a moment before the appropriate theme spoke out from the appropriate instrument or instruments, apparently wholly by its own volition, and absolutely without any effort of composition on my part. At once I found myself spontaneously released from the dream-state, and went to work in the ordinary way, developing the theme which the "universe" had given me. This process I repeated for months, obtaining immediately, and in rapid succession, the themes I required, which always fitted precisely my expressed need.[29]

Kreider's letters to Farwell contain numerous references to the role of inspiration in the creative process, which he nearly always referred to as something coming from outside. In a letter from 1935 he wrote, "I reached here full of high resolve to put down as many of my little dots as the gods see fit to grant me ideas."[30] On another occasion he wrote, "Yesterday several ideas, so called inspirations, came to me."[31]

Like his fellow composer, Kreider expressed a child-like wonder at the way ideas came to him. In one letter from the 1930s he wrote, "This morning I have been composing, writing a new piano comp. At present there is a surging of sounds so great within me I can hardly think."[32] He described the genesis of another composition in this way: "The new Prelude gives me pleasure in going over it. It has no key being as impersonal as nature. I feel very strange about it; it came to me without the least desire to write. Generally I think of a work for a short time at least before putting it on paper; but this I just wrote and not without [sic], as usual, a whipping process."[33] This sense of inspiration was not typical for him, though. He wrote to Farwell on another occasion, "Since my return two piano works have come to me. I wish I wrote easier. I dread composing as I do nothing else."[34] Like many pianist composers, he found it necessary to segregate these two aspects of his life. He wrote to Farwell, "I am not writing but practising [sic]. I sway between these two points thinking each is all that counts and then I am at the other. At present I am at the other."[35]

The close friendship between these two composers and the affectionate tone of their letters seem more typical of the nineteenth than the twentieth century. Both men came to maturity during the waning years of the Romantic Era, and neither embraced the experimentation of twentieth-century modernism. For Kreider, his friendship with Farwell must have helped him cope with the isolation of being on the fringes of a Mennonite community. Curiously, not one of Kreider's letters uses the word Mennonite, although there are numerous references to Goshen College and to Mennonite students and acquaintances. It is perhaps ironic that nearly half a century after his death, Kreider is remembered fondly by his Mennonite students but entirely forgotten by scholars and audiences of mainstream American music.

Notes

[1] Box 36 folder 32 of the Arthur Farwell Collection at the Sibley Music Library contains sixty-five letters from Kreider to Farwell and two letters from Farwell to Kreider. Box 39 folder 60 contains an additional seven letters from Kreider to Farwell. They are quoted courtesy of the Ruth T. Watanabe Special Collections, Sibley Music Library, Eastman School of Music, University of Rochester. Charles Burkhart holds an additional seven letters from Farwell to Kreider: one from August 25, 1906, and the rest from 1945 to 1948. They are quoted courtesy of Professor Burkhart. In a letter to the author dated July 2, 2004, he stated that he had donated these seven letters to the Sibley Music Library.

[2] Letter dated "Home, Friday morning," box 36 folder 32.

[3] Kreider's obituary in the *Goshen News* states that he studied "in the Black Forest sector of Germany and in France," but I have found no independent verification of this. According to records of the Stuttgart Conservatory, Forsyth was a student of organ there from 1888 to 1890.

[4] Reprinted in Arthur Farwell, *"Wanderjahre of a Revolutionist" and Other Essays on American Music*, ed. Thomas Stoner (Rochester: University of Rochester Press, 1995), 133.

[5] Evelyn Davis Culbertson, *He Heard America Singing: Arthur Farwell, Composer and Crusading Music Educator*, Composers of North America, No. 9 (Metuchen, NJ and London: Scarecrow, 1992), 138.

[6] Former students who shared their recollections were Lois Bender, Charles Burkhart, Miriam K. Byler, Carolyn W. Hertzler, James A. Miller, and Karl Stutzman.

[7] The keyboard score was published by Hatch & Loveland in 1914. A manuscript note in the copy in the New York Public Library states "Composed Pasadena/Nov Dec. 1913." Further information may be found in Gillian B. Anderson, *Music for Silent Films, 1894–1929: A Guide* (Washington: Library of Congress, 1988), 105 and in the Internet Movie Database http:www.imdb.com.

[8] Letter dated "Home, Wed. p.m.," box 36 folder 32. The letter mentions

marital problems between Farwell and his first wife Gertrude, meaning that it probably dates from the mid 1930s.

[9] Arthur Farwell to John Tasker Howard, April 19, 1931, box 36 folder 15.

[10] Letter dated "Home, May 14th 1935," box 36 folder 32.

[11] Letter on stationery of the Park Tavern, Wadsworth, Ohio, dated simply "Tuesday," box 36 folder 32.

[12] Culbertson, *He Heard America Singing*, 164.

[13] Arthur Farwell to Arne Oldberg, August 31, 1906, Oldberg Collection box 88 folder 39, Library of Congress Music Division.

[14] Letter dated "Home, Sunday morning," box 36 folder 32.

[15] Letter dated "Home, Wed." box 36 folder 32.

[16] Letter dated "Home, Sunday a.m." ["1930" added in pencil], box 36 folder 32.

[17] Letter dated "Home, Wed. Evening" ["1935" added in pencil], box 36 folder 32.

[18] Arthur Farwell to Noble Kreider, October 27, 1946, Charles Burkhart personal collection.

[19] Letter dated "Home, Monday noon" ["1930 or '31" added in pencil], box 36 folder 32.

[20] Letter dated "Home, Tuesday a.m.," box 36 folder 32.

[21] Gilbert Chase explores this isolation at some length in "The Wa-Wan Press: A Chapter in American Enterprise," introductory essay to *The Wa-Wan Press, 1901–1911*, ed. Vera Brodsky Lawrence, 5 vols. (New York: Arno Press and The New York Times, 1970), 1: x–xi.

[22] Letter to Edward N. Waters, quoted in Waters, "The Wa-Wan Press: An Adventure in Musical Idealism," in *A Birthday Offering to Carl Engel*, ed. Gustave Reese (New York: G. Schirmer, 1943), 217.

[23] The difficult task of assessing the influence of Farwell's efforts on behalf of American composers is undertaken in Waters, "The Wa-Wan Press," 228–31.

[24] Arthur Farwell to Noble Kreider, May 26, 1948, Charles Burkhart personal collection.

[25] Arthur Farwell to Noble Kreider, May 21, 1946, Charles Burkhart personal collection.

[26] Letter dated "Home, Sunday P. M." ["1930" added in pencil], box 36 folder 32.

[27] Personal interview with Charles Burkhart, New York, June 21, 2003.

[28] Further information on these and other religious leanings may be found in Culbertson.

[29] Quoted in Culbertson, *He Heard America Singing*, 341–42.

[30] Letter dated "Home, Wed. Evening" ["1935" added in pencil], box 36 folder 32.

[31] Letter dated "Home, Wed." The letter contains comments on the Christmas gifts he received, placing it sometime in late December or early January.

[32] Letter dated "Home, Wed. a.m." ["1931" added in pencil], box 36 folder 32.

[33] Letter dated "Jan 17—'32" in pencil, box 36 folder 32.

[34] Letter dated "Home, Sunday morning" ["1931" added in pencil], box 36 folder 32.

[35] Letter dated "Home, Friday p.m.," box 36 folder 32.

Appendix: Noble Kreider Works

After his death in 1959, Kreider's surviving manuscripts were catalogued and donated to the New York Public Library (NYPL) by Charles Burkhart. A descriptive catalog of this collection may be found at http://digilib.nypl.org/ dynaweb/ead/music/muskreider. Additional manuscript scores are in the Arthur Farwell Collection of the Sibley Music Library (AF) and the Detroit Public Library (DPL). The following list provides publication information for the published works and manuscript locations for unpublished works.

Published Works

Legend, op. 1 no. 1 (composed before August 1906; published by Boston Music, 1911)

Legend, op. 1 no. 2 (composed before August 1906; published by Boston Music, 1911)[1]

Ballad, op. 3 (Wa-Wan, 1906)

Nocturn, op. 4 no. 2 (Wa-Wan, 1907)[2]

Impromptu, op. 5 (Wa-Wan, 1907)

Study, op. 6 no. 1 (Wa-Wan, 1908)

Study, op. 6 no. 2 (Wa-Wan, 1908)

Six Preludes for pianoforte, op. 7 (composed before August 1906; published by Wa-Wan, 1908 [2, 3, 5] and 1910 [complete])

Prelude, op. 8 (Boston Music, 1911)

Three Moods, op. 9 (Schirmer, 1913)

Samson (composed November/December 1913; published by Hatch & Loveland, 1914)

Unpublished Piano Works

Poem, op. 10, NYPL

Nocturn, op. 13, NYPL[3]

Three Waltzes, NYPL, AF (No. 1, dated 1915)

Moderato (1923), AF

Andante (1929), AF

Prelude: Lento [no key signature] (1932), NYPL

Transfiguration (1934), NYPL, AF

Theme (August 31, 1935), NYPL

Bagatelle (1936), DPL

Sapphic [based on *Nocturn* below] (1937), NYPL, AF

Prelude in B Major: Vivace ma tranquillo (1938), DPL, NYPL

To Betty: Moderato (1939?), AF

Prelude (Jan. 12, 1940), DPL [not seen—may be identical to one of the preludes below]
Prelude in A Major: Con moto (June 1952), NYPL
Memory of Katherine Clayton (October 1958), NYPL
Gavotte in G Major: Allegro moderato, NYPL
Lento, NYPL
Minuet, AF
Ode to Evening, NYPL
Prelude in A Major: Largo, NYPL
Prelude in B-flat Major, NYPL
Prelude in C-sharp Minor: Assai lento, NYPL
Prelude in E Major: Andante, NYPL
Prelude in E Major: Con moto, NYPL
Prelude in E Minor: Allegro, NYPL
Prelude in E-flat Major: Allegro giocondemente, NYPL
Snowflakes, NYPL
Study in G-sharp Minor: Presto, NYPL
Wedding March, NYPL
[100] Exercises for Fingers, NYPL

Unpublished works for solo voice and piano

Russian Peasant Song (November 1913), NYPL
To Celia (1927), NYPL, AF
Avenging and Bright (1930), NYPL
Why? ("Feb. 1st, 1930, Goshen—Mishawaka"), NYPL
Nocturn (1931), NYPL, AF
Tristesse (1940?), NYPL, AF
I Sought my Beloved, NYPL
In the Garden, NYPL
In the West, NYPL
Ein Schwann, NYPL
To Sleep (based on Prelude in B Major above), NYPL
When the Day Darkens, NYPL, AF

Unpublished works for violin and piano

Waltz in A Minor (1935), NYPL
Berceuse in C-sharp Minor (1946), DPL, NYPL
Prelude No. I in C-sharp Minor: Hommage a Tschaikowsky, NYPL
Prelude in E Minor, NYPL
Song without Words in G-flat Major, NYPL
A Swan (transcription of *Ein Schwann* above), NYPL

Unpublished works for cello and piano

A Little Serenade, NYPL
Mazurka (Homage to Poland) with unidentified sketches on verso of NYPL copy, NYPL, AF
Study in B Minor, NYPL
A Swan (transcription of *Ein Schwann* above), NYPL
Waltz (transcription of violin waltz above), NYPL

Unpublished choral works

Sound the Trumpets for our Feet! (March 24, 1943), NYPL
King David and King Solomon (sketch for *Avenging and Bright* on verso), NYPL
O God, the Refuge of our Fear, NYPL

Notes to Appendix

[1] In his first letter after Kreider's visit in August 1906, Farwell raises the issue of publication: "It remains to choose what to put in the next issue. A book is supposed to have ten pp. of music, and on a pinch we go up as high as fifteen. I propose one of the following—

    Legends No. 1 and No. 3. (about 15 pp)
    Preludes in Maj. Keys (I think will go into 15 pp.)
    Ballad op. 3 (Ossian) (about 10 pp)

I rather incline to the Ballad, as it's about time for us to come out with another single strong work filling up a book." The Ballad, op. 3 was in fact the first Kreider work published by the Wa-Wan Press. The Legends, op. 1 nos. 1 and 2 were eventually published by Boston Music Company, but the whereabouts of No. 3 is not known. It is possible that Farwell was in error and meant to say No. 2.

[2] I have found no evidence of op. 4 no. 1.
[3] I have found no evidence of opp. 11 and 12.

Rebel with a Cause: Innovation and Grace in the Music of a Reinfeld Boy

Judith Klassen

The increasing influences of globalization on the creation and dispersion of popular music, via new technological media and the advent of transnational recording companies, have sparked a new interest among ethnomusicologists in the tensions between local and global contexts for music.[1] Some have championed the ways local musicians have maintained aspects of community tradition within transnational media. Others have stressed diversity within communities, arguing for the role of "micromusics" in multicultural societies.[2] While related to these initiatives, my questions are somewhat different. What happens, for example, when we encounter a musician whose musicking seems neither explicitly local nor global? One who remains an integrated member of the immediate community, while challenging its conventions? And what happens when this musician is also Mennonite—a member of a religious group that values community but whose churches enact this value in myriad ways?

Abram M. Friesen (1909-2002) used music as a joyful expression of his Christian faith throughout his life.[3] Born in Reinfeld, Manitoba, he was an active pastor, musician, and producer, working with four different radio stations in Canada and the United States before hosting Videon Cable Television's *Happy Home* program in Winnipeg for twenty-five years.[4] Influenced by the sentimental songs of popular musicians like Hank Snow and Jim Reeves, and fascinated by new media technologies, Friesen's musical style and television persona took shape. While his name and performance style—when coupled with the thematic content of the *Happy Home* telecasts—may seem to allow an easy placement of Friesen's music,[5] his musical pathways take on new meaning in the context of his Old Colony Mennonite heritage and subsequent affiliations with other Mennonite denominations. Herein we encounter the tension between religious devotion and popular musical style, as Friesen utilized precisely the tools that his home church initially rejected (guitar, electronic recording devices, television, and radio) to follow his "calling" to Christian witness.

Methodology

When I began this project, it seemed obvious that in order to become better acquainted with A. M. Friesen, a twenty-five-year icon of public access television in Manitoba, it would be necessary to immerse myself in the video recordings of the *Happy Home* telecasts. I soon discovered, however, that Shaw Communications Inc.—the company that took over the Videon Cable network in 2001—no longer holds any of the programs in its archives, having "recorded over" or otherwise disposed of them in the roughly ten years since Friesen's last broadcast.[6] Thankfully, Edna Friesen (A. M. Friesen's widow) has kept some telecasts from the late 1980s and early 1990s in her possession. These recordings, along with some home video footage and a few cassette tapes generously loaned to me by other family members, have formed the primary material for this study, supplemented by interviews and various articles written by or about A. M. Friesen.

Roots

A. M. Friesen's early encounters with music were in no small part affected by his Old Colony Mennonite upbringing. In his own words: "You see, I grew up Old Colony—*Alt Kolonien*—and they didn't believe in music, so we didn't have music."[7] Friesen's passion did not go unrecognized, however, and he notes that it was his father who bought him his first guitar: "My dad, he thought that I could go into music and he bought me a guitar, and from there I went!"[8] The love for music that Friesen developed in the years that followed seems to have been matched only by his evangelical fervour, and the two have become intertwined in his life story such that one is rarely separated from the other. Friesen recalled the night in 1937 that he first discovered the "joy of salvation," and it was this experience that he cited as pivotal for his life choices:

> In 1937 I went to an evening service. My uncle had an evening service in Winkler Manitoba, and he was the kind of man you couldn't help but love him.[9] Lovable and likable. And his preaching was just—well like one person who wrote to me and said, "it's so simple the way you tell it to us." Well, that's the way he used to do it. And during the service I just got to my feet and I walked to the front and I said "Uncle, if anybody wants to go to heaven when he dies it's me. Can you tell me how?" And he said to me in simple words "I can tell you, and I can pray for you, but

there's nothing that I can *do* for you. That's between you and God." And he explained to me. And friends, after that I had the joy of salvation. I went home and the same thing happened in our home. Then I went to a lot of neighbours and told them the story and after that we started an evening service, we started a choir, and I started going from place to place, telling the people the good news.[10]

Grace

Friesen's evangelical vigour was expressed in many ways, especially through his service as a pastor and later on radio and television. After moving away from the Old Colony Church and becoming ordained into ministry with the Rudnerweider Church north of Winkler, Manitoba,[11] Friesen eventually founded the Winkler Gospel Mission Church in 1954, a fellowship that emphasized mission and evangelism, and included frequent participation in gospel revivals around Manitoba and later "from coast to coast."[12]

When speaking with Friesen or reading articles written by him, however, it is not his ordination or specific church affiliations that are emphasized; instead, we find stories of starting a Sunday school, a church choir, and a young people's group. Motivated by what he saw as a misunderstanding in "most churches" as to the centrality and nature of grace and salvation, Friesen embarked on his life path, albeit with some resistance from those around him. In his own words:

> I believe in grace. By grace are you saved. And the churches wouldn't go for that. They thought it was grace plus. There is no salvation "grace plus." It's only grace. And you see, that's why I started a choir, I started a young people's meeting, started in radio and television, and all this met with great opposition. But, finally, finally, finally they gave in and I had the privilege of visiting many, many, many different churches with *great* results.[13]

Rebellion

Notably, it was not just Friesen's emphasis on grace that created controversy in the congregations in which he was active. His children recall an incident when, after starting a church choir, he carried a piano into the sanctuary (where it stayed) because he felt that instruments were useful tools of worship, not agents of distraction as they had been commonly understood.

Friesen's strong views on music and worship were equally matched by an evangelical vigour behind the pulpit. Remembering her father's preaching style at that time, daughter Marion Penner recalls a "fire and brimstone" approach, stating that "he was out to convert!"[14]

While such recollections attest to Friesen's commitment to his personal convictions, he was nevertheless held accountable by his community. When asked whether he was aware of the responses his father received from the church, Friesen's son Abe asserts that he was "too young" to notice. Abe's sister Marion, however, tells a different story:

> Oh, yes. We had a lot of *prediger gäst* you might call them—"preacher visitations" [laughter]. We'd see the car come on the yard and mother would say *"Ach, prediger gäst mal wada"* [laughter]—"another issue to discuss."[15]

When asked what sort of "issues" were discussed, she goes on: "Whatever Dad had done. Maybe he was a little too flamboyant on stage... didn't stand strictly [behind the pulpit]...."[16]

Innovation

In addition to holding theological convictions that were radical in the context of Old Colony and Rudnerweider beliefs, Friesen was "always on the cutting edge" of technological developments.[17] His children remember cutting "rose-coloured plastic records" of guests to their home,[18] and their father's construction of a motorized, propeller-driven "snowflyer" used to take the country doctor on winter house-visits.[19] His fascination with new recording and visual technologies is evidenced in his obituary, which states: "At the age of ninety-three he was still operating his computer and taking and printing pictures of friends and family using his digital camera."[20]

I mention these things not merely to celebrate Friesen's endearing characteristics, but because of the challenges they present to assumed notions about what it means to be Mennonite, what it means to be an amateur, and what it means to be ninety-three. By emphasizing the sometimes radical stances taken by A. M. Friesen during his life and ministry, we discover that in many ways, Friesen worked outside of the boundaries of "a Mennonite boy from Reinfeld."

Using his guitar, electronic media, and television—precisely the tools that would have been questionable in his home church—Friesen sought to follow his "call" to Christian witness. In so doing, he embodied an innovation that was consistent with his theology of grace—a belief that the love of God and the salvation of humankind is not contingent on one's actions or musical preferences, but is rather a gift freely given to those who believe.

Reciprocity

A. M. Friesen, as depicted on the *Happy Home* telecasts of the 1980s and 1990s, maintained a passion for sharing the love of Jesus; however, he showed little sign of the fiery preacher previously described. What we find in the host of *Happy Home* is a gentle performer who seeks a relationship of reciprocity with his audience by writing, receiving, and reading letters; who greets the camera staff while on the air; and sends "hellos" and "thank-yous" to his viewing audience. Friesen also placed much emphasis on friendship in his telecasts, speaking to viewers by name and mentioning specific weekly celebrations, meals, or other events to which he had been invited. Commenting on a similar technique used in some religious radio broadcasts of the southern United States, Howard Dorgan writes: "I was often amused by such program episodes. Later, however, that amusement was changed to a deep respect for the tradition, recognizing the role such reporting played in the lives of the listeners."[21]

This mutual intimacy bears much in common with the model of community radio offered by Lewis and Booth in their 1990 text, *The Invisible Medium*, wherein the listener is understood to participate as both subject and participant, allowing the station (or in this case, a particular broadcast) to "break through the isolation of separate constituencies."[22] In so viewing this relationship, frequently assumed binaries between active media performers and passive audience members are challenged.[23]

The intimacy afforded by this manner implies an openness and connection between Friesen and his audience, foregrounding familiarity —a characteristic that one might associate with a local performer. But does this reciprocity indicate locality?

Reflecting on the show in 1985 (after 840 telecasts), Friesen remarked on the letters he had received from such places as Africa, Trinidad, the Philippines, the United States, and London, noting that "by the grace of God, *Happy Home* has been a blessing to people in all walks of life, all ages, and many different nationalities."[24] Friesen's introduction to one episode encapsulated his interest in cross-cultural dialogue clearly, as he began by welcoming the viewing audience to the show in five different languages. When we look at the numerous and overlapping constituencies represented by viewers, we realize that reductive assumptions about a homogeneous response to Friesen's work are misleading. To borrow from Abu-Lughod, "Television, in short, renders more and more problematic a concept of cultures as localized communities of people suspended in shared webs of meaning."[25] But how is this played out musically?

Music

When examining Friesen's performance repertoire, we find that it is comprised primarily of original compositions.[26] This is not to assert, however, that Friesen was disconnected from his own musical climate. Indeed, the influences of various musicians and musical styles—both sacred and secular—can be heard in Friesen's compositions and seen in his telecasts.

Friesen's music and television persona, for example, reflected the influences of popular artists like Jim Reeves and Hank Snow, two musicians who were identified by Friesen's children as prominent in their father's record collection. While Friesen's gentle vocal production, shifting periodically between singing and the spoken word, could be compared to some of Jim Reeves's later recordings,[27] the white cowboy hat that Friesen sported on episodes of *Happy Home* in the late 1980s and early 1990s aligns him with the country persona espoused by artists like Hank Snow.[28]

Instrumentally speaking, the guitar and electronic keyboard were prominent throughout the *Happy Home* telecasts while the harmonica, prominent in earlier years, is not featured in the episodes of the late 1980s and 1990s. Furthermore, whereas both Snow and Reeves use a more extensive instrumental accompaniment (often featuring a fiddle, and in the case of Reeves, a chorus of back-up vocalists) than does Friesen, a careful outlining of chord progressions with root notes clearly spelled out in the bass line, as well as the use of a constant rhythmic ostinato, may be heard in the music of all three performers.

The influences of his church affiliations on Friesen's telecasts and compositions, in which themes of travel, hope, perseverance, and faith in a loving and grace-filled God, are pervasive. The final two lines of "Young Man in His Thirties," a quotation from the refrain of the gospel song "What a Fellowship, What a Joy Divine" (Example 1), for instance, comprise a sort of coda. While Friesen's performance asserts a minor rhythmic deviation, both the text and melody of these lines can be found in *The Mennonite Hymnary*, a hymnal first published in 1940.[29]

Example 1 "Young Man in His Thirties," text[30]

A young man in his thirties, driving through the land
A guitar on his shoulder, a Bible in his hand
I told the congregation, about the Promised Land
Driving, singing, going down the trail.

This happy driving preacher, through mire and the mud
Told the congregation, of Noah and the flood
I preached the way to heaven, you must be born again

Singing, driving, going down the trail.
Leaning, leaning, safe and secure from all alarms
Leaning, leaning, leaning on the everlasting arms.

Friesen's use of the same melody for more than one text, as well as his frequent use of particular themes, key signatures, and chord progressions, has been understood by some to indicate a "monochromatic" character in his presentation style.[31] *Winnipeg Free Press* writer Ted Allan, for example, described Friesen in 1980 as "perhaps the most lachrymose performer since Buster Keaton," with a tendency to underlay "everything with obligato guitar and harmonica noodling."[32] Such assertions, however, ignore one of the primary factors that makes each of Friesen's performances unique; namely, his interaction with these patterned, periodic elements in his music.

The combination of electronic drum-beat patterns and pre-recorded keyboard accompaniments with the poetic rhyme schemes of his texts do not serve to impose a rigid temporal structure and form upon Friesen's performances. Though he was aware of and interacted with the framework presented by the ostinato, Friesen was not bound by the time structure that it asserts. A transcribed excerpt from "A Young Man in His Thirties," wherein Friesen accompanies a solo song with his guitar, exemplifies this autonomy (Example 2). The independent treatments of the voice and the guitar (mm. 7-9), for example, create a sense of momentum through the musical phrase. Whereas Friesen emphasizes the downbeat of m. 8 with his voice, the guitar has already moved towards a new three-beat grouping beginning with the last beat of m. 7. By implementing this shift while crossing the barline, Friesen displaces the downbeat and momentarily divorces the instrument from the voice, pulling along the ear of the listener. Furthermore, Friesen varies his choice of time signatures and treatment of cadence points, sometimes adding beats to a repeated melodic motive (m. 12) or moving into a new phrase without the pause expected by the listener (mm. 8-9).

While this provides but one example, the consistent ease with which Friesen shifted from one rhythmic pattern to another during his performances seems to indicate a competence with his musical vocabulary, such that structure may be variously implied without hindering his ability to deviate from it and without binding his creativity.

Meaning

How do we begin to draw meaning from Friesen's music, given the stylistic influences of other musicians and musics upon both him and his audience?

We have already identified elements of reciprocity and familiarity in Friesen's work, but the determination of a local context is—as we have already discovered—complicated by the numerous affiliations that he held and from which he lived. Is Friesen's world ethnically, religiously, or geographically defined? Do age and class figure into this discussion? Once

Example 2 "Young Man in His Thirties," opening stanza[33]

again, layers of affiliation and points of reference indicate a musical location that is not easily pinned down. While Friesen identified Reinfeld as his home town and the Old Colony Church as his faith community of origin when asked, he did not affiliate himself with a particular church or denomination during his telecasts, and we can assume by the names signed to the letters he read that his audience was not a homogeneous religious group.[34] Given his radical views within his own church communities, his extensive travel, and his diverse musical influences (having played with the likes of Wilf Carter),[35] we find a musician who is decidedly *not* confined by Old Colony or Rudnerweider affiliations—a musician who is perhaps not local.

But how, then, do we define "local"?

In looking more closely at how Friesen's music was created and performed, received and used, it appears that the local might be best understood *relationally*. Jocelyne Gilbault—whose comments refer to world music but are nonetheless apt—has noted that cultural bonds, political allegiances, or economic necessities may impact experiences of "the local" in music even more than "genealogical heritage or the sharing of a particular geographic location."[36] Jan Fairley puts this succinctly when he writes that "global and local aren't simply contrasting descriptive terms. They suggest, rather, different perspectives of the same process."[37]

To what extent do our points of reference dictate our notions of what constitutes locality? We might, for instance, look to the *Vorsaenger* of the Old Colony Church to account for Friesen's temporal freedom at cadence points.[38] His vocal quality and composition style, however, point our gaze in the direction of the country artists dotting his record collection—artists geographically removed from the Mennonite communities of southern Manitoba. Yet if we refocus our gaze on the "sincerity" of Friesen's performances, wherein friendship is extended from television screen to living room, we find technological media enabling an intimacy between Friesen and his audiences in such a way that a "local" community of listeners is easy to imagine. But does a public access channel present an inherently local production?

Clearly, the simple equation of *intimacy* with "local-ness" is inadequate in this context, as it disregards the intricacies of Friesen's musical constitution, and the values—both personal and communal—by which it was shaped. Furthermore, while the media through which Friesen expressed himself speak to his worldview, the texts of his compositions and the words spoken on his telecasts are equally vital to our understanding of his music and ministry. What do we make of the fact that Friesen's message of grace is "simple" yet miraculous? Dare we connect Friesen's spontaneity of performance to his theology of grace, wherein belief, rather than a fixed and perfectly manicured form, is central to one's assurance of salvation?

One might argue—with good reason—that such readings superimpose layers of meaning onto Friesen's music that cannot be verified. However, if we are to assert, with Ingrid Monson, that layered musical practices may be (carefully) conceived as analogies for social and cultural practices, then perhaps this is a risk worth taking.[39] In so doing, we may find that the significance of musical inquiry lies not so much in our ability to decipher unerring truths as it does in challenging the boundaries which shape, guide, and sometimes misguide our readings of music.

In A. M. Friesen, we find not the "electronic individualist" that *The Winnipeg Free Press* would have us imagine,[40] nor do we find a "rural Mennonite boy from Reinfeld." Instead, we discover a musician whose compositions, while repetitive, are not replicable; while local, are not "very local"; whose music offers a unique example of the multiple levels of influence engaged in both the creation and interpretation of musical production and performance.

Notes

[1] See for example Arjun Appadurai, "Disjuncture and Difference in the Global Cultural Economy," *Public Culture* 2, no.2 (1990):1-24; Georgina Born and David Hesmondhalgh, eds., *Western Music and its Others: Difference, Representation, and Appropriation in Music* (Berkeley: University of California Press, 2000); Veit Erlmann, "The Politics and Aesthetics of Transnational Musics," *The World of Music* 35, no.2 (1993):3-15; Simon Frith et al., eds., *The Cambridge Companion to Pop and Rock* (Cambridge: Cambridge University Press, 2001); George Lipsitz, *Dangerous Crossroads: Popular Music, Postmodernism and the Poetics of Place* (New York: Verso, 1994); Ingrid Monson, *The African Diaspora: A Musical Perspective* (New York: Garland, 2000); Ronald Radano and Philip Bohlman, eds., *Music and the Racial Imagination* (Chicago: University of Chicago Press, 2000); and Timothy Taylor, *Global Pop: World Music, World Markets* (New York: Routledge, 1997).

[2] Mark Slobin defines "micromusics" as "the small units within big music cultures." *Subcultural Sounds: Micromusics of the West* (Hanover, NH: University Press of New England / Wesleyan University Press, 1998), 11.

[3] While "Abram M. Friesen" is Friesen's full name, and he is referred to as "Abe" in familiar settings (when signing letters, or when referred to by his widow, Edna Friesen), it seems that Friesen most often self-identified as "A. M. Friesen" when signing his name to articles and other official documents. I have chosen to follow suit for the purposes of this paper.

[4] When writing about his experience in broadcasting, Friesen refers to having worked with "four different stations." While he doesn't name these stations in the written materials that I accessed, two of his children, Marion Penner and Abe Friesen, recall Friesen broadcasting from KFGO (North Dakota, USA), and CJOB (Winnipeg, MB). Abe Friesen and Marion Penner (Friesen), interview by author, 5 January 2004, Steinbach, MB, tape recording.

[5] Although Mennonite church congregations are comprised of a diverse membership worldwide, surnames (e.g. Friesen) often signal a cultural Mennonite heritage in Canadian Mennonite communities.

[6] Marv Thiessen, telephone conversation with author, 2 January 2004, Winnipeg, MB.

[7] A. M. Friesen, telephone interview by author, 9 February 2002, Winnipeg and Toronto. Friesen's suggestion that the Old Colony church "didn't believe in music" likely refers to the type of singing that was deemed appropriate in his congregation. Whereas unison congregational singing would have been common in Old Colony worship services, the use of instruments was forbidden. Part-singing or the solo performance of sacred songs—often heard in the services of

other Mennonite denominations—was also excluded. Because worship was to be a communal experience of openness and humility before God, the use of musical instruments threatened not only to distract the congregation from worship, but also to invoke a sense of pride in the performer, hindering the development of a humble spirit. (Judith Klassen, "*Well wie noch een poa Leeda singen?* Family Music Making and Particular Experience Among Mennonites in Southern Manitoba," MA Research Paper [York University, 2003], 23).

[8] Ibid. While humility remained an important aspect of home life, the use of instruments in home music was not forbidden in Friesen's family.

[9] The uncle to which Friesen refers is possibly I. P. Friesen, a preacher who was instrumental in the formation of the Rudnerweider Church in Manitoba. While this has not been confirmed, A. M. Friesen's daughter Marion Penner asserts that "he [I. P. Friesen] was certainly a relative... an uncle or a cousin." (Marion Penner, e-mail correspondence with author, 27 August 2004). Furthermore, literature about the early Rudnerweider Church points to I. P. Friesen's involvement with evangelical activities in the Prairies during this time period. The Rudnerweider movement began in the early 1930s and emphasized personal salvation, with revival meetings described as "a movement of the spirit" by those involved. Rev. Isaac P. F. Friesen, "The Beginnings of the Rudnerweider Mennoniten Gemeinde in 1936," in *Church, Family and Village: Essays on Mennonite Life on the West Reserve*, trans. Helen Ens, ed. Adolf Ens, Jacob E. Peters and Otto Hamm (Winnipeg: Manitoba Mennonite Historical Society, 2001), 229-242.

[10] Transcribed by author from *Happy Home* telecast, personal collection of Edna Friesen.

[11] Unlike Old Colony worship, the Rudnerweider Church (now affiliated with the Evangelical Mennonite Mission Conference), included part-singing in its worship services.

[12] A. M. Friesen, interview, 9 February 2002.

[13] Ibid.

[14] Marion Penner, interview, 5 January 2004. It has been my experience that when asked about A.M.Friesen, members of his extended family, as well as other southern Manitoba Mennonites, remember him as "a rebel."

[15] Ibid.

[16] Ibid.

[17] Abe Friesen (son of A. M. Friesen) offers the following anecdote about the Polaroid camera: "Well, when that first came out, he was, I think, the first one in southern Manitoba to have one. We had to go to Walhalla [a small town 'across the border' in the United States] to buy the film!" Abe Friesen, interview, 5 January 2004.

[18] According to Tim Stafford and Richard Blaustein, home disc recorders enjoyed great popularity in North America between the late 1930s and early 1950s. Although the model and origin of Friesen's machine can not be confirmed, and I have not found specific mention of "rose-coloured" plastic discs in descriptions of home recording technology, home disc recorders were marketed in the Sears catalogue starting in 1940, with blank records and recording needles sold well into the 1950s. Tim Stafford and Richard Blaustein, "A Short History of Home Disc Recording," booklet accompanying *Down Around Bowmantown: A Portrait of a Musical Community in Northeast Tennessee, Then and Now*, produced by The Center for Appalachian Studies and Services in cooperation with the Tennes-

see Folklore Society (Now and Then Records LP 1001, 1989), 16-18.

[19] Essentially, this was an enclosed sled on runners, the construction of which Friesen had improvised.

[20] "Family Notices: Rev. Abram M. Friesen, 1909-2002," in *The Winnipeg Free Press*, 6 September 2002, C10.

[21] Howard Dorgan. *The Airwaves of Zion: Radio and Religion in Appalachia* (Knoxville: University of Tennessee Press, 1993), 11.

[22] Peter M. Lewis and Jerry Booth, *The Invisible Medium: Public, Commercial and Community Radio* (Washington, DC: Howard University Press, 1990), 191.

[23] Ideas surrounding the complex relationships between radio stations and their listeners are further developed in the recent work of Charles Fairchild, *Community Radio and Public Culture: Being an Examination of Media Access and Equity in the Nations of North America* (Cresskill, NJ: Hampton Press, 2001), 101.

[24] A. M. Friesen, "Happy Home," in *Reflections: Winnipeg's Public Access Newsletter*, May 1985.

[25] Lila Abu-Lughod, "The Interpretation of Culture(s) after Television," in *The Fate of 'Culture': Geertz and Beyond*, ed. Sherry B. Ortner (Berkeley: University of California Press, 1999), 123.

[26] The decision to compose his own music was, in Friesen's estimation, a matter of practicality, as it enabled him to avoid issues of copyright and royalties in his performances. A. M. Friesen, interview, 9 February 2002.

[27] Hear, for example, Reeves's recording of "This is it" on *Jim Reeves: Anthology*, produced by Rob Santos (BMG Heritage, compact disc 82876 54849 2, 2003), track 30.

[28] See the images of Hank Snow presented on the liner notes to *Hank Snow: RCA Country Legends*, produced by Rob Santos (Buddha Records compact disc 74465 99789 2, 2001). Of course, Snow is not the only country musician to have been pictured with cowboy paraphernalia, but our knowledge of Friesen's respect for his music makes this comparison apt. It should be noted, however, that it was extremely important to Friesen that his appearance not come between him and his audience. While the cowboy hat mentioned here was a gift from then-mayor of Calgary, Ralph Klein (accompanied by a certificate naming Friesen an "Honourary Calgarian"), Friesen stopped wearing the hat on the air when a viewer suggested that it was a symbol of pride. Edna Friesen, conversation with author, 3 January 2004.

[29] Elisha A. Hoffman (text) and Anthony J. Showalter (tune), "What a Fellowship, What a Joy Divine" in *The Mennonite Hymnary*, 9th ed. (Newton: General Conference Mennonite Church of North America, 1955), no. 489. Although we cannot be certain that the melody used on the telecast is the "original" used by Friesen in 1937, the textual incorporation of "leaning on the everlasting arms" remains a clear indication of this continuity.

[30] Transcribed by the author from *Happy Home* telecast, personal collection of Edna Friesen.

[31] For example "My Darling Dear" and "I Am Thinking of You" (found on some of the *Happy Home* telecasts used for this study) are two songs whose tunes are nearly identical, each bearing a striking resemblance to the gospel hymn "My Jesus, I Love Thee." Instrumental numbers are most often recorded in C major, with vocal pieces sung in G major. While this consistency of key signatures may be related to technical ability and the ease with which Friesen was able to perform,

it also made it possible to use the same pre-recorded bass line or accompaniment for more than one occasion, and likely made improvisation more comfortable.

[32] Ted Allan, "Video's Land of Nod: Electronic Individualists Like Abe Friesen Make VPW Channel 13 an Unforgettable Experience in Free-form TV," *Winnipeg Free Press*, 26 September 1980, 39.

[33] Transcription by author. Source: *Happy Home* telecast, personal collection of Edna Friesen.

[34] During one of the *Happy Home* telecasts from the late 1980s, Friesen prefaced a song by reminiscing about growing up in Reinfeld, Manitoba. Russian Mennonite surnames like "Sawatzky" were read from time to time on the program, but they do not appear to make up the majority of respondents. The song, titled "Nobody Answered Me," uses imagery from the biblical narrative of the Prodigal Son. However, in Friesen's text the small boy who returns home finds nobody there to welcome him. While it would be interesting to examine the relationship between Friesen and his home village implied by this story, any inferences would be speculative and perhaps dishonest in the absence of his own explanation or other points of reference.

[35] Friesen and Penner, interview, 5 January 2004.

[36] Jocelyne Gilbault, "On Redefining the 'Local' Through World Music," *The World of Music* 35, no.2 (1993): 40.

[37] Jan Fairley, "The 'Local' and 'Global' in Popular Music," in *The Cambridge Companion to Pop and Rock*, ed. Simon Frith et al. (Cambridge: Cambridge University Press, 2001), 273.

[38] The *Vorsaenger*, translated literally as "front singer," leads congregational singing in Old Colony churches. Because hymnals in this Mennonite denomination include song texts only, the *Vorsaenger* stands at the front of the sanctuary during services of worship, and "lines out" the melody to be sung with a particular hymn. The congregation joins him soon after, and the singing (usually quite slow, rhythmically flexible and melismatic in nature) continues in unison.

[39] Ingrid Monson, "Riffs, Repetition, and Theories of Globalization," in *Ethnomusicology* 43, no.1(1999):31-65.

[40] Allan, "Video's Land of Nod," 39.

Mennofolk Manitoba: Cultural, Artistic, and Generational Perspectives in a Music Festival Setting

Allison Fairbairn

My goal in this paper is to look at Mennofolk Manitoba as a place where young Mennonites can explore who they are in the context of Mennonite culture and the broader Mennonite community, free from the perceived constraints placed on them by organized religion and an older generation of Mennonites. I will begin by outlining the context of Mennofolk, a Mennonite-organized music and art festival in Winnipeg, its relationship to the original MennoFolk in Ontario and to the Mennonite Church Manitoba conference. After describing the typical group of young people who participate in the festival, I will look closely at the experiences and opinions of one particular performer, Jan Braun, and discuss how her work challenges and tries to make sense of the contradictions present in her everyday life as a Mennonite. Through her work Braun creates a new place for herself "in between" the binary oppositions she faces and has been raised to understand.

In "Beyond the Binary: Re-inscribing Cultural Identity in Mennonite Literature," Hildi Froese Tiessen addresses what she sees as a Mennonite tendency to view the world in terms of binary categories or opposites such as community/individual or insiders/outsiders.[1] This penchant for binary thinking has led Mennonites to create the monolith that is the "Mennonite community," whose opposite would be the "wordly world" beyond the community.[2] Froese Tiessen asserts that Mennonite poets and writers, in trying to understand where they have come from and who they are in this world of binary understandings, have been adept at exploring a middle ground, a grey area in between the typical "black or white" Mennonite understanding of the world.

This grey area is one that Mennofolk Manitoba is able to inhabit. However, I do not feel as though the tendency to think in terms of the binaries identified by Froese Tiessen is restricted to the way Mennonites view their surroundings. As one who has been both an insider and an outsider in the Mennonite world (my own family is decidedly WASP, but I attended Mennonite schools and have a large network of Mennonite friends), I have observed that many Mennonites actively work to construct divisions between the Mennonite world and the so-called "worldly world." Mennofolk is in some ways an example of this deliberate construction, as are the typical MCC (Mennonite Central Committee) relief sales held across central and western Canada. Although these events are certainly open to anyone, their secondary (some would argue primary) function seems to be one of fellowship with the local Mennonite community.³

In the following discussion, I will use the phrase "Mennonite community" to refer specifically to the network of Mennonites on the Canadian prairies. I will be dealing primarily with those Mennonites who until recently were referred to as General Conference (GC) Mennonites, a group whose cultural ancestors were mainly Russian-German Mennonites. Although they came to Canada from Russia, these Mennonites retain a German-influenced cultural heritage resulting from prior emigrations through Europe; speaking Low German is often part of this heritage, especially (but not exclusively) among people who were themselves immigrants, or whose parents were immigrants. Whether they know each other through blood relations, marriage, congregational communities, hometowns, volunteer experiences, or college experiences—to name just a few ways—these Mennonites have formed a network of connections that defies the generally individualistic experiences of the average North American lifestyle. To be "Mennonite" on the Canadian prairies means more than simply having a religious affiliation; it also connotes a cultural identity, with traditions that have been passed down through generations.

Many Mennonites choose to remain a part of the Mennonite community—that network of friends and family where they feel most comfortable—but may or may not attend a Mennonite church. For the sake of clarity, I will refer to those Mennonites who are involved in the church as "faith-based" Mennonites, and those who are not directly involved in the religious side of things as "cultural" Mennonites. "Cultural" Mennonites may appreciate the values of the Mennonite church and/or the cultural traditions of one or more lineages of the Mennonite heritage, but they may not be involved in church organizations or perhaps are struggling with their beliefs.

Mennofolk Manitoba began in 1999 as a response to the remarkably large number of young people connected to Mennonite Church Manitoba

(MCM) congregations who were making original music outside of the church. Although this event was initiated by the MCM conference, organizers felt the music did not really fit in a church setting but that it still grew out of a faith context and deserved the support of the Mennonite church community—that part of the network that remains tied to the church and the provincial conference.

The planners of Mennofolk Manitoba drew on the philosophy of Ontario MennoFolk, which had originated in 1987. The Ontario festival's statement is framed by the following set of polarities or perceived opposites:

A. Mennonite-Based vs. Ecumenical/Secular
B. Amateur Musicians vs. Professional Musicians
C. All Ages vs. Young Adults Only
D. Group Performers vs. Individual Performers
E. Outdoor/Camp Setting vs. Indoor Setting
F. Musical Variety vs. One Style (only Folk)
G. MennoFolk as an Ongoing Process vs. MennoFolk as a One Weekend Event[4]

In their statement, the organizers of Ontario MennoFolk acknowledge the grey area between these polarities and refer to it as a continuum, but express definite "leanings" toward the first of each set of opposites. Thus, the philosophy emphasizes amateur musicians over professionals, groups over individuals, and a variety of musical styles over uniformity. The philosophy also promotes music in "good taste," which is defined as musical genres and lyrics that are not offensive to the largest number of listeners. Although Ontario MennoFolk is coordinated by the Student and Young Adult Commission of the Mennonite Church Eastern Canada (MCEC) conference and most performers are young adults, performers are drawn from all age groups and an effort is made to bring in music for children to make it a family event. It is primarily a camping event, where outdoor activities can be enjoyed.

What is interesting here is that the Ontario MennoFolk statement appears to take the religious meaning of "Mennonite" (as opposed to the cultural meaning) for granted through the direct involvement of the MCEC conference and through the unquestioned inclusion of explicitly Christian music such as worship bands. For example, the statement's first set of polarities—"Mennonite-Based vs. Ecumenical/Secular"—and the definition that follows point to a target audience that is intricately linked to Mennonite churches and the MCEC conference:

> The "Menno" part of MennoFolk is important to us. Our primary constituency in terms of performers, audience and advertising is Mennonite. It's where our roots are...we are not

saying that all lyrics need to be Christian, simply in good taste. We want to strengthen our visibility and the participation of the wider MCEC community.[5]

"Mennonite" in this context is set apart from the "secular," as well as from other Protestant or Christian denominations, which suggests a faith-based meaning of the word rather than a broader cultural meaning. There is also a strong suggestion of catering to those who keep the festival financially afloat: as long as funding comes in the form of Mennonite advertisers and the MCEC conference, it makes sense to curb controversy that might arise from vulgar language, for example. At the same time, the Ontario festival encourages original music and creativity in a variety of styles. It is a fine balance.

Initially, Mennofolk Manitoba also took place in a camp setting and drew performers through the religious community.[6] Unlike Ontario's event, Mennofolk Manitoba was meant primarily for youth and young adults. There were no strong ties to the local college community at this time, so connections were made through congregations. The Mennonite Church Manitoba (MCM) conference gave the festival minimal financial support of about five hundred dollars. In 2002, responsibility for planning the event was handed over from the original conference-sponsored committee to a new committee representing the current generation of young Mennonites associated with the greater Winnipeg Mennonite church community, including the post-secondary schools.[7] A year later, Mennofolk Manitoba moved from Camp Assiniboia (a conference-supported camp located a short distance outside Winnipeg) to the West End Cultural Centre in Winnipeg, a site that MCM hoped would encourage more people to attend, including those outside both "cultural" and "religious" Mennonite circles. Goals were set to welcome Mennonites of all ages, not just youth and young adults.

Both groups—the Mennofolk organizers and the MCM conference—have similar goals: each wants to bring young Mennonites back into the Mennonite world. Unlike the conference, however, the Mennofolk committee is not as interested in bringing estranged Mennonites back into the Mennonite church as it is in inviting them back to the broader Mennonite cultural community and trying to help them feel accepted. The Ontario MennoFolk festival's philosophy focuses on Mennonites in terms of performers, audience, and advertising, yet gives no firm definition of the term "Mennonite." However, its mandate implies that the organizers are seeking Mennonite musicians who are directly tied to churches in the MCEC conference. By contrast, a look at Mennofolk Manitoba's "Identity and Mission Statement" soon reveals that the church, like the conference, is kept somewhat at arm's length:

> Mennofolk is a festival celebrating music and art from people associated with the Mennonite community....
>
> Mennofolk seeks to provide a welcoming atmosphere for people regardless of age and level of connectedness to the Mennonite Church to come together and appreciate the music and art of the Mennonite community....
>
> We realize that some people feel estranged or disconnected from the Mennonite Church. Mennofolk seeks to help bridge the gap by providing an atmosphere and contexts for art that may not be "acceptable" in the church.[8]

Mennofolk Manitoba's statement makes it clear that its organizers are concerned with providing a welcoming atmosphere for those who feel distant from the greater Mennonite cultural community (including but not limited to the church-going community), and that the emphasis is on "Mennonite" as a network of friends and family, rather than "Mennonite" as a faith-based group. The intent is fellowship, not pressure to be devout or even to worship God, although the organizers do not feel compelled to hide religion in any way.

When I assert that Mennofolk Manitoba keeps religion at a distance, I mean organized religion, not Christianity or spirituality. In fact, spirituality is intensely important to many of the artists and organizers, as are the core values of the Mennonite church. However, many Mennofolk artists feel as though the Mennonite religious community is not appreciative of their art, often because it challenges acceptable behaviours or familiar taboos, or reacts against expectations—as art should. As noted in its mission statement, Mennofolk Manitoba seeks to give artists appreciation without prejudice, and without pressure to conform to the expectations of organized religion. "[The festival] is an effort to be a welcoming community . . . to demonstrate that our God can be recognized (and worshipped) in a variety of ways."[9] This openness toward various views of God in a decidedly "Mennonite" setting appears to grow out of the grey area between the "worldly world" and the "Mennonite world," and between the younger generation's new perspectives on the Mennonite faith and the traditions and expectations of their parents' and grandparents' generations.

The typical crowd that attends Mennofolk Manitoba is an under-thirty group of current or former Canadian Mennonite University (CMU) and Canadian Mennonite Bible College (CMBC) students, many single and some young married couples, typically a General Conference group. Although I attended CMBC in 1997 and 1998, I have been away from the greater Mennonite Bible college community for some time. Yet when I attended

Mennofolk Manitoba in February 2004, I was soon struck by the feeling that almost everyone—in a group of possibly 200 young people—knew each other.[10] There is also a typical mode of dress for the people at Mennofolk, one that is strikingly uniform in spite of admirable attempts at originality and difference. Clothes are simple and low-maintenance, typically from thrift stores and for the most part without name brands, reflecting their wearers' adherence to cultural-religious values of simple living and concern for environmental impact, whether or not they attend church. I will generalize here and assert that the politics of Mennofolk and of most of its performers and attendees are considerably leftist. Pacifistic ideals come through in the t-shirts (sold at the festival) that proclaim, "Make borscht, not bombs," "Make pie not war," and in the social commentary of song lyrics that are direct reactions to the war in Yugoslavia and the disappearance of traditional rural life.

Mennofolk Manitoba is a unique combination of cultural celebration in the context of the outside world, and worldly challenge issued by Mennonite youth to the Mennonite world. Froese Tiessen notes that the lines between "insiders" and "outsiders" blurred as a post-World War II Mennonite "oneness" dissolved during the later twentieth century, thanks to factors such as urbanism, evangelicalism, and a greater access to travel and information. Even so, "Mennonites insist on referring to something they call 'the Mennonite community' and persist also in accepting the notion that any voices that do not emerge from what they have conventionally regarded as 'the centre' must be perceived as 'marginal' at best."[11]

To the young Mennonites involved with Mennofolk I talked to, the "centre" of the perceived Mennonite community is associated with the older generation, likely people their parents' or grandparents' age, who run the church. The younger generation's perceptions of the older powers-that-be is on the surface fairly typical—the older generation is too conservative, too willing to dismiss the concerns of the younger generation, conspicuously disinterested in and absent from the Mennofolk festival and, in turn, apparently disinterested in and unsupportive of the art they are making. The younger generation—the Mennofolk generation—often perceives its own place in this Mennonite community as minimal, a group on the margins whose opinions are not heard and whose needs are often not addressed.

Yet the entire premise of the festival is based on the concept of a "oneness" among Mennonites, and the community atmosphere of Mennofolk—the fact that those who go there know they will be surrounded by friends and family of a similar ethnic background—is taken for granted and celebrated. When the festival was held at Camp Assiniboia, a Mennonite

Bible camp that drew only a Mennonite crowd, supper consisted of a barbeque. Nothing notably Mennonite about that. But when I attended Mennofolk on a Sunday at the West End Cultural Centre—a venue not tied to Mennonite culture in any perceptible way and one that invited the attendance of more cultural outsiders—I was pleasantly surprised to find that organizers were serving *Faspa* around suppertime. *Faspa* is defined in Herman Rempel's *Mennonite Low German Dictionary* as "a traditional Mennonite light meal between lunch and supper,"[12] but my own understanding of the meal is that it is was typically served on Sundays and involves no cooking, so the women did not have to work on the day of rest. Buns and cold cuts, pickles and veggies, cheese and cookies would not be so notable at a smaller, non-Mennonite and non-young adult event, but the enactment of this Mennonite cultural tradition in a group of 150 to 200 young people is interesting. Organizers baked dozens of cookies and buns, and someone's parents donated the pickles and cheeses. That the cultural tradition of *Faspa* on Sundays is celebrated while the organized religion is kept at arm's length is significant, I think. In the same vein, the visual art component of the festival included items of folk art such as a quilt, a painted chair, and handmade clothing displayed among the more "modern" paintings and collages.

The large community that is covered by the umbrella of "Mennonite" in Winnipeg makes for a pool of vastly different musicians and artists. At the same time, musical style and genre at the 2004 festival was, for the most part, conventional. The afternoon consisted of folk and bluegrass music, and the evening featured pop and rock music, poetry, and spoken word. For the remainder of this paper I want to focus not on genre choice, but rather on an interesting example of cultural perception and mediation that I witnessed during my day at Mennofolk, demonstrated in the performance of Jan Braun.

Braun grew up on a farm near a small prairie town that is still predominantly populated by Mennonites. Her family is very active and, I would say, powerful in her home congregation, a General Conference church. She laughingly told me in my interview with her that she feels like an "outsider" in her own family, and that she was labeled the non-singer in her family along with her dad.[13] This, she feels, made her shy about singing, although she can read music and feels comfortable singing an alto line if she stands near a confident singer. I asked her if she thought that singing should come naturally for her, being a Mennonite, and she replied that it does not necessarily feel as though it should be natural, but rather that there is something about the choral music of the religion and the culture tied to the religion that feels so important. Jan was raised to feel a close relationship between her spirituality and the music traditions of the Mennonite church, and although other music may prompt an emotive reaction from her, no other music hits her on this spiritual level, or is so closely linked to the history of her people—of which there are no known non-Mennonites. When she attended Canadian Mennonite University, Jan immediately felt the inclusiveness of music and was asked to participate in spontaneous music-making by non-judgmental friends, who encouraged her not only to participate but also to help create. This typically took place in a lounge around one or two guitars, but she also experimented with found objects, creating percussion ensembles with friends. Jan felt that this inclusiveness, in spite of her skill level, increased her musical abilities and made her less shy about music.

At the 2004 Mennofolk Manitoba, as part of the duo Teacup, Jan performed spoken word poetry together with Mike Petkau's rhythmic electric guitar and vocal backup.[14] Jan's poetry is deeply affected by her faith, which she struggles with but still finds very important. Her poetry is also influenced by the Mennonite cultural community she has grown up in, its strong literary tradition, her rural prairie upbringing, and her homosexuality—including her family's struggle to accept it. She feels that art should challenge and seeks to do exactly that by addressing a hierarchy she perceives within the Mennonite literary world and the taboos around sexuality in Mennonite culture and religion. Having been active in several churches across Saskatchewan, Manitoba and Ontario—including presenting sermons and acting on several boards—Jan feels that the main problem with the old guard of the Mennonite church is their refusal to admit new ideas, and in her opinion, that is what is pushing young people away. She asserts that maybe young people are not anti-religion as such—maybe they still carry with them the values and tenets important to the Mennonite faith but are simply not finding a place for themselves in the church.

Jan's poetry becomes a powerful performance art on stage. Although practiced to a certain extent, there is a feeling of in-the-moment improvisation and dialogue between Jan and Mike, with her words suggesting the direction of each piece and his guitar style, which varies from poem to poem, setting the general tone. For example, Jan's poem "Slam" appears in print as follows:[15]

> slam my body
> against the body
>
>   my prayer
>   hope

> to retain hope
> i will slam my body
> against the body
> if only to smash my heart
> if it hardens one day
>
> be peaceful
>
> obey:
> your parents
> the body
>
> deny:
> yourself
> the body

As a poem, "Slam" is a powerful work in its own right, and when it is presented by Teacup, Jan's frustration and anger hits the viewer/listener on a visceral level. Repetitions of the phrase "slam my body / against the body" are spoken quietly, shouted into the microphone, *performed* in such an immediate way as to make very real Jan's situation in the so-called "Mennonite world," expressing her struggles to find a certain level of comfort and happiness with sex and sexuality in a framework so dominated by traditional religious values. The "body"—the human body, the church body—becomes a one-word tug-of-war between desire and liberation (in the form of sexuality and anger), and obedience and peacefulness (the expectation a Mennonite should be "quiet in the land").

Jan came to the February 2004 Mennofolk with an agenda, one of presenting her challenges to a group of people who would understand to a large degree where she was coming from and what she was reacting to, a group who would likely be more welcoming and supportive than a random audience in a murky bar. Her performances with the now-defunct Teacup gave her a certain level of notoriety not only in the Mennonite cultural community, but also in the greater Winnipeg music and literary community. Arts and university newspapers took notice of the group, which had some radio exposure as well as a tour through Ontario (with Mike Petkau and Dave Quanbury) before calling it quits in May 2004. Through her performances with Teacup, Jan carved out a unique place for herself in the world of Mennonite music-making. She was able to take an active part in music, something she feels is so important to the culture she holds dear, yet in a manner in which she could feel confident to explore her own passion for words and the effect the Mennonite world has had on her life and her writing. In these ways, Mennofolk offered Jan the opportunity to create a place for herself where she could be appreciated and accepted by the Mennonite community for who she is, rather than for who she is expected to be.

As Froese Tiessen notes, the master narrative, an idea rooted in binary thinking, is an essential resource for the artist on the margins to rally against.[16] Without, for example, the taboos around sexuality in the religion and culture that I perceive to be a major part of the Mennonite master narrative and a point of contention for young Mennonites today, the challenges Jan put forth would lack meaning. Jan found a place in the middle, between the younger generation and the older guards of the culture, between a disappearing ethnic rural culture and the urban "of-the-world" life she now lives, between music and poetry. Froese Tiessen asserts that by writing about the world that exists between binary oppositions, Mennonite poets reveal the complexity that lies beyond the typical monolithic generalizations of their culture. In the same way, organizers, artists, performers, and audience members at Mennofolk experience and create an "in-between," a site where they can celebrate aspects of their culture and heritage with very little pressure to conform to ideas of religion that they may or may not be struggling with; a site where cultural rituals can be observed and the complexity of the meaning of "Mennonite" can be addressed at whatever level participants feel comfortable. That Jan's personal, political, and often controversial work was welcomed by the festival and the audience with open arms (and vigorous applause) suggests the beginning of a changing of the guard and a new narrative that combines traditional Mennonite values and cultural rituals with a gradually shifting world-view. And Jan's personal insights as a lesbian artist who passionately wants to celebrate both her religious and cultural "Mennoniteness" find their place in that undefined grey area between the "Mennonite world" and the "worldly world" surrounding it.

Notes

[1] Hildi Froese Tiessen, "Beyond the Binary: Re-inscribing Cultural Identity in the Literature of Mennonites," *Mennonite Quarterly Review* 72 (1998): 491-501.

[2] The expression "the worldly world out there" is borrowed from Di Brandt, "how I got saved," in *Why I Am a Mennonite: Essays on Mennonite Identity*, ed. Harry Loewen (Scottdale, PA: Herald Press, 1988) and cited in Froese Tiessen, "Beyond the Binary," 492.

[3] Relief sales are one- or two-day festivals of Mennonite arts, crafts, and food

that are organized to raise money for MCC and affiliated organizations for their charity and relief work around the world.

⁴ See Appendix 1 for complete statement of the "Ontario MennoFolk Philosophy." Additional MennoFolk materials consulted in the research of this paper include past programmes (2000, 2002); "Student and Young Adult Minister Report (1990, 1991); letter to MennoFolk performers (20 May 2003); and performers' schedules (2002, 2003); all supplied courtesy of Mark Diller Harder, Mennonite Church Eastern Canada. Further information on Ontario MennoFolk can be found at http://www.mcec.on.ca/youngadult/mennofolk.htm.

⁵ Ontario MennoFolk Philosophy, Appendix 1.

⁶ Thanks to Brendu Grunau, chair of Manitoba Mennofolk planning committee, 2003-2005, for her insight, access and endless help in researching Mennofolk Manitoba. More information on the event can be found at http://www.mennofolk.bestmusicpages.com/home.html.

⁷ These include the (General Conference) Canadian Mennonite Bible College, the (Mennonite Brethren) Concord College, both of which joined Menno Simons College in 1999 to form the Canadian Mennonite University. For a clearer picture of this merger, see http://www.cmu.ca.

⁸ "Mennofolk Manitoba Identity and Mission Statement." See Appendix 2 for a complete version.

⁹ Ibid.

¹⁰ Observations based on fieldnotes, interviews, and film footage from February 29, 2004. I want to thank Heather Peters for her considerable help in video-recording this event and in providing me with constructive feedback on the interviews that I conducted.

¹¹ Froese Tiessen, "Beyond the Binary," 495.

¹² Herman Rempel, *Kjenn Jie Nock Plautdietsch?: A Mennonite Low German Dictionary*, second ed. (Rosenort, MB: PrairieView Press, 1995).

¹³ Interview with Jan Guenther Braun, with input from Mike Petkau, on Saturday, February 28, 2004.

¹⁴ Petkau is an up-and-coming Winnipeg singer/song-writer/producer. A familiar face at Mennofolk, he too spent time at CMBC with Jan and me before embarking on a full-time career in the music business. See http://www.mikepetkau.com.

¹⁵ Jan Guenther Braun, "Slam," *Ach Veit Nuscht* (unpublished booklet, 2002). My analysis of Teacup's performance of "Slam" is based on film footage from Mennofolk, February 29, 2004, and on a CD recording of Teacup, with music by Mike Petkau (Head in the Sand Records, 2004).

¹⁶ Froese Tiessen, "Beyond the Binary," 494.

Appendix 1

*Ontario MennoFolk Philosophy*¹

The MennoFolk committee met recently. We spent most of the meeting talking about the whole philosophy of MennoFolk. We realized that we keep bumping up against this in most of our decisions. We also realize that it is more difficult to define exactly what MennoFolk is. Maybe it's more a cluster of understandings. We decided that the most helpful way to define MennoFolk is to set up a series of polarities representing the key MennoFolk issues. MennoFolk will lean in certain directions along a continuum in each of these polarities. Each of these leanings results in concrete ideas for how we set up MennFolk. This format recognizes that MennoFolk is a fluid evolving event, but gives us some directions in our planning. We used 7 different sets of polarities. We've listed the pole we lean towards first. This is followed by some explanations, rationale and outcomes.

A. Mennonite-Based vs. Ecumenical/Secular

The 'Menno' part of MennoFolk is important to us. Our primary constituency in terms of performers, audience and advertising is Mennonite. It's where our roots are. This does not mean that MennoFolk is exclusive to others, simply where its focus is. We want to encourage Mennonite musicians to perform and encourage original compositions. We are not saying that all lyrics need to be Christian, simply in good taste. We want to strengthen our visibility and the participation of the wider MCEC community.

B. Amateur Musicians vs. Professional Musicians

MennoFolk is primarily for amateur musicians. We want to give a forum for amateur musicians to play in front of people. We don't want musicians to feel intimidated by playing at MennoFolk. At the same time, (semi-) professionals are welcome to play at MennoFolk, if they are comfortable with the philosophy and format. All performers volunteer their time and talents rather than some being paid. Musicians can sell their own recordings. All performers are given similar time slots (no 'headline' groups or individuals).

C. All Ages vs. Young Adults Only

Even though MennoFolk is planned by the Student and Young Adult Commission it is an event open to all ages. While performers tend to be young adults, there are no age restrictions. (We've had both high school groups and older groups). The weekend is intended for all age groups. This means deliberately planning some family-focused (children's) music. The camp setting is conducive to all ages. It means we are open to the CMC youth conference joining us.

D. Group Performers vs. Individual Performers

We would like to move more towards group performers than individuals, even though we will still have individuals perform. Groups utilize the talents of more people and give more people the chance to participate in

MennoFolk. They also tend to be more interesting for the audience. We usually give longer time slots to groups. This leaning towards groups means trying to shoulder-tap and encourage groups to form for MennoFolk.

E. Outdoor/Camp Setting vs. Indoor Setting

MennoFolk is an outdoor event that works best in a camp setting. The atmosphere of MennoFolk is informal and relaxed. There needs to be space to camp and enjoy outdoor sports/leisure (ex. volleyball, baseball, swimming). The stage is outside where people can choose to sit and listen or simply enjoy the Stratford arena or grass parking lot.

F. Musical Variety vs. One Style (only Folk)

MennoFolk is intended to have musicians perform a wide variety of musical styles with various combinations of instruments and voices. MennoFolk has included acoustic guitar, rock, hammered dulcimer, a cappella vocals, traditional folk instruments and more. The only concern would be that music be in good taste (for example, not an abundance of vulgar language). For the sake of neighbours, we may also need to have some volume control.

G. MennoFolk as an Ongoing Process vs. MennoFolk a One Weekend Event

We decided that MennoFolk need not be only a One Weekend a Year Event. MennoFolk could take on added dimensions throughout the rest of the year. Part of the purpose of MennoFolk is to nurture and encourage Mennonite musicians and artists. One way would be to sponsor occasional development workshops (ie. Composing, jamming etc) and additional coffee houses (Blaurock). We want to encourage people to learn how to play in groups and compose their own music. Much of this culminates in the MennoFolk weekend.

Appendix 2

Mennofolk Manitoba Identity and Mission Statement[2]

Mennofolk is a festival celebrating music and art from people associated with the Mennonite community.

Mennofolk seeks to provide opportunity for expression for those art forms that may not ordinarily be found in church.

Mennofolk seeks to provide a welcoming atmosphere for people regardless of age and level of connectedness to the Mennonite Church to come together and appreciate the music and art of the Mennonite community.

Recently the Mennofolk committee met to re-visit who we are and what makes us unique and why we should continue to hold Mennofolk. Something that gives Mennofolk identity is the fact that it is Mennonite. It is rooted in tradition, but provides outlets from the traditional to explore new artistic ideas stemming from the Mennonite culture. We realize that some people feel estranged or disconnected from the Mennonite Church. Mennofolk seeks to help bridge the gap by providing an atmosphere and contexts for art that may not be "acceptable" in the church. It is an effort to be a welcoming community. This is not to say that Mennofolk is a new kind of liberation movement, but rather to demonstrate that our God can be recognized (and worshipped) in a variety of ways.

This approach refers to both the performers and artists as well as the people attending the event. Mennofolk has typically been advertised as an all ages show. This still remains the case. Most of the performers will be young amateurs, but (semi) professionals are welcome, and may be invited to perform.

Notes to Appendices

[1] Ontario MennoFolk Philosophy used with the permission of Mark Diller Harder and the Ontario MennoFolk committee. The philosophy was written following a committee meeting in spring, 1998. That year, MennoFolk was invited to take place in Stratford, ON, in conjunction with the July annual meeting of Mennonite Church Canada. However, the committee ultimately decided to hold MennoFolk at nearby Hidden Acres Camp instead. *[personal communication from Mark Diller Harder, 1 September 2005 – ed.]*

[2] Found on Mennofolk Manitoba's website: http://www.mennofolk.bestmusicpages.com/home.html; used with the permission of Brenda Grunau and the 2004 Mennofolk Committee.

Voices of Performers, Composers, and Singer-Songwriters

Fraser Valley String Orchestra

Leonard N. Neufeldt

Our tightwad violin teacher, also conductor,
would hitch his pants twice *larghetto*
ritardando so they could settle down
to where they'd been,
and then his hands were over us like a holy man's,
benediction that could hush any audience,
even Yarrow's berry pickers,
loggers, hopyard slashers, dairy farmers,
and volunteer firemen,

and music streamed from us.
We moved together in a breath
like an endless field of grass in wind
or quiet rollers of an earthquake
in the schoolyard, the stage floor
near the cellos and double bass alive.

At intermission we couldn't remember
a single entry or note in advance,
but we were unafraid.
Take those nights when mosquitoes
wheedled through my bedroom window screen,
tuning in the dark in twos and threes
and starting together as one,
exchanging melodies, positions, tempo
like new orchestra members practicing
face to face in the wings.

Sound in the Land

Too warm in bed after the final concert
I could hear violins singing out
with the mosquitoes to the edge of town,
across the U.S. border, through the mountains,
under the faint arc of the Lion's Gate
suspension bridge, beyond the Pacific
toward a small blue planet, well-lit overhead,
revolving slowly with sounds, resinous
with open notes, double stops,
crescendos, muted refrains, *ritardandos*,
perfect vibrato in the upper positions,
and six cellos indistinguishable,
the way I dreamed for years of playing,
without teacher

or conductor. Out there,
everything memorized in the dark blue
of the new world, fingers came down
where they pleased, no matter how much was left
of our former life. No one
could stop us.

No one.

(On) Being Mennonite, Being a Composer, and Composing "Mennonite Music"

Anna Janecek

The fascinating work of North American Mennonite composers is often overlooked within academic circles—indicative, perhaps, of prevailing attitudes concerning what constitutes "Mennonite music." While many, both within the academy and beyond, immediately think of robust and hearty four-part congregational singing, others turn first to particular hymn texts and tunes that have come to signify or characterize this rich singing tradition: "Nun danket alle Gott," for instance, or the popular anthem "Praise God from whom all blessings flow." Some make a short leap from these ecclesiastical roots to more formal choral singing, including church and school-based choirs, while a few others turn to those professional musicians within our midst including vocalists, conductors, pianists, and, occasionally, other classically trained instrumentalists. A brief survey of the academic literature confirms this perception. In a search of several music research indices, nearly 75 percent of citations addressing Mennonite music dealt with hymnody, hymn singing, hymn writing, or some similar aspect of congregational song in worship whether past or present.[1] Half of the remaining articles dealt with choral singing, choirs and choral festivals, while the remainder covered a variety of topics ranging from classical vocal soloists to popular music among Amish youth to a folk group which performs "Amish, Mennonite, Brethren, and other traditional styles." Yet as the 2004 Sound in the Land festival so amply demonstrated, "Mennonite music" is in fact a richly variegated panoply featuring all manner of musical styles, mediums, instruments, technologies and ideologies, both sacred and secular. To some extent, this may have always been the case, but it is particularly valid in the reality that is twenty-first-century North America. The range of music being performed, listened to, or composed by North American Mennonites is indeed vast and diverse.

The place of Mennonite composers within this diversity is particularly interesting, for it is here that pivotal questions of identity, influence, and the definition of "Mennonite music" intersect. To what extent is the music written by Mennonite composers "Mennonite," and to what extent do their experiences as "Mennonites" influence their compositional craft? At an even more rudimentary level, what constitutes "Mennonite music" in the first place, and what experiences, backgrounds or beliefs make one "Mennonite?" These are but a few of the issues raised in a recent survey of North American Mennonite composers soliciting reflections on the experience of being both Mennonite and a composer.[2] Central to the discussion is the question of whether Mennonite composers have an identifiable "voice"—whether any unifying identity, be it stylistic, aesthetic, cultural, or ideological, can be said to exist among them.

Five of the most well-established composers of the North American Mennonite community were invited to participate in this survey: Esther Wiebe, professor emerita of Canadian Mennonite Bible College (CMBC, now Canadian Mennonite University); J. Harold Moyer, professor emeritus of Music at Bethel College (North Newton, Kansas); Carol Ann Weaver, Associate Professor of Music at Conrad Grebel University College (Waterloo, Ontario); Larry Warkentin, recently retired Professor of Music at Fresno Pacific University (Fresno, California); and Leonard Enns, Professor of Music at Conrad Grebel University College (Waterloo, Ontario).[3] Together, these five composers exemplify the diversity of musical voices present within the North American Mennonite community today. Esther Wiebe and J. Harold Moyer may be called the pioneers of Mennonite composition in Canada and the United States respectively and as such, each has made important and lasting contributions to this field, influencing many younger composers through their teaching and writing. Both are known primarily for their vocal and choral writing, whether original or arranged, ranging from large-scale operas, oratorios, and musical dramas,[4] to extensive collections of hymns and sacred choral selections suitable for smaller school and church-based choirs. While between them they have also written numerous instrumental works, Moyer in particular made important strides in this medium, writing works for orchestra, chamber ensemble, concert band, and instrumental solo, at a time when this was virtually unheard of among Mennonites.[5] Wiebe's and Moyer's compositional style tends towards the traditional and diatonic, but both have also ventured beyond into more dissonant or popular sounds when necessary or desired.

Weaver, Warkentin, and Enns all represent a slightly younger generation of composers, though one no less established than the previous generation.

Carol Ann Weaver, raised and educated in the United States, has spent much of her professional life in Canada. Trained as a concert pianist, Weaver has primarily composed instrumental works, featuring large ensembles and a variety of instruments ranging from the traditional to the electric and synthesized. She has also written a number of vocal and choral works, often with substantial instrumental accompaniment. Weaver's writing displays the influence of both her upbringing (classical, vocal) and her education (atonal, minimalist, experimental). More recent works also demonstrate an increasing interest in world and popular musics and the limitless possibilities of fusions of various musical styles.[6]

Larry Warkentin was also raised and educated in the United States, remaining there for much of his professional life. His works cover a broad range of media, though works for solo voice and other vocal groupings (including hymns and choral settings) predominate. Among his purely instrumental compositions are works for orchestra, chamber ensemble, solo piano, and carillon.[7] His musical style may be called at once modern and traditional; though primarily diatonic and tonal, it is not without dissonance and incorporates many non-traditional compositional techniques.

Leonard Enns has spent most of his life in Canada, with the exception of a few years spent pursuing a PhD at Northwestern University (Evanston, Illinois). His background in choral music and choral conducting has greatly influenced his compositional work, such that the vast majority of his works are for this medium, both accompanied and a cappella.[8] His compositional style further reflects this influence, being largely tonal and diatonic.

The composers' reflections and responses to questions posed in the survey fall into three broad categories. The first category addresses matters pertaining to their experiences as Mennonites, particularly in their youth and early childhood, but also in regards to their present connections to the Mennonite community. The second addresses matters relating more specifically to their experiences as composers including their earliest compositional explorations, the musical language(s) with which they have become most comfortable, and the styles, genres, and mediums in which they have worked over the years. The third category addresses connections and points of divergence between their experiences as Mennonites and as composers, with specific attention given to the ways in which their Mennonite backgrounds and/or current associations may have influenced or continue to influence their compositional expression. Issues raised in each of these categories touch upon various aspects related to the central question guiding this paper—namely, is there any unifying, identifiable voice among Mennonite composers?

Being Mennonite

While these five composers have come to represent a vast array of educational, professional, and personal life experiences, their earliest musical and personal origins are remarkably similar. All were raised in Mennonite homes, both culturally and theologically, whether in small, rural farming communities or in larger, more urban settings. Perhaps not surprisingly, each composer grew up surrounded by music beginning at an early age. Many lived in households where music, primarily sacred, frequently classical, and only rarely "popular" held a central role. Larry Warkentin notes,

> My earliest musical influences . . . came from my family. My grandfather, Herman Janzen, played guitar, autoharp and piano as a folk musician. . . . My mother, Marie (Janzen) played piano, but not in public. . . . And my father, Pete, always encouraged us in our interests, although he found little satisfaction in classical music. Their hope was that I would become a competent church pianist. When I became more interested in Chopin than in "Heavenly Sunshine" they were a little concerned, but by then it was too late to change course.[9]

Carol Ann Weaver cites four-part a cappella singing as "the only form of live ensemble music we were able to have in my early days." While jazz and popular music were forbidden in her childhood home, music was nevertheless always present, particularly in the form of her grandfather's vast classical record collection, covering the works of composers such as Bach, Beethoven, Mozart, Haydn, and Schubert. Outside the home, numerous musical influences could also be found in the predominantly Mennonite communities, churches, and schools that similarly defined their early years. As Leonard Enns comments:

> I grew up with choral music, not so much in the home but certainly in the church and the schools—our little village school in Arnaud, Manitoba; the Mennonite Collegiate in Gretna, Manitoba where I finished high school; and the Canadian Mennonite Bible College in Winnipeg. . . . Choral music—that was my "textural environment," and it clearly impacted my writing. It was a cultural influence of growing up Russian Mennonite, and a heritage of teachers who had introduced it to the school system in the Mennonite villages in nineteenth-century Russia.

These settings provided the original impetus and venues for early compositional explorations. Esther Wiebe writes, "Since the age of four, when a piano was brought into my farm home, I played by ear and improvised freely. This led to the first composition I have a faint memory of— a piano solo—*Northern Lights*." Carol Ann Weaver's early compositional attempts were also largely in the home: ". . . my extended family was very long-suffering. My Grandpa, Grandma, Mother, and Aunt, plus my sisters were frequently captive audiences for my first musical experiments." Others cite Mennonite educational institutions as places where their compositional inclinations were first tested. Leonard Enns remembers trying his hand at "a few choral compositions" with Esther Wiebe at what was then CMBC, and J. Harold Moyer recalls, "My first compositional experience was theory class assignments [at Bethel College]. While some students struggled with this, I enjoyed it thoroughly and received affirmation from my instructors."

If Mennonite communities and institutions were foundational in the early lives of these composers, their influence has been no less important throughout their compositional careers. All five have been employed, at one time or another, by a variety of Mennonite higher educational institutions including Canadian Mennonite Bible College, Mennonite Brethren Bible College (later Concord College), and the newly amalgamated Canadian Mennonite University (Winnipeg, Manitoba); Conrad Grebel University College, Bethel College, Fresno Pacific University, Eastern Mennonite University (Harrisonburg, Virginia), and the United Mennonite Educational Institute (Leamington, Ontario). Most have also maintained close ties to the Mennonite church locally, nationally, and internationally. In addition to their personal involvement as members of Mennonite congregations in both Canada and the United States, these composers have played a central role in the production and content of many Mennonite hymnals. J. Harold Moyer, for example, served as vice-chairman on the Joint Hymnal Committee for the 1969 *Mennonite Hymnal*, a position he found both challenging and rewarding:

> [Serving as vice-chairman] kept me in the "real world" of the congregational hymn, selecting, harmonizing and creating usable, singable hymns, technically very limiting, compared to composing for advanced level performers. I learned to accept and enjoy the challenge of composing within narrow limitations.

In addition, numerous hymns written by these composers grace the pages of hymnals used by North American Mennonite congregations, including *Hymnal: a Worship Book* and *Covenant Hymnal*.[10] This is something many find deeply rewarding, as reflected in comments by Larry Warkentin: "It is also encouraging to me as a composer to know that each Sunday several hundred thousand people are holding some of my music in their hands." Furthermore, many have had works commissioned for and premiered at national and international church conferences, often resulting in some of their most consciously "Mennonite" writing, at least thematically. Works such as Esther Wiebe's *Maranatha*, an extended work for choir and orchestra, Larry Warkentin's symphonic essay *Koinonia*, Leonard Enns's *Other Foundation* for choir and congregation, and Carol Ann Weaver's *Spirit Dance* for choir, soloist, mandolin, keyboards, and dancer were all composed for this purpose.

The culture and theology of the Mennonite community, therefore, has profoundly influenced the lives of these five composers not only from their earliest days, growing up in Mennonite homes and communities, but also in their professional lives as providers of music for Mennonite schools, conferences, and churches. This was the environment of their first musical experiences, the venue of their first compositional explorations, and thus also a profound source of influence and encouragement in their earliest attempts as composers. Indeed, this influence has followed them throughout their careers, in both their personal and professional lives. But to what extent this influence has shaped their respective compositional voices, and to what extent it has resulted in a coherent "Mennonite voice," remains to be seen.

Being a Composer

Like many composers of the late twentieth and early twenty-first centuries, Mennonite composers, such as those profiled here, have come to embrace a wide range of musical styles, genres and mediums for their musical expression. Composers of this era are in a relatively unique position, being able to experiment with a wide range of compositional techniques, incorporating both ancient and modern, in their quest for a compositional voice. Larry Warkentin likens the process to a culinary adventure:

> I like to think that all the techniques and styles of the past are like herbs and spices that can flavor the music I write. When a particular emotion needs to be expressed, I try to find the most effective technique to create it.

When asked to describe her musical style, Carol Ann Weaver's response evokes similar sentiments:

> There are different ways to label the fusions of styles I write in, but the labels change from place to place, and usually contain more hyphens than are grammatically acceptable. Maybe we can just begin to call it "twenty-first-century music" and expect it to have fusions of jazz, pop, alternative, folk, avant-garde, world, classical, traditional, [and] experimental. In fact, the one trademark of most current music is that it is able to borrow, beg,

and steal from many ongoing styles all at once or all within one piece.

Indeed, none of the surveyed composers used one particular style or genre to describe their music. Rather, as Larry Warkentin suggests above, their musical styles are determined, at least in part, by the particular needs of each piece. Esther Wiebe, for instance, indicates that many of her stylistic decisions have resulted from such practical considerations:

> My early writing style was traditional because my music was meant to be suitable for singers and congregations within the traditional Mennonite church—in other words, much of it was *Gebrauchsmusik* written to suit a particular need or theme. [While] my classical music background influenced all my early writing ... I also began writing more popular music when the traditional church was "invaded" by contemporary new styles, attempting to give an example, through my writing, of good quality in that style. Several of my larger works also include some mild rock sections ... to have appeal for the generation absorbed with this style.

J. Harold Moyer calls his particular compositional style a blend of two approaches, traditional and neo-classical, adapted as needed to accommodate particular performers and contexts: "The style choices come from a combination of practical considerations and personal preference." He further suggests that these choices are also influenced by his Mennonite background, commenting:

> As a Mennonite I have a cultural inheritance fostering simple, direct communication. I have been comfortable with this. I could have rebelled against this and moved into a more avant-garde expression.

Leonard Enns, too, connects his earliest musical experiences with his later stylistic choices, suggesting simply:

> My earliest writing was strongly influenced by my choral background, and reflects what might be called traditional choral texture in a diatonic, tonal idiom. Clearly the church and church-based singing (congregational and choral) is behind all of that. I continue to find the choral idiom my most comfortable cloth.

If these composers' compositional styles reflect trends common among other twenty-first-century composers, their choice of media and instrumentation is perhaps more unique. While each composer's oeuvre includes an assortment of works for virtually any instrumentation, all have composed extensively and, in some cases, almost exclusively, for voice. Even Carol Ann Weaver, who considers herself "an instrumental composer," has always written some choral music and today increasingly finds herself returning to vocal music as "possibly the most satisfying medium, simply because it has been my first musical expression." Among Larry Warkentin's eclectic collection ("I have tried to write in every medium," he writes), the medium found most frequently is that of solo voice and piano, followed closely by selections for choir and various hymn tunes and settings. He comments, however, "I don't think this [the predominance of vocal music] resulted from any Mennonite predilection or influence. It is simply easier to find performers for solo voice."

Choral music in particular forms a substantial portion of the collected works of J. Harold Moyer, Esther Wiebe, and Leonard Enns and again, has often resulted from practical considerations. Esther Wiebe has written mostly choral music (both a cappella and with piano accompaniment) because her earlier writing primarily responded to the needs of the fledgling music department at CMBC: "Choral singing was a very vital part of the educational and outreach component of not only the music department but of CMBC as a whole." She later comments:

> My opportunities [to compose] were almost always with and for Mennonite organizations and my choice of media I used in writing would depend on what was available in the situation for which I was writing. In later years, when CMBC's music program had been more fully developed and there was a larger enrolment and there was a larger number of fine instrumentalists, my writing grew in "complexity" and interest and more frequently included instrumental parts.

J. Harold Moyer's choice of media was similarly influenced by the context for which he was writing: "Teaching at a Mennonite college has tended to move me more toward choral, vocal, and music drama expressions." Leonard Enns' writing too, particularly with his earlier pieces, was dictated by circumstance: "Much of my early music was written for the choirs I conduct(ed), and was from the start either for worship or concert settings." Though he, too, has written for a variety of media, the non-choral works tend to be informed and influenced by his choral writing. He states,

> While I have also studied piano for a number of years, writing for piano has always been much more challenging than for voice. Admittedly, it's more work—more notes to put down; but I find that my imagination speaks to me most naturally in choral textures, and I have to work harder for compelling ideas when I'm writing for piano.... I have, of course, written a good bit for piano as part of larger textures (choir/piano; chamber ensemble, etc.), but I'm simply saying it is a more difficult task.... I also love writing for other instruments that I have never played; I have written several large works for choir and orchestra in recent years, and am very satisfied with the results. So, I guess my starting point was choral, and that is likely the window through which I

continue to imagine much of the music I write, regardless of instrumentation.

Being a Mennonite Composer

Numerous allusions have already been made to the various points at which these composers' experiences as Mennonites and as composers intersect, yet these points of contact deserve further consideration for it is precisely here that we may begin to discern a "Mennonite voice"—should one exist—among these composers. While responses to questions concerning whether and how background, confessional stance or community values have impacted compositional work were varied, each composer readily acknowledged at least some level of influence. Differences were evident only in the extent of such influence and in the ways in which it was perceived to be manifest. Examples already mentioned demonstrate the wealth of possibilities, yet there are also several commonalities that may be discerned amongst their responses.

One striking example is the concern demonstrated by these composers for the communities within which and for whom they are writing. As a people defined by both faith tradition and ethnic identity, Mennonites are very community-oriented people, a perspective perhaps rooted in the ideals of believer's baptism and the priesthood of all believers, and refined through the realities of repeated, forced relocations. This orientation becomes evident in the work of these composers in that both what and why they have composed is frequently motivated by the communities around them. Sometimes this is manifest in very concrete ways, such as the commissions and requests for works that these composers regularly receive from others within the Mennonite community. Leonard Enns, for instance, has described himself as "a challenge-driven composer," commenting:

> Those who have encouraged me are really the reason for my continuing involvement in composition, and the stage I am at today... Very, very much of the reason I am writing today lies with the fact that others have chosen and promoted my music, encouraged and supported me, and requested and commissioned works from me. They have taken the risk for me. I feel very fortunate in this.

Both Esther Wiebe and J. Harold Moyer similarly note that many of their works have been written with particular situations and performers in mind. Choral and vocal music occupies such a prominent place among their collected works precisely because this medium occupies such a prominent place in the Mennonite church and the institutions and organizations for which they have been writing. Both composers recall

Hindemith's conception of *Gebrauchsmusik*: music written for a particular time and place.[11] J. Harold Moyer writes, "I like Hindemith's encouragement for *Gebrauchsmusik* or 'utility music,' composing for a specific individual or performing group. I have almost always known who will do the first performance." Other times however, this orientation is less concrete—less evident in the particular works themselves, but more so in the overall approach. Carol Ann Weaver, for example, alludes to the unexpected influence the Mennonite community has had on her compositional writing:

> My sense of community values has shaped my composing in subtle ways. In my atonal days when my Grandma would say, "Why don't you just write something pretty?" I began to think about who was able to benefit from my music. And if I continued to write music which lay beyond the aesthetic levels of so many people in my life, was my music doing what I really wanted it to do? . . . [S]urely the Mennonite community has served as a testing ground for my music [but] rather than feeling restrained by this community, I feel honoured to have such a community to whom I can relate. And the more I respect this community, the more I want to write music which speaks to, moves and relates to these people. . . . Possibly, my returning to tonal and accessible forms of music is one way of expressing respect for this community. . . . I care about the people who are within these Mennonite communities and I want them to feel my love for them within the music I write.

This community-oriented approach frequently means remaining outside the realm of mainstream composition. Larry Warkentin, for example, wonders if being Mennonite has caused him to be "less commercial," recounting:

> I have an older composer friend in Fresno who has made a fortune writing commercial band and choral music. When he heard my first string quartet he asked, "How many string quartets do you think there are in America? And how many elementary school bands do you think there are? You owe it to your family to write for the best market."

J. Harold Moyer remembers a similar situation: "I recall a conversation with my University of Iowa composition teacher. He learned that I had entered a hymn tune in a national contest. 'Why are you wasting your time writing a hymn tune? That's for amateurs!'" Moyer, however, had already learned to find enjoyment in the challenge of composing within these narrow limitations, particularly within the context of composing for the church, and therein lies an important consideration. These composers have chosen to dedicate their art to this community because of the intrinsic value and satisfaction that they derive from it and not because of any inability to compete in the mainstream marketplace—quite the contrary.[12] But while

On Composing "Mennonite Music"

many have received prestigious honours and recognition for their compositional work from outside the Mennonite community, this has not been the primary objective, as Esther Wiebe explicitly asserts:

> If I would continue writing twentieth-century classical compositions and promote them in the larger public, my "voice" might become recognizable in the way that composers in general are known for their style. My reasons for composing however—for better or for worse—have almost always been to fulfill requests and needs for particular church/conference-related situations. I do not recall any conscious strivings to become a recognizable voice in the larger musical world.

This approach to composition is not without its challenges. Many of the surveyed composers acknowledge distinct musical discrepancies between what is accepted in the church community and what is expected of a twenty-first-century composer; what may be appropriate in musical circles is frequently considered too "avant-garde" for the church, whereas what may be acceptable in the church community is too "traditional" for the musical world. The prevailing challenge facing these composers is to write music that resonates with the community and the congregations for whom they are writing and yet is stylistically, musically, and aesthetically "authentic" for them personally. Esther Wiebe and J. Harold Moyer have responded to this challenge by consciously choosing to write in a more traditional style, even as they are comfortable with more mainstream compositional approaches. Other composers candidly describe their uneasy struggles to find an honest, personal musical expression that still speaks to their community. For Carol Ann Weaver, this has been particularly true:

> I [was] haunted by the esoteric nature of the world so many atonal composers inhabit. This "difficult music" began to feel like a shield or a barrier rather than a bridge between people. I became weary of the distance between the accessible music I would do in various church and community settings, and the "concert" music I would compose for the new music audiences. In certain ways this felt dishonest.

This search for an integrity of musical expression also guides Larry Warkentin in his attempts to bridge the musical and church worlds:

> In one sense I have tried to do what I love. In Mennonite circles my music may seem modern and dissonant, while in university settings I seem to be a conservative. In both settings I try to be honest.

Quite apart from questions of musical style, genre, or compositional orientation, however, the point at which these composers believe their Mennonite background may be most apparent is in their choice of texts for vocal music. It is to these texts that most of the surveyed composers immediately turn when asked for examples of Mennonite influence in their compositional craft. As Larry Warkentin quipped, referring to one of his earliest works, a cantata for voice and orchestra entitled *The Word*, "Who else would set texts by Menno Simons?" Upon further reflection he continues:

> The number of texts in my music which have a Christian message is also the result of my Mennonite commitment. Being Christian and being Mennonite have much in common but being Mennonite puts a unique overlay on faith. I do deal with peace issues more than many Christian [composers].

Esther Wiebe and J. Harold Moyer echo these sentiments. Wiebe writes, "I would say that all the music with sacred texts that I have written is linked with my faith/belief stance. Most of it was intentional in efforts to communicate the message being sung." Similarly, Moyer claims his Mennonite background has "indirectly affected my choice of texts and kept vocal music primarily church-related." He goes on to say:

> My personal faith would be most evident in the choice of texts for vocal music. Occasionally it has related to Mennonite history. In the 1970s James Juhnke and I wrote a musical, *The Blowing and the Bending*, based on Mennonite experience during World War I.

Carol Ann Weaver, by contrast, has turned to more contemporary expressions of Mennonite experience, citing recent collaborations with various Mennonite poets and writers:

> I feel bonded to these writers in a wonderful way. They have been trying to find verbal ways to create new connections and communities within and beyond their own Mennonite roots. Their routes have often paralleled my own, thus my ongoing desire to join their words with my music.

Leonard Enns, conversely, appears less concerned with particularly Mennonite themes, theologies, or references in individual texts or text settings of his works, addressing, rather, his attraction to the setting of text in a more general sense. He muses, "I love working with text; whether that reflects an emphasis on the 'word' in the [Mennonite] tradition is an open question... an interesting one too, for those called the silent in the land."

Composing "Mennonite Music"?

We return then to the central question guiding this paper: do Mennonite composers have an identifiable voice? Those surveyed overwhelmingly believe they do not. Their responses can be summarized in the following comments by J. Harold Moyer:

> The Sound in the Land experience [of May 2004] demonstrates that Mennonite musicians are involved in a great number of musical settings, with a great variety of idioms and styles, without obvious unified identity.

Stylistically, the music of Mennonite composers appears to be no more unified than is the music of Catholic composers, Canadian composers, or twenty-first century composers. Each of those surveyed approaches his or her music in his or her own way, incorporating whatever media, genres, and styles best convey each individual's voice.

And yet, as outlined above, in the midst of this rich diversity there remains a common heritage and a common (community-centred) orientation. Each of these composers has been profoundly influenced by the Mennonite culture and community of faith personally, spiritually, and musically. Thus, in striving to find authentic musical expressions of their identities and life experiences, they write "Mennonite music" for they themselves are Mennonite and perhaps could not do otherwise. Larry Warkentin expresses this idea most succinctly:

> I don't tend to think about writing Mennonite music. I do like to think about being Christian, Anabaptist and Mennonite in my faith and actions. Then I try to make my music an honest, personal confession. At its best I suppose this results in Mennonite music, but I don't think that writing like a Mennonite should be the initial goal.

The diversity of voices among Mennonite composers reflects a similar diversity to be found within the Mennonite population in general. And yet, in each instance, a unity within the diversity can be found, however subtle or indirect. Among these composers, it is a unity arising from honest attempts to give expression to a common heritage on one hand, while serving the musical needs of a common community on the other; a unity evident not so much in the music itself as in the perspectives and approaches guiding the act of composition.

It is also, however, a unity based upon a rapidly disappearing precedent. While it may be true that the composers surveyed here represent a common heritage, it is also true that an ever-increasing percentage of Mennonites today do not share this cultural background. If some sense of unity may be found among this generation of composers, what will unite future generations when the term "Mennonite" no longer denotes primarily ethnic, western Mennonites and the cultural experiences and religious perspectives assumed therein? Leonard Enns comments on this conundrum:

I'm not a big fan of the idea of "Mennonite music"; I believe there are styles that grow out of particular geo-historical environments, and that Lutherans or Mormons or Mennonites etc. may or may not be connected with a myriad of possibilities of such. Russian-Mennonite music has some meaning as an historic style signifier; but in the twenty-first century, I find "Mennonite music" to be a problematic term, and I am bothered by the assumptions implied. If one accepts the real world-wide face of the Mennonite church, then how can Mennonite music be different from the music of any other well-meaning people and peoples?

What constitutes "Mennonite influence" is becoming increasingly difficult to quantify as the balance shifts from primarily culture-derived elements to more faith-derived ones. The trend is already apparent to these composers, particularly to Carol Ann Weaver:

> As our children grow up in the internet world, with "Mennonite" becoming an increasingly side-lined facet of their lives, the music they write can hardly reflect the limited parameters which gave so many of us a common sense of identity and struggle. Possibly our children will deal with the fact that much of their Mennonite culture has been lost to them, and in order for them to regain it, they will have to re-invent some of the very restrictions and limitations we so bravely fought against. In which case, their music may be the complete inversion of our current sonic creations!

As the definition of "Mennonite" changes, so too will any unifying voice among Mennonite composers. However, as this definition becomes less culturally overt and less externally apparent, it will be no less influential. Indeed, the ideological and theological characteristics that will come to define twenty-first-century Mennonites will be no less significant than were the cultural characteristics that distinguished this faith community in the past. The challenge will be in discerning the underlying similarities, the new unified voice, and for this we will need to turn to the voices of the next generation of composers.

Notes

[1] Indices surveyed included the *International Index to Music Periodicals (IIMP)*, the *Music Index Online*, and the *RILM Abstracts of Music Literature (1967-Present)*. The results presented here were compiled on August 26, 2004, and were obtained by entering the term "Mennonite" into the online search engines of these three indices.

[2] A seven-question survey was initially e-mailed to respondents, with opportunities for follow-up discussion in response. See Appendix 1 for a copy of the survey questions. All correspondence took place via electronic mail or telephone

On Composing "Mennonite Music"

during the months of July and August, 2004.

³ The experiences of other younger or less-established Mennonite composers would provide an interesting counterpoint to the observations expressed here but unfortunately must await another study.

⁴ Large-scale choral or dramatic works by Moyer include *Job* (1967), an oratorio for choir and orchestra, *The Blowing and the Bending* (1974), a musical, and the musical for children, *Galilean Picnic* (2001). Wiebe's larger works include two operas, *The Bridge* (ca.1973) and *Crossroads* (1989), and several cantatas for choir and orchestra or instrumental ensemble such as *Maranatha* (ca. 1970), *Make Me an Instrument* (ca. 1972), *Thy Kingdom Come* (for the 1978 Mennonite World Conference in Witchita, KS), and *The Abiding Place* (for the 1984 Mennonite World Conference in Strasbourg, France).

⁵ Published works include two arrangements for concert band, *Crown Him* (1993) and *Christ the Lord* (1994), and another for flute quartet, *What Child is This?* (1993); (all publications by David Smith Publishers).

⁶ Consider, in particular, works from her recordings *Awakenings* (2003), *Dancing Rivers* (2001), *Journey Begun* (1999) and *Daughter of Olapa* (1996).

⁷ Works of note include *Academic Variations* for piano, which was awarded first prize by the California Music Teacher's Association in 1978, the choral cantata *Ruth*, and the symphonic essay *Koinonia*, commissioned by the Mennonite World Conference.

⁸ Among his more prominent works are *Te Deum* (1997) for choir with optional piano, *The Silver Chord* (1994) for choir, baritone solo, and orchestra, the cantata *Logos* (1991) for choir, oboe, and organ, and *Songs of Innocence* (1979) for choir, piano and flute, which was performed in Vienna, Austria for the First World Symposium on Choral Music by the Elmer Isler Singers. Significant instrumental works include *Hammer and Wind* (1999) for saxophone and piano, premiered at the 12th World Saxophone Congress, and *Duo* (1985) for oboe and piano, second prize winner in the Manitoba Mennonite Historical Society 1985 Composer's Competition.

⁹ Unless otherwise stated, all quotations in the following text are drawn from survey responses and personal conversation with the composers. I am most grateful to these individuals for their willingness to participate in this project and for the enthusiasm and candour with which they responded to my inquiries.

¹⁰ Examples from *Hymnal: A Worship Book* (Elgin, IL: Brethren Press; Newton, KS: Faith and Life Press; Scottdale, PA: Mennonite Publishing House, 1992) include "God, whose purpose is to kindle" (no.135) by Esther Wiebe; "With all my heart I offer" (no.432) by Carol Ann Weaver; "What does the Lord require" (no.409) and "When grief is raw" (no.637) by Larry Warkentin; "My soul proclaims with wonder" (no.181), "Lord of our growing years" (no.479), and "I sought the Lord" (no.506) by J. Harold Moyer; and "O Holy Spirit, Root of life" (no.123) by Leonard Enns. *Covenant Hymnal: A Worship Book* is published by the Evangelical Covenant Church of America (Covenant Press, 1996).

¹¹ See also Esther Wiebe's comments, above.

¹² Larry Warkentin, for example, received first prize for his piano composition "Academic Variations" in the California Music Teachers Competition and, since 1990, has received an annual award from the American Society of Composers, Authors, and Publishers, while Carol Ann Weaver, in addition to having seved as president of the Association of Canadian Women Composers, has re-

ceived commissions and performances from some of the leading new music ensembles in Canada, including ARRAYMUSIC, Hemispheres Orchestra, Blue Rider Ensemble, and Inde'85 Dance Festival.

Appendix 1

Survey Questions

1. Please outline your compositional career, how you started writing music, what were early venues for your music, why have you continued to compose and how have you received affirmation in this, etc.

2. What were initial influences in your career? What influences have come later?

3. Within what media have you most frequently worked—choral, instrumental, solo voice, orchestral, other? Comment briefly upon the instrumentation with which you have chosen to work over the years—is there anything about your community values, perspectives, Mennonite background, etc., which has affected your choice of musical instrumentation or media?

4. Within what musical styles have you most frequently worked—traditional, classical, avant garde, popular, jazz, etc? Comment briefly upon the reasons for the musical styles which you have chosen over the years—is there anything about your community values, perspectives, Mennonite background, etc., which has affected your choice of musical expression?

5. Has being a person of Mennonite background shaped and/or coloured your compositional work, and if so, in what ways has it been an influence?

6. In what ways are your musical compositions linked with your confessional stance or personal belief system? Have you felt your music to be "with" or somewhat "ahead" of the Mennonite church or community within which you live? Comment, explain.

7a) Where do you see your music going? Where do you see so-called "Mennonite music" going?

7b) Do Mennonite composers have an identifiable "voice," or is Mennonite-composed music sufficiently varied as not to have a unified identity?

Encountering (Mennonite) Singer-Songwriters: J. D. Martin and Cate Friesen

Jonathan Dueck

I first encountered J. D. Martin's music as an eight-to-ten year old kid, through the green *Sing and Rejoice* book that sat in the pews at Altona Mennonite Church in southern Manitoba alongside the red *Mennonite Hymnal*. I first heard Cate Friesen sing at the Electric Brew Café, in the Mennonite Church mecca of Goshen, Indiana. Both memories key a whole network of associations for me—people, routes and ways, beliefs, sounds, and more. Each of these music-related memories might be understood as a geography — a collection of places, connected and made meaningful in my memory.[1] This chapter will take the form of two musical life histories, recounting the stories of J. D. Martin's and Cate Friesen's lives in music on the basis of interviews that I pursued with them both in the fall of 2004.[2] There are a few central themes that I will bring out in this re-telling. The first is the idea that a musical life story is geographic in nature, so that places, people, and musical sounds are linked together and experienced, remembered, and even performed together. The second is the overlapping, sometimes conflicting relationship of the economic sphere of life to the spheres of personal relationships and musical creativity, as described to me by these two singer-songwriters. The third is the place of the individual relative to the community, especially the Mennonite community.

Why choose to talk formally about these stories as "geography" rather than talking more colloquially of "influences," as has often been the case in writings on popular music? Recent ethnomusicological and hermeneutic work suggests that an individual's memory and life history could be thought of as a kind of network of people and places, which are later re-imagined by the individual. In this re-imagination, music can play a key intermediary role.[3] The spatial image which arises from this understanding is that of a fractal or web, branching out and returning as memories of place, understood in part through the intense and sensual experience of music, re-map the past onto understandings of the present and even expectations of the future.

More broadly, as Keith Negus argues, popular music is made and experienced through social intermediaries—chains of production and consumption, music-making and music-listening—and the intersections of these intermediaries become the sites where musical meaning happens.[4] In the stories of music-makers, and specifically of singer-songwriters, the sociability of musical production and consumption—in other words, how and why people come together at a particular place and time to make music—becomes an important carrier of meaning.[5]

Instead of listing important individuals as influences on Martin's or Friesen's songwriting, then, I intentionally relate their stories as geographic in order to bring into sharp focus the networks of people and places that together make up a complex of influences, relationships, and overlapping stories, located in time and later remade in memory and in song.

Story Songs and Tightrope Tensions: Cate Friesen

I met Cate Friesen at the Nook, a small breakfast place near her home in Winnipeg's Wolseley area. Her young son Chester accompanied her and enthusiastically ate some of his pancakes while we talked. Friesen currently works as a radio journalist and variety program director for the Canadian Broadcasting Corporation (CBC) in Winnipeg. She interviews local musicians, covers music performances, and researches and works with other local journalists on various stories. The geographic and creative movements by which Cate Friesen travelled from a southern Manitoba farm to Toronto as a singer-songwriter and then to Winnipeg as a radio journalist highlight the push-and-pull between public (but personal) creative work and private relationships and family. Friesen's responses to these public/private tensions are both constrained by and appear as creative responses to the economic systems in which songwriting in Canada takes place.

Friesen grew up on a farm not far from the U.S. border in Gretna, Manitoba, a rural community she describes as "very Mennonite." Her father was the minister of the town's Mennonite church, and she sang in church choirs from age six and on. Although a fine choral singer, she was more interested in the folk musicians of the 1960s and 1970s such as Carole King and John Denver, received through her older sister's record collection and guitar-playing.

Strongly encouraged to continue her musical development by studying church music at Canadian Mennonite Bible College in Winnipeg, Friesen wanted to write her own songs instead. However, because of the pragmatic

Mennonite understanding of work she had inherited, she did not see this as a career option, and chose to study occupational therapy at the University of Manitoba. Although she enjoyed the program, four years of study were enough to convince her that this was not her vocation.

While working as an occupational therapist in London, England, Friesen bought a guitar, wrote some songs, and played them in local folk clubs. It was here that it became clear to her that she wanted to make her way as a singer-songwriter. When I asked what her parents thought of the idea, Friesen described her father's feeling at the time that music—with the exception of choral church music—was all about drugs, sex, and rock'n'roll. "I played where people were drinking!" she said. As she has pursued her career, she reflects, her family, including her father, has been very supportive; however, at the time she was not sure her decision would receive family approval.

After six months of living in London and travelling, Friesen returned to Manitoba in 1985 just long enough to pack her bags and move to Toronto, where she would live for the next eighteen years. If people wanted to make it in the music business at that time, Friesen notes, Toronto was one of the places to which they went.

In Toronto, conversations with a friend about the music business convinced Friesen that going to music school was not the best way to become a singer-songwriter. Instead, she had to get out there and play her songs. When Friesen told her friend she was going to give this singer-songwriter business a year to see if it worked out, he laughed. After a year, she understood that it would take much more time and much more work to "make it" as a musician, especially as a folk musician.

Friesen began applying for small grants to record demo tapes. Her first independent cassette was a compilation of three demo tapes; this achievement supported applications for further funding to record her first CD, *Tightrope Waltz* (1993). This professional recording gave her access to performance opportunities in folk clubs and house concerts. These spaces were especially attractive to her because—in a humourous contrast to her father's initial estimation of her music—bar owners were not eager to book folk artists, calling Friesen's audience "tea-drinkers" more interested in listening than drinking.

When I asked how a singer-songwriter succeeds in Canada, in a day-to-day economic sense, Friesen laughed and said that she was almost too good at this business: she booked her own shows and tours, and ran her own publishing company, Wide Eyed Music, through which each of her albums has been released. Friesen explained that the option of using an agent to do this frustrating and time-consuming work is not usually available to singer-songwriters, especially to folk-style singer-songwriters, because most agents prefer to handle more commercially remunerative genres. Friesen also worked hard to gain bookings at folk festivals, which are timed in summer in Canada to form a national "circuit." This circuit connected her to local folk music clubs across the country: if you play at the Calgary folk festival, she told me, then you can get booked in a Calgary folk club.

The folk festival network carries with it genre expectations that can influence the songwriting process. Friesen's second album, *Wayward* (1996), which focuses on what Friesen describes as "storytelling" songs, produced a good deal of activity for her within this circuit and in CD sales. This resulted in concomitant pressures to continue writing similar songs, and also to perform music from this commercially successful album later in her career. Friesen doesn't like performing her old stuff just to promote the sales of her albums, wanting the music to be "true" to her experiences at the time she's singing, and she pursues this goal in her songwriting and performances despite its economic ramifications.

The structure of the folk music business in Canada encouraged Friesen to pursue songwriting and performance as a solo artist. "That's the only way to make it financially," she told me, because there is not a great deal of money to be made performing at folk venues, and it becomes even more difficult when the revenues are split among several band members.

Friesen described some of her experiences of songwriting: sitting at home every morning at the keyboard with a sheet of lyrics, playing composition and piano exercises, and waiting to see if melodies for the lyrics would arise. It was quite difficult to reserve time for this, as other work and other distractions beckoned. However, the songs came after weeks and weeks of solitary work.

Grants have played an important role, Friesen emphasizes, in allowing her time to work at songwriting and recording in order to produce an album. She has received assistance from the provincial Ontario Arts Council and the Canada Council, as well as with Canada's FACTOR loan program. Comparing the influence of granting agencies on the process of songwriting and song content with that of the American music industry's marketplace, Friesen feels that the Canadian system of artist grants left her very free to do as she saw fit. Unlike the popularity-driven market, arts grant proposals are evaluated by a peer group of other artists. Friesen's music, not mainstream enough for major commercial success even though it was critically acclaimed, was well-placed for evaluation by other artists.[6]

Friesen has always worked at other jobs in addition to music, trying to find time to write and perform in the margins of these other jobs. She mentions in particular playing guitar and singing in retirement homes. Echoes of this experience surface on the album *Wayward*, in the song "Passionately fond of you." Here, the melodic sound of a clarinet, evoking a bygone jazz era, accompanies a first-person narrative describing love from an older person's perspective: "Passionately fond of you / Every moment I'm with you is a joy / for seventy years, since I was just a boy / I've been passionately fond of you." Friesen recently wrote a song while walking to work at the CBC in Winnipeg: "I'd write as I'd walk and I'd write in the rhythm of the walk, and it was about my walk to work every day, on Portage Avenue." Friesen's "other work" not only provides her with basic economic means, but also, through her creative engagement with the world of work, its stories, its people, and its sounds, offers material for writing songs.

Friesen's Mennonite background was a part of the songwriting process for her third album, *Joy's Disorder* (1999), through a version of the "Mennonite game," whereby through triangulation of relatives, last names and towns, two Mennonites find how they are related. During her first few years of living in Toronto, Friesen found the book *Flicker and Hawk*, by then Winnipeg-based poet Patrick Friesen, in the bargain bin of a bookstore.[7] Taken by the poetry, she used a few lines of the poems in her song "Several sides to love," written for the album *Wayward*. When she called Patrick Friesen to ask his permission to use the lyrics, he replied that he had just bought her recent CD—on account of their shared last name. A cross-country songwriting collaboration was begun, a turning point from solo songwriting to collaborative work for Cate Friesen. She and Patrick worked together via e-mail and occasional visits during this process; Patrick for the most part producing lyrics and Cate writing the music. However, Patrick also listened to the melodies that Cate was composing and wrote lyrics in response to them. He also provides spoken vocals on one song on *Joy's Disorder.*

Friesen intentionally played with melody, tempo, and the tone of her voice to reflect the tone and the metre of Patrick Friesen's lyrics: "I worked a lot to work with his words, and not shift the line, so one of his songs I wrote in 7 [beats per bar]." This collaboration was exciting because it sparked new kinds of melodic creativity for Friesen, and also because she could give voice to poetry that she found very meaningful at that time.

I asked Cate Friesen if she considers herself to be a "Mennonite singer-songwriter. "I would never choose to call myself a Mennonite singer-songwriter . . . [or] a female singer-songwriter," she told me, "but I don't mind if people want to own me that way." For Friesen, her Mennonite background is an indispensable element of her songwriting—images and stories from the place she grew up become part of her songs.

However, Friesen found it necessary to make a break with the Mennonite church, to "fight against... that whole sense of community that we grew up with, that sense of, the community and family come first and individual needs come second," in order to make space for her own creative work as a songwriter. And further: "to go out and write from my own voice and tell my own story, and put myself on stage, not as part of a choir, which is totally, totally acceptable... but as my own voice, this is my own story... That was a big resistance to get over... because [according to] my values as a Mennonite... that was not right." In southern Manitoba, the choir was "the only choice"; coming to terms with her desire to write songs and tell her individual story was not easy for Friesen. Even the musical structures of Mennonite singing had to be overcome; she has worked hard to expand her rhythmic flexibility as her background did not prepare her to "clap on the two and on the four"—a rhythmic freedom that is clearly perceptible in the songs of *Joy's Disorder*.

While in Toronto, Friesen joined a Quaker meeting. She explained its appeal in terms of its engagement with aspects of the Mennonite faith that she particularly values—peace and community—but significantly, free of what she described as relatively inflexible religious "dogma."

The interval between *Wayward* and *Joy's Disorder* saw the birth of Friesen's first son, Sam. This aspect of her life created some tensions concerning the time required to be a (mostly) self-employed singer-songwriter: in a 1999 interview, she described her life as eight musical tracks on a recording, of which her son had seven.[8]

Holding together a touring schedule and caring for her son was possible until he turned three. At that point, Friesen made the decision to tour less and pursue more local work as a radio journalist. "It started to get hard to love what I was doing. I was resenting the time away, and I started to resent making music.... If you're not doing it for the love of it, you're not doing it for the money either." This decision dovetailed with the commercially lukewarm reception of *Joy's Disorder*: the darker and more experimental album was well-received critically but did not sell as well to the folk market as had her earlier work.

Friesen describes this market response in terms of the constraints of the folk music media economy in Canada. Albums are primarily sold through performing and touring "relentlessly." Friesen's decision to make what she described as an "inward"-sounding album oriented toward the recorded medium, stretching vocal tone and metrical time, rather than an album of storytelling songs that worked in the live and very "outward" contexts of folk clubs and festivals, left fans of her earlier work disoriented. "It wasn't the storytelling, folksy Cate Friesen; a lot of people didn't react, not that they didn't react favourably, they just didn't know what to think of it."

Friesen feels the transition from touring songwriter to radio journalist has been a good one. It has also been personally freeing to focus on "telling other people's stories" for employment, rather than telling her own story. She describes journalistic work as similar to songwriting: "[Freelancing] was a natural second passion for me, because I was doing documentaries and interviews with musicians.... It was storytelling, it was still connecting with community, it was getting other people's stories out, I was supporting independent musicians. So it was all those things that I valued."

At the same time, her choice to pursue collaborations has allowed her to push her songwriting well beyond storytelling. She has recently performed a multi-media collaboration with writer Bonnie Loewen and visual artist Monica DeJonge. She continues to create music; a room in her Winnipeg house is devoted to music-making. She and her partner have started a band with several other musicians who have also recently moved to Winnipeg from Toronto—"We just sort of outgrew Toronto!" she laughs. This band is not only an enjoyable social group but also a way of "keeping up [her] chops," musically speaking. Collaborations also provide deadlines— inflexible demands to produce music. The social connections and creative impetus of musical collaboration have become a way for Friesen to mediate the push-and-pull between the personal and the economic spheres of life.

Friesen also still sings in a choir: "I have to sing. That's a part of me. [I sang in choirs] all through my childhood, and then on and off in Toronto. But singing is really essential, I just have to do it, it's just part of my chemistry." Singing in choirs — group performance— is not the same as the individual or collaborative space of songwriting. But these experiences are rooted in her childhood memories and they find expression in her voice. Friesen's broad life experience, her family, her Mennonite background, her work, and her travels all contribute to her continued re-membering, story-telling, writing, and singing.

Bigger and Bigger Containers: J. D. Martin

I spent two evenings talking on the telephone with J. D. Martin, who was speaking from his home in the Colorado mountains. A particular theme that emerges in Martin's story is the way in which geographic moves to different centres correlate with an expansion of his songwriting palette, and with parallel enlargements of his worldview, his professional networks, and his social communities.

Among his early childhood memories from Harrisonburg, Virginia, where his father was a Mennonite minister, Martin remembers plain-clothed and cape-dressed Mennonites singing in church, and his parents singing church music at home. He also remembers hearing white gospel quartet music on the radio, which was acceptable "adult" repertoire in the Harrisonburg Mennonite community, and other musical sounds that articulated a small rupture with the community's norms. When Martin was nine years old, a friend showed him a collection of pop and country music records hidden under his bed "like he was introducing me to drugs or something." His mother became an accomplice to these musical explorations, warning of his father's approach as he lay on the floor, listening as quietly as possible to the radio, his ear pressed against the speaker.

Martin credits the beginnings of his basic skills as a songwriter to the piano lessons he received at the age of eight in Harrisonburg from a local (Mennonite) teacher named Norman Kreider. Martin told me, "I was always good at picking out things by ear, like a melody, you know, sit at the piano and pick out a melody, but he showed me how to play chords with that, and that was, oh, a wonderful thing to find out about." To perform the popular music he heard on the radio Martin would remember the melody and transpose it in his mind to the key of C, so that he could visualize it and form chords for it. This was a physical, embodied understanding of the melody, rooted in the experience of playing the piano; when I asked Martin whether he visualized "notes on a page or fingers on a keyboard," he replied, "More like fingers on a keyboard." Even today, Martin continues to write songs in this way, conceiving the melody in his mind and the chords as "fingers on a keyboard."

From the relatively conservative environment of Harrisonburg, Martin and his family moved briefly to Elkhart, Indiana, and then to Eureka, Illinois, where his father worked as pastor of a local church. Popular music was more acceptable here, so that while Martin's hymn-singing activities in church continued, he could also buy and listen to LP records. He remembers especially the records of rockabilly legend Johnny Horton and the close folk-and-country harmonies of the Browns. When Martin told his high-school conductor that he wanted to be a pop music singer, the conductor advised him to consider becoming a music teacher "because it's really hard to be a singer."

Martin pursued this career recommendation in college, beginning at Hesston College (Kansas) in 1966, then at Millsaps College (Jackson, Mississippi), and finally at Goshen College (Indiana). He took music education classes and classical voice lessons, singing art songs and other classical repertoire, as well as in choirs. His move "out of the box," in his words, to Millsaps and the American South brought him into contact with many non-Mennonites. Martin's senior year at Goshen College (1970) saw the beginning of an enduring love he bears for the vocal sounds and the piano styles of African-American gospel music. Martin particularly remembers hearing a choir from Chicago's Lawndale Mennonite Church with both Latino Mennonite and white Mennonite members, singing with that "gospel sound."

Martin's "fooling around" with pop music was applied to songwriting in earnest at Goshen College, when noted Mennonite hymnologist and music professor Mary Oyer gave him a songwriting assignment. Martin wrote a melody and chorded at the piano to complete the song; he described this process of bringing melody, chords, and lyrics together as "finding a feel on the piano (it had that gospel 'thing') and then letting the words come out gradually." This song was subsequently recorded by the Hallam Street Band as "Pentecost."

Oyer later asked him to write a song for the Festival of the Holy Spirit. The Festival took place at Goshen College three times between 1972 and 1974, a time when the church was "torn apart, fragmented in some way," Martin remembers. The charismatic movement and the concomitant use of popular music in churches inspired the Festival, through which the Mennonite church tried to accommodate some aspects of this worship so as to hold the church together. "The church was having to loosen up, [because] people were having experiences that didn't fit in the old way of doing things." Martin's song "Unity," written in response to Oyer's request, was among the most-used popular songs in Mennonite churches in the 1980s, and it continues to be frequently sung today.[9]

After college, Martin and several friends decided to volunteer with Mennonite Voluntary Service (MVS or VS), but not in the usual way of working with a social-services or non-profit group. Instead, they started a VS unit in Aspen, Colorado, whose work was music, and from this emerged the Hallam Street Band (other members included Jim Yoder and Randy Noe). Over the course of a year, Martin spent a good deal of time writing songs with and for the band, as well as working hard to "unlearn" the classical vocal "stiffness" he'd acquired in college. He wryly described for me intentional processes he used to lend some roughness to his voice, including such tried-and-true methods as smoking cigarettes, drinking whiskey, and more experimental methods such as eating a good deal of peanut butter right before a recording session. The band played locally and toured in Mennonite church coffee houses, at larger events such as the Mennonite youth convention, and also in some non-Mennonite venues.

Although the band considered themselves to be part of the "radical Mennonite movement," influenced by hippies and political radicalism, their main focus was writing and singing songs that asked, "What does it mean to be a follower of Jesus?" In other words, this band was well-situated within the Mennonite church networks of the 1970s.

Following VS, Martin moved to Indiana to work as a teacher. Teaching was difficult for Martin: "It was hard for me to live without the creative outlet . . . being a schoolteacher was good, but it was so different, I didn't have a really good chance to write songs." At the end of this year, he returned to his friends from the VS unit in Colorado and joined their new band, Tanglefoot.

Martin describes the difference between the Hallam Street Band and Tanglefoot as not so much a conscious move away from a singular focus on Christian reflection in songwriting as a move toward simply writing good songs, becoming a successful band, and enjoying life. This "open[ed] up the ceiling" for Martin's work as a songwriter. Again, the band lived together in a house in Aspen. "Everyone was a songwriter," recalls Martin, in this "hothouse" environment, and nearly everything that was written by a band member was eventually performed. Tanglefoot's main performance networks were popular music venues, such as clubs and bars, rather than Mennonite venues. However, one of the most meaningful memories for Martin from this time is of a song he co-wrote with Ellen Stapenhorst, called "One more home," which required a cello part as accompaniment. When Tanglefoot played at Goshen College in 1979, Martin and the band wrote out the cello part for Mary Oyer, rehearsed with her, and then performed together for the Goshen College community. Martin describes this as "a wonderful kind of homecoming for those of us that had gone there [Goshen College]."

In 1980, Martin moved to Nashville, Tennessee, to become a professional songwriter. There he worked as a staff writer for several music publishing companies, first with MCA Music (now Universal), and then with Warner/Chapell. This was a time for "going to school," a time for the craft of Martin's songwriting to be developed. Martin worked in an office writing songs and if the song was promising, he would go to a studio in the same building and record it. An intermediary, or "songplugger," would promote the song to recording artists in the hope that they would record and perform the song. As a result, rather than writing songs that expressed his own feelings, he worked to write songs with good melodic and lyrical ideas that were likely to find their way to an artist. Martin enjoyed success with songs he co-wrote for artists like Reba McEntire and The Oak Ridge Boys.

Eventually, Martin signed a record deal with Capitol Records. His musical interests lay with pop-country music, but his style of writing was very different from the Randy-Travis-influenced sound popular in the early 1990s. When the market for his music in Nashville dried up in 1993, Capitol Records dropped him. This precipitated a question for Martin: "What do I really want to say?" Martin describes the experience as a kind of re-enclosure and re-rooting, because "[it] got me back into my own body."

While places can be thought of in terms of their musical and social content, Martin's story of movement between major centres of the music world resonates with Arjun Appadurai's characterization of the world as a set of overlapping "scapes," routes that are travelled rather than places that are inhabited.[10] Appadurai defines five "scapes": finanscapes (money), ideoscapes (ideologies), mediascapes (sounds and images), technoscapes (technologies), and ethnoscapes (people). These various "scapes" have an impact on the lives of people, but they are disjunct—they are not moved through at the same time. For Martin, the mediascape in which Nashville was once placed—where his songwriting ideas had once fit well—re-routed him once again.

Martin moved to Los Angeles on January 1, 1994, immediately after a major earthquake. When I asked him what the experience of Los Angeles was like, he responded that the "lid [was] blown off, personally, spiritually ... [like] jumping into a much bigger container." On a prior visit to Los Angeles, he had stayed at the house of his friend Jamie Houston, where he had a powerful dream. This dream provided the impetus to co-write "One heart" with Houston and Wendy Waldman, a song about connecting with the world of the spirit despite complex and sometimes negative experiences with organized religion. This song became part of his landing a job in Los Angeles, again with Warner/Chapell.

His personal and religious life also developed in new ways in Los Angeles: here he met Jan Garrett in 1995 and co-wrote a song with her, "beginning to write our own love story." As their relationship deepened, she too moved to Los Angeles and they collaborated again on Garrett's solo CD, *Gypsy Midwife* (1999), which Martin co-produced.

Openness to other religious traditions and a commitment to peace came together with elements from Martin's accumulated soundscape, especially gospel music, when Garrett and Martin connected with the Agape International Spiritual Centre, a Religious Science church. Martin explained that Religious Science is part of a larger movement called New Thought churches, which began in the nineteenth century. These churches are universalist, believing that Christ or the creator is in everyone, and that every spiritual path can lead to God. Agape has over 7,000 members rooted in various faith traditions—Jewish, Christian, Muslim, and Buddhist, among others—who both meet in separate faith groups and come together for worship. Martin talked about Agape's minister, Michael Beckwith, whose fiery preaching style reminded Martin of southern African-American Baptists, though his sermons focused on peace and brotherhood—"very Mennonite," concluded Martin with laugh. The choir performs new music in the African-American gospel style, which Martin loved. Garrett and Martin became (and remain) members of Agape, where they occasionally present music.

In 2001, they moved together to Aspen, Colorado. When I asked Martin about this decision, he told me about a recent visit to Los Angeles where he read several "pitch sheets," advertisements from artists who were looking for material. About three-quarters of these pitch sheets described what they were looking for with the same word: "edgy." When I asked what that meant, musically, Martin said, "You have to be part of that world, and I'm not," explaining that he was not angry but peaceful these days; nor was he writing for the twenty-year-old market but for his own reflective, middle-aged peers. What Martin himself wanted to say and what the market wanted were again at odds. He responded in part by writing and recording his own album, *One Heart* (2001), near the end of his time in Los Angeles; on the jacket of the CD he notes that "In the twenty years I have been writing for other artists, these songs have felt like 'mine.'"

Martin and Garrett, now married for five years, had just purchased a house when I interviewed Martin. The house has big windows, a feature that is not good for soundproofing but one that nevertheless provides a "nice space to be creative in"—a songwriting room of their own. Martin continues to travel to Los Angeles and to Nashville to write. However, the business of establishing a niche for his and Garrett's musical collaborations now takes the majority of his time, leaving relatively little time for writing new material.

The duo recently co-wrote and produced an album entitled *I Dreamed of Rain* (2003), which they are touring to promote. They handle their own bookings, in part through connecting with a network of spiritual communities, including New Thought churches and Mennonite churches. They also run their own web site and handle all order fulfillment for their albums. This is the first time Martin has worked so closely with the business aspect of popular music. He talks about it being particularly difficult to ask for money for what he does as a labour of love, and about his attempts to re-imagine the business aspect of his work as providing him with the means to give an artistic and spiritual service.

An agent would alleviate much of this work, but agents are hard to come by until you are an established artist. However, Martin sees his future in singer-songwriter work, because of the relationship between his own and Garrett's creativity, and the marketplace for songwriting. Perhaps the most important thing he's learned about songwriting over the years, Martin tells me, is to be "emotionally honest." That honesty may be a liability in the marketplace for songwriting, where tastes change rapidly. Despite the risks of beginning their own business as a singer-songwriter duo, Martin sees a stable future in creating music and finding his own audience for that music.

Co-writing music with Garrett threw a particular light on each of their own songwriting processes, and demanded some accommodations. Martin describes his own process as making an appointment with someone, going to meet them, and obstinately working and waiting until they have written a song. Garrett, on the other hand, waits until she is inspired by hearing a melody in her mind, and then works on the song. To write together, Martin waited until she came up with a germ of a lyrical or musical idea; they then alternated between working together intensively on the idea, and taking time and space to work on their own.

At one point in the interview, Martin said that love songs could be called "secular ... I hate that word." I asked what it was about that word he objected to, suggesting that the sacred/secular dichotomy could be seen as a particularly Mennonite, church-versus-the-world construct. Martin responded that where he grew up, even Catholics were seen as "the world," to say nothing of Buddhists and beyond. As a result of his discomfort with this viewpoint, he does not claim to be Mennonite, feeling it might be too limiting a label. However, he is pleased to be claimed as Mennonite, as he has been recently, by being invited to sing at Mennonite churches and conferences. The big containers of Martin's religious openness and his musical activities continue to hold his Mennonite roots. And these containers include many other people, relationships, beliefs, places, and sounds. As he later explained, "A large part of my reaction to the word 'secular' is also because I've come to see all of life as 'sacred.' Songs about human love and work and play are no less important or less sacred than songs about the mystery."

Conclusions

Given the obvious contrasts which might be drawn between them—woman and man, Canadian and American, Russian Mennonite and Swiss Mennonite—there are remarkable commonalities in the stories of Cate Friesen and J. D. Martin. Both are the children of Mennonite ministers, from relatively small towns; both were encouraged to continue in the world of Mennonite music as conductors and teachers of choral music, though both subsequently moved out of their Mennonite towns to large urban centres to work as singer-songwriters; and both moved to a smaller urban centre later in their careers. Both describe a process of individuation and creative development culminating in an ethic that Martin described as being "emotionally honest," a goal of honest representation of their feelings and thoughts in the music that each of them makes.

One important contrast can be drawn between the music economies, or to use Appadurai's term, the finanscapes of the United States and Canada. While Martin moved between two large centres (and one small centre) for popular music, Friesen remained for the most part in Toronto, reflecting the differing contexts of a relatively multilateral economy of popular music centres in the United States, and the dominance of Toronto in Canada. While Martin fought to sell his music in a highly competitive marketplace, working for major record labels, Friesen competed for grants and successfully produced her own independent albums. And although both artists have released CDs as independent productions, the grant economy and the major-label songwriter economy were contrasting economic contexts for their development as songwriters.

On the other hand, while contrasting economic frames were a strong factor for both songwriters' careers, they did not entirely determine the geographic or creative paths of either. When the market for songwriting in Los Angeles took a downturn, J. D. Martin decided to move to Colorado and work on his own albums instead of writing songs for a music publishing company. This economic decision also afforded him more creative control over his songwriting process, allowing him to write songs that reflected the peaceful place he'd found in his life. When Cate Friesen found that the economic demands to promote her albums through constant touring were too great for her family life, she began to pursue collaborations that allowed her to experiment with and expand her artistic voice. Both artists were constrained by the market; but the personal and musical meanings which correlate with their economic frames are not determined by those frames but rather arise (are "emergent") in their retelling of the stories of their creative and personal lives in relation to this economic frame.

Encountering (Mennonite) Singer-Songwriters

A final connection between these two stories might be the relationship of Friesen and Martin as individuals to their Mennonite communities. Martin described an experience while driving in Nashville and hearing on the radio that a Mennonite had been jailed for protesting a government action. He pulled his vehicle over and started to cry, feeling a profound sense of connection. This story suggests that Martin's recent re-connection to Mennonites is the surfacing of a long-standing, sometimes latent, sometimes cultivated connection to his roots. As part of this re-connection, Martin read Jeff Gundy's recent book, *Scattering Point*, in which Gundy recounts his travels from his Mennonite home out into the world, his need to ask questions, and his fascination with and love for "worldly" things such as the immense and beautiful Catholic churches in Europe.[11] These two experiences underline Martin's connection between his own experience and that of persons remaining within the Mennonite church.

Friesen told me that her favourite song on *Tightrope Waltz* is "Baptized (Prodigal daughter)" and quoted these lyrics: "I'm half a child of farmer's fields / but I'm all the distance I have come / and I may be sowing different seed." She said this song was well-liked, especially by Mennonite audiences. When I asked if Mennonite audiences or community were a major part of her "fan base" in Toronto, she told me that they were not, and that her social community in Toronto was for the most part not Mennonite. However, individual Mennonites in audiences all over the country would approach her after shows and mention that they recognized the name "Friesen," then talk about how the music resonated with them and about how nice it was to see a Mennonite at a folk festival. Friesen always loved being approached in this way and enjoyed that sense of continuing connection, of being "owned" as a Mennonite, though at that same time she was in the midst of building broader networks.

In the stories of both Friesen's and Martin's geographic and creative moves, and in the musical and social enlargements that accompanied them, there is the paradoxical sense that at the same time as their individual voices as songwriters are emerging, that identity is dispersed over broader networks of people and places. The strengthening of individual identity in these stories does not mean the erasure of group identity and structure. Nor can Martin's or Friesen's voice be said to be solely a "Mennonite" voice, or that of any other single group, since they both maintain connections with and are philosophically open to many groups and communities.

In these stories, social identity and musical voice do not seem to arise primarily either through breaking away from groups to construct an identity apart from the group, or from deep roots in a particular group with strict social boundaries. Rather, as Ruth Glasser has argued, when the individual is made the centre of research, identities can be seen as repertories of performative norms and signs that are deployed situationally by individuals *in relation to the connections drawn to those individuals by others*.[12]

In the stories of J. D. Martin and Cate Friesen, the group as a monolith that exists by virtue of "holding" a stable group of members seems untenable. Yet the group and its boundaries remain important to both Friesen's and Martin's identity. This is only true, however, if these boundaries are understood as being composed of folkways, performances, and acceptable behaviours ("the Mennonite game") which, when accumulated as a repertory, allow this identity to be performed meaningfully and situationally. The memories of "farmers' fields" that appear in Friesen's songs are an instance of this kind of performance. On the other hand, the "claiming" or "owning" of Friesen's and Martin's songs by Mennonites—a process of which this chapter is itself no doubt a part—is equally part of this performance of identity, and it is not fundamentally unlike the "claiming" or "owning" of Martin's songs as "Nashville country" or Friesen's as "Toronto folk." In other words, Mennonite is only one of a range of performed and received identities.

Why then do Mennonites receive Martin's and Friesen's songs as "Mennonite"? The breadth of this reception may well suggest that just as Martin understands Gundy's story to be like his own, each Mennonite—and any member of any social group—strains at and differs from the group's norms, engages ambivalently with the expressive practices of the group, yet sometimes loves to be "owned" by the group all the same; the group then exists in situational intersections of social performances and interactions rather than as a bounded entity unto itself. But this is the flip side of the stories I've re-told in this chapter, and it is probably better sung than said: "What to do with the ways of the ones / That have been planted in my bones / How to live in the spirit of their lives / Yet live a life that is my own" (Friesen, "Prodigal daughter," 1993).

Notes

[1] J. D. Martin's contributions to church song have continued; in the 1992 Mennonite *Hymnal: A Worship Book*, he contributed number 515, "Jesus, Rock of Ages" (under the name M. Gerald Derstine).

[2] I interviewed J. D. Martin via the telephone on September 20 and 28, 2004; Cate Friesen on October 3, 2004 in person in Winnipeg and on October 26, 2004 via telephone.

[3] Paul Ricoeur, *Memory, History, Forgetting*, trans. Kathleen Blamey and David Pellauer (Chicago: University of Chicago Press, 2004), see especially chapters 1-3;

Sara Cohen, "Sounding Out the City: Music and the Sensuous Production of Place," in *The Place of Music*, ed. Andrew Leyshon, David Matless, and George Revill (New York: Guilford Press, 1998), 269-290.

[4] Keith Negus, *Popular Music in Theory: An Introduction* (Hanover and London, Wesleyan University Press, 1996). See especially ch. 3.

[5] Here I draw on Suzel Ana Reily, *Voices of the Magi: Enchanted Journeys in Southeast Brazil* (Chicago: University of Chicago Press, 2002); see especially chapter 1. Reily's concept of "enchantment" includes the argument that sociability is one of the key aspects of making music together as a ritual practice, because it is sociability as experienced in making music together which allows a moral community, in the lived-in, present, local place, to be imagined and enacted in the act of music-making.

[6] It might be argued that artists form a very particular kind of audience as well, whose tastes are well served by the combination of critical acclaim and incompatibility with mass culture.

[7] Patrick Friesen, *Flicker and Hawk* (Winnipeg: Turnstone Press, 1988).

[8] Jay Vanderhorst, "Cate Friesen: Totally in the Moment" in Tower of Babel, February 1999. Accessed 25 October 2004 at http://www.towerofbabel.com/sections/music/troubadours/catefriesen/

[9] See *Sing and Rejoice* (Scottdale: Herald Press, 1979), no. 129 (under the name Gerald Derstine).

[10] Arjun Appadurai, *Modernity at Large: Cultural Dimensions of Globalization* (Oxford: Oxford University Press, 1996).

[11] Jeff Gundy, *Scattering Point: The World in a Mennonite Eye* (Albany, New York: SUNY Press, 2003).

[12] In *My Music is My Flag: Puerto Rican Musicians and their New York Communities, 1917-1940* (Berkeley, Los Angeles and New York: University of California Press, 1995), Glasser describes the lives of Puerto Rican musicians in New York City, where they are variously recognized by their white audiences, and sometimes by Hispanic audiences, as African-Americans, Cubans, or Puerto Ricans; in the end, these multiple receptions are not only a constraint, but also a kind of repertory of identities which can then be used by individuals in building broad social and musical networks.

Experiences of Singing Today

The Music of What Happened

Jeff Gundy

"The sweetest music of all
Is the music of what happens."
-Irish folk saying

So after two days drenched, swimming, drowning in music
I woke early and headed out to run. Nobody on campus

but the geese and crows. I dodged the goose crap and found
Columbia Lake, blue on the map but mainly mud in truth,

a little water threading through. A catbird chased the robins,
a redwinged blackbird muddled in the long grass,

two goldfinches darted away from the dirt track and led me
to the real creek, spring-strong and almost clear.

A pair of willows, grasses, boot prints and the rush of water
down a rocky riffle. The music of what happens

in a sweet glade not far from the power lines: clamors,
chords, voices loud and sweet and slow, solo and chorus.

This music is not soul or fingers, not breath through brass
or cords of flesh, not mind or heart. It is the whole being,

blood and tendon, neuron and electron, mitochondria
and muscle, darting eye and spinning dream, all tuned

and tuning, turning, dancing, portals, ports in the storm,
gifts offered and accepted, maps and instruments,

instructions and provisions, salt pork and molasses,
barley and cider for the winter, the oil and the lamp

for burning, the cabin in the clearing and the path
that leads home to the music, the music that is the path.

Waterloo, 30 May 2004

What are U. S. Mennonites Singing in Sunday Morning Worship?

Stephen Jacoby

The Impetus for the Study

Fall 2002 marked the tenth anniversary of the initial publication of *Hymnal: A Worship Book* (*HWB*),[1] intended for use in worship in "churches in the believers church tradition," including those that now comprise Mennonite Church USA. This anniversary marked an appropriate point in time to examine the impact of this resource on the worship life of the church.

One year earlier, in 2001, Herald Press published *Singing: A Mennonite Voice*, by Marlene Kropf and Kenneth Nafziger. This volume was admittedly (even proudly) anecdotal rather than data-based. Witness the foreword by John Bell: "What this book does is to provide that kind of necessarily anecdotal evidence that some scientific researchers may scorn, but that people of good sense recognize as essential. Percentages, graphs, and theories may be derived from accumulated information, but the life of faith is not easily put in a box or shown in a pie chart."[2]

While I do not respond to anecdotal evidence with "scorn" (and I am not a "scientific researcher" in the strictest definition of that term), nonetheless I believe there are important insights to be gained from an examination of data. At the time of its publication, *HWB* was thought to be "progressive." It was noted for its diversity of styles, its non-gender-specific texts, and its music representing the worshipper in the pew rather than the musicologist in the library. Now, more than ten years after its publication, how many congregations have purchased and used this resource? How many continue to use the previous *Mennonite Hymnal*?[3] How many did not purchase *HWB*, but purchased some other hymnal or songbook instead? Within those congregations that use *HWB*, which hymns are regularly sung? More than 40 percent of *HWB* is "new" in relation to the previous hymnal—have these new hymns become a part of the church's worship repertoire?

The answers to questions such as these may reveal changes that have occurred since the 1992 publication of *HWB* and may also suggest projections for the future. The anecdotal evidence in *Singing: A Mennonite Voice* clearly demonstrates the importance of congregational singing to Mennonites. Is this tradition changing? Is it in jeopardy?

Procedures

In an attempt to address some of these questions, 207 Mennonite Church USA congregations were selected randomly in June 2003 to serve as a sample for data collection. Mennonite Church USA comprises 21 area conferences. These area conferences are basically geographical subdivisions, but because they existed as entities within either the Mennonite Church or the General Conference Mennonite Church prior to the creation of Mennonite Church USA in 2002, area boundaries sometimes overlap. The conferences vary in size from several with fewer than 20 congregations, to 203 congregations in the Lancaster Conference, the largest of the area conferences.

The method of random selection was simply to choose every fifth congregation listed in *Mennonite Church USA: 2003 Directory*. There were two exceptions to this procedure. First, if a congregation listed "0" members, it was skipped. Second, in a few cases an additional congregation was selected to ensure that each area conference was represented by at least three congregations. Since congregations are grouped together in the directory by area conferences, this procedure provided a fair distribution among conferences and geographic regions. The *2003 Directory* lists a total of 992 congregations in 45 states; the 207 congregations selected for the sample represent 21 percent of that total, distributed over 34 states.

The 207 congregations received "Survey One" by United States mail. Survey One requested information about a) what resources are used for congregational singing; b) how congregational singing is led; c) how congregational singing is accompanied; and d) who is involved in the selection of congregation hymns and songs.[4] 104 congregations returned a completed copy of this survey, a 50-percent return rate. The 104 responding congregations represent 10.5 percent of the 992 congregations in the *2003 Directory*.

In August 2003, the 104 congregations that had responded to Survey One were sent a second survey, via e-mail when possible. "Survey Two" asked respondents to estimate the familiarity and frequency of five different styles in their congregational singing.[5] Survey Two also requested a tally of all hymns and songs sung by the congregation in worship on the four Sundays in September 2003. 81 congregations responded with answers to this second survey. These 81 congregations represent 78 percent of the 104 congregations that received the second survey, 39 percent of the initial random sample of 207 congregations, and 8 percent of the 992 congregations in the *2003 Directory.*

This paper will consider the survey results under three categories: a) resources used for congregational singing (from Survey One); b) the relative familiarity of various musical styles among the congregations (from Survey Two); and c) the contents from *Hymnal: A Worship Book* commonly sung by congregations (from Survey Two). I will then summarize what these results imply regarding singing in Mennonite congregations in the United States.

Resources Used for Congregational Singing

71 of the 104 congregations that responded to Survey One use the 1992 *Hymnal: A Worship Book*. But only eight of those congregations use *HWB* exclusively (including the supplemental "Hymnal Subscription Series" issued as part of *HWB*). The large majority of congregations—63 of 71—use *HWB* along with other resources. 33 of the 104 congregations that responded do not use *HWB* at all. Stating these numbers as percentages, out of the 104 respondents:

- 68% of the congregations use *HWB*
  - 8% sing from *HWB* exclusively
  - 60% use other resources, along with *HWB*
- 32 % of the congregations do not use *HWB*
- 92% of the congregations do not limit what they sing to the contents of *HWB*

Among the 92 percent of the congregations that do not limit their singing to the contents of *HWB*, a great variety of resources are used. More than 30 hymnals or songbooks were reported, including sources as old as *Church and Sunday School Hymnal* (1902),[6] and as recent as *Songs for Praise and Worship* (1992; later editions from 2000 and 2002).[7]

The most commonly used resource for congregational singing (other than *HWB*), reported by 61 congregations, was words projected on a screen or wall. (It should be noted that using a published source and singing "off the wall" are not mutually exclusive. It is quite possible for a congregation to project a page of a hymnal onto a wall or screen, as well as a contemporary praise chorus.) 37 congregations continue to use the 1969 *Mennonite Hymnal*; 13 use *Sing and Rejoice*, intended to supplement the 1969 hymnal with more twentieth-century hymns and songs;[8] and nine congregations use *Life Songs*

#2, designed as a "Sunday School hymnal" to supplement the 1927 *Church Hymnal*.[9] Stating these last numbers as percentages of the 104 respondents:
- 59% sing from words projected on a screen or wall
- 36% use *The Mennonite Hymnal*
- 12.5% use *Sing and Rejoice*
- 8.5% use *Life Songs #2*

Thus, in answer to the question, "What resources do Mennonite congregations use for singing?" we can say that most Mennonite Church USA congregations use the 1992 *Hymnal: A Worship Book*, but not exclusively. The range of other resources is quite wide in terms of the date of the resource and the styles represented.

Musical Styles

Survey Two asked respondents to estimate the degree of familiarity of five different styles in their congregational singing, according to frequency of use. It is admittedly a somewhat arbitrary task to define styles. In this case, the attempt was to emphasize performance or singing styles, rather than musical styles per se. These five styles were not meant to be comprehensive; surely additional styles could be identified. Nonetheless, the five styles used were defined on the survey as follows:
- "Traditional Hymns," usually sung in four-part harmony ("My faith looks up to Thee" or "Oh, for a thousand tongues to sing")
- "Contemporary Praise and Worship" music, usually led by a praise team ("O Lord, our Lord, how majestic is Thy name" or "Shine, Jesus, shine")
- "Modern Hymns," often sung in unison, with written keyboard accompaniment ("New earth, heavens new" or "God is working his purpose out")
- "Folk Hymns," written in unison, accompanied by acoustic folk instruments ("There are many gifts" or "You are the salt for the earth")
- Hymns and Songs in "non-Western" styles ("Santo, santo, santo" or "Here, O Lord, your servants gather")

For reporting purposes a five-point scale was used, where 1 signified "rarely or never" and 5 signified "regularly, every Sunday." Using the five-point scale, averages for the 81 congregations that responded to Survey Two were as follows:

Traditional	Contemporary	Modern	Folk	Non-Western
4.35	3.21	2.44	2.13	1.80

The numbers suggest that "traditional" hymns are sung more often than "contemporary" songs by a ratio of about 4:3, while the ratio of "traditional" to the other three categories is about 2:1.

Hymns and Songs Sung in September 2003

Survey Two also asked congregations to report every hymn or song sung during Sunday morning worship on the four Sundays of September 2003. Again, 81 congregations responded. These congregations, in summary, sang a total of 258 hymns from *HWB* and 426 other hymns or songs during worship that month.

While it would be presumptuous to assume this data can identify a "favourite hymn" with statistical validity, nonetheless the following list shows hymns and songs sung by at least ten congregations during that one-month period:

Hymn or Song	Number of congregations	Percentage of 81 respondents
Come, let us all unite to sing (*HWB* 12)	15	18.5%
Come, now is the time to worship (Doerksen)[10]	13	16%
Will you let me be your servant (*HWB* 307)	12	14.8%
God is here among us (*HWB* 16)	11	13.6%
You are the salt for the earth (*HWB* 226)	11	13.6%
Praise, I will praise you, Lord (*HWB* 76)	11	13.6%
I sing the mighty power of God (*HWB* 46)	10	12.3%
Be thou my vision (*HWB* 545)	10	12.3%

Of further interest from the data reported on Survey Two is the degree to which the contents of *Hymnal: A Worship Book* were used. The 258 items from *HWB* sung by the responding congregations during the four Sundays of September 2003 represent 39 percent of the 658 musical items in the hymnal. While it's difficult to appraise the significance of this figure, it seems to suggest broad usage of the hymnal's contents by the responding congregations during one month, especially considering that most of those congregations were not limited to music from the hymnal.

Furthermore, these congregations sang many hymns and songs that were new to this hymnal. A little more than 40 percent of the 658 musical items in *HWB* were "new" in the sense that they were not in the previous *Mennonite Hymnal*. Of the 258 hymns sung in September 2003 by the 81 reporting congregations, 124 (48 percent) were in this "new" category, and thus most likely have become part of the congregations' repertoires within the last ten to twelve years.

Thus it would seem clear that *Hymnal: A Worship Book* has had a strong impact on the church's repertoire of congregational song.

Summary

The data collected in these two surveys suggest the following conclusions:

1) Congregations in Mennonite Church USA are singing from the denomination's hymnal by a ratio of about 2:1.
2) Congregations in Mennonite Church USA continue to sing traditional four-part hymns more than anything else.
3) Most of these congregations are also singing a new repertoire of hymns and songs learned from this hymnal.
4) At the same time, most of these congregations (more than 90 percent) are not limiting themselves to the repertoire in the hymnal, but use many other sources as well.

To put it succinctly, Mennonites in the United States sing a whole variety of things in worship on Sunday mornings, from traditional four-part hymns out of the hymnal at one extreme, to unison praise choruses from words projected on the wall at the other. Does this matter?

It may matter more for Mennonites than similar data would matter to other denominations.

For congregations in Mennonite Church USA, singing in a traditional four-part, unaccompanied style has become part of our self-identity. When the person next to you on the airplane discovers that you're a Mennonite and asks you exactly what that means, you're likely to respond with something like, "Well, we believe in peace, we do lots of service projects, and we have beautiful four-part a cappella singing!"

Indeed, Kropf and Nafziger suggest that singing has become sacramental for North American Mennonites: "It may be that Mennonite detachment from the sacramental tradition has caused us to overlook what is the most obvious and powerful locus of God's presence in Mennonite worship: hymn singing."[11] If this is true, it matters greatly what we sing. And what we sing is slowly changing. While we continue to sing in four parts, much of our newer music isn't written in parts. Indeed, there may be no written music for the congregation to see at all. Sometimes, instead of a congregation being joined together as one in song, members may find themselves mostly listening to the leadership of a worship band.

And while it may be easy to credit the secular culture with changes in congregational song, the official hymnals of the church affect what we sing.

Thus *Hymnal: A Worship Book* has impacted the church's song, and so will its much-anticipated supplement volume.[12]

Notes

[1] *Hymnal: A Worship Book* (Elgin, IL: Brethren Pres; Newton, KS: Faith and Life Press; Scottdale, PA: Mennonite Publishing House, 1992).

[2] Kropf and Nafziger, *Singing: A Mennonite Voice* (Scottdale, PA: Herald Press, 2001), 9-10.

[3] *The Mennonite Hymnal* (Newton, KS: Faith and Life Press; Scottdale, PA: Herald Press, 1969).

[4] Survey One is appended to the end of this paper as Appendix 1.

[5] See Appendix 2.

[6] *Church and Sunday School Hymnal....Compiled and published under the direction of a Committee appointed by Mennonite Conferences.* J. D. Brunk, musical editor (Elkhardt, IN: Mennonite Publishing Co. and Freeport, IL: J.S.Shoemaker, 1902).

[7] *Songs for Praise and Worship* (Word Music: Waco, Texas, 1992, 2000, 2002).

[8] *Sing and Rejoice* (Scottdale, PA: Herald Press, 1979).

[9] Mennonite Publishing House, 1938.

[10] Copyright 1998 by Vineyard Songs. This song was printed in the program and sung at the Atlanta Mennonite Church USA Assembly, July 2003, which may account for its frequency of use in congregations in September of that year.

[11] *Singing: A Mennonite Voice*, 132.

[12] *Sing the Journey*, Hymnal: A Worship Book — Supplement I (Scottdale, PA: Faith and Life Resources, 2005). A second supplement volume is forthcoming.

Appendix 1: Survey One "What Are Mennonite Congregations Singing?"

Church Identification
Name of person completing this survey:

Worship Services

How many Sunday morning worship services does your congregation have on a regular basis?
    One / More than one
If more than one, are the services identical or each unique?
    Identical / Unique
    (If unique, please complete the bottom half of this form for each service.)

Congregational Singing

What resources does your congregation use for singing? (Check all that apply.)
    (*Note well: This question is in reference to what the* congregation *sings, not music that may be done by soloists, ensembles, choirs, et al.*)

    Hymnal: A Worship Book, 1992/*The Mennonite Hymnal*, 1969/*Sing and Rejoice!* 1979/Other published hymnals (please identify by title an date):

locally produced song books or song sheets / words projected on a screen/ no books or words—all singing done "by heart"

How is congregational singing led in worship? (Check all that are commonly used.)
> by a chorister, who conducts the music / by a leader who stands in front of the congregation and sings, but does not conduct / by a worship team of musicians who sing and play various instruments / by a piano or organ / Other

What instruments accompany congregational singing? (Check all that are commonly used.)
> None—all singing is a cappella / Organ / Piano / Guitar(s) / Other

Who selects the congregational songs and hymns?
> a pastor / a staff person with a title (e.g. "Chorister" or "Music Director") / various congregational volunteers, assigned to specific Sundays

> Comments:

Appendix 2: "Survey Two"

Style Familiarity Survey

How frequently does you congregation sing various musical styles?
For each style, respond with a number between 1 and 5, where 1 means "rarely or never" and 5 means "regularly, every Sunday."

Simply enter your numbered response at the beginning of each style description.

"Traditional Hymns," usually sung in 4-part harmony (such as "My faith looks up to Thee" or "Oh, for a thousand tongues to sing")

"Contemporary Praise and Worship" music, usually led by a praise team (such as "O Lord, our Lord, how majestic is thy name" or "Shine, Jesus, shine")

"Modern Hymns," often a unison melody, with written accompaniment (such as "New earth, heavens new" or "God is working his purpose out")

"Folk Hymns," written in unison, accompanied by acoustic folk instruments (such as "There are many gifts" or "You are salt for the earth")

Hymns and Songs in "Non-Western" styles (such as "Santo, santo, santo" or "Here, O Lord, your servants gather")

(Comments in relation to your responses above are welcome.)

"Gutierrez is Also a Mennonite Name": Issues of Identity and Hymnody in Contemporary Southern Ontario Mennonite Churches

Anna Janecek

In 1992, the General Conference Mennonite Church, the Mennonite Church in North America and the Church of the Brethren witnessed the culmination of a long and fruitful collaboration with the publication of a new joint hymnal. It was a significant project in many respects: not only was it an important cooperative effort involving these three distinct conferences, it was also the first major hymnal project to be attempted in nearly twenty-five years, a period that had witnessed significant demographic and ideological shifts among Mennonites both within North America and abroad. *Hymnal: A Worship Book,* or "the new hymnal" as it is still often called, was an attempt to provide an updated collection of hymns that not only recalled the historic traditions of each of these groups, but also exemplified their contemporary and increasingly global identities. As Managing Editor Rebecca Slough wrote in her introduction, "Our singing reveals much about who we have been and who we are as Anabaptists and Pietists. *Hymnal: A Worship Book* was prepared with the goal of continuing and expanding our singing tradition."[1] Towards this end, many new hymns were added, supplementing the core of traditional hymns common to all three conferences. Most noticeable among these were newly-composed hymns, contemporary songs, and hymns drawn from non-western countries with an emerging Mennonite presence.

Yet *Hymnal: A Worship Book* was not greeted with unanimous acclaim upon its distribution. Whereas many did welcome the new additions found within, regularly relying upon them in their worship services, others criticized the omission of particular historic favourites (such as "How great Thou art") while questioning the value of including hymns in languages and musical styles seen to be foreign and/or inaccessible to most "traditional" Mennonites. More than ten years after its publication, it is important to examine the role played by the new hymnal in the worshipping life of contemporary Mennonite churches, and the degree to which these new hymns have been accepted as part of an ever-evolving Mennonite identity. To what extent have the emergent voices of other nationalities and experiences been adopted into the wider body of Mennonite hymnody, and to what extent does our Sunday morning hymn singing still rely upon the traditional canon drawn from our western, European, and Germanic roots?

In seeking an answer to these questions, I devised an initial program of research that would attempt to identify what Mennonite congregations in Southern Ontario are singing during weekly worship services and examine how hymn selection trends have changed since the introduction of *Hymnal: A Worship Book*. Six congregations were selected for this initial case study: St. Jacob's Mennonite Church, Vineland United Mennonite Church, Toronto United Mennonite Church, Poole Mennonite Church in Milverton, Nith Valley Mennonite Church in New Hamburg, and Tavistock Mennonite Church. Congregations were selected on the basis of several criteria to ensure as balanced a survey as possible. The selected congregations therefore include both rural and urban settings, large and small memberships (where large is defined as greater than 300 members, and small as less than 200), and represent formerly Amish, Mennonite Conference, or General Conference backgrounds. Furthermore, an attempt was made to include congregations that are primarily mono-ethnic in makeup and those that are either more culturally diverse or that are closely associated with another ethnic congregation: St. Jacob's, for example, shares worship space with a Laotian Mennonite church as does Toronto United Mennonite Church with an Hispanic congregation.

The primary source of research material was published church bulletins from the years 1990 through to 2003.[2] Select years from the period in question were examined: 1990 was chosen as a representative year prior to the introduction of *Hymnal: A Worship Book* for all six churches, followed by the first full year with the new hymnal and then alternating years up to and including the year 2003.[3] Hymns listed in weekly service bulletins were examined as were those from select additional services including Good Friday, Christmas Eve, and other similar mid-week services.[4] It must be acknowledged that a survey such as this does not reveal the full extent of a given congregation's hymn repertoire, as it does not include a host of both formal and informal settings in which hymn singing may also occur such as community events, hymn sings, Sunday school programs, and church retreats. Nor does it necessarily reflect the particular tastes of individuals within a congregation, as anyone who has ever held responsibility for hymn selection can probably attest. But it does provide a vital window into the musical life of a congregation and, in particular, into how the hymnal is being used, since the act of gathering for weekly worship is one of the most central and defining acts of any congregation.

Since the primary objective of this research was to determine how emergent voices of other nationalities and experiences are being incorporated into regular Mennonite hymn singing, it was important to first identify and define which hymns represented these emergent voices. For this initial case study, I chose to focus specifically on international or global hymns, defined as those hymns that had originated in countries and cultures outside of Western Europe and North America. Of the 658 hymns included in *Hymnal: A Worship Book*, I identified forty-four international hymns; approximately 7 percent of all hymns in the hymnal.[5] This group included eleven hymns from Asian countries (including Japan, Indonesia, Taiwan, China, and India), nine from Latin American countries (including Venezuela, the West Indies, Uruguay, Nicaragua, and Colombia), and thirteen from African countries (including Nigeria, South Africa, Zambia, Tanzania, Ghana, Kenya, and Zaire). In addition, three hymns from Native North American communities were included, as were ten drawn from Eastern European nations and the Greek or Russian Orthodox liturgies.[6] Of the forty-four international hymns identified in *Hymnal: A Worship Book*, three (all of Asian origin) had been included in the previous *Mennonite Hymnal* of 1969: "Here, O Lord, your servants gather" (*HWB* 7), "God created heaven and earth" (*HWB* 160), and "Heart and mind, possessions, Lord" (*HWB* 392).[7]

To determine how these forty-four international hymns were being incorporated into Mennonite worship, they were cross-referenced against a list of hymns produced from each church's weekly bulletins. Statistics were tabulated on the basis of which hymns were being sung, how often and when. Furthermore, eight additional hymns, four of which had been retained from the previous hymnal and four of which were new, were also surveyed as a means of comparing usage of international hymns versus usage of western hymns either new or familiar.[8]

A number of interesting trends and tendencies can be found in the survey results. For the purposes of this paper, however, I will focus on three particular issues. First of all, which of these forty-four international hymns are being sung in Southern Ontario Mennonite congregations, as exemplified by these six churches, and how often are they being sung? Which hymns, styles or regions have become particularly popular with these churches? Second, how has congregational utilization of international hymns changed since the introduction of the new hymnal: has usage become more frequent or less over time, have congregations continued to incorporate a greater variety of international hymns into their worship, or have they become more discriminating in their selections? And third, on what occasions are these hymns included in Sunday morning worship: are they primarily relegated to services with an international focus, or are they also incorporated into so-called "regular" services? By examining these three issues, it will be possible to begin reconstructing the mosaic that is Mennonite congregational hymn-singing today, insofar as it exists in Southern Ontario, and from there to examine how Mennonite identity in this region, as demonstrated through music, is being influenced by this hymnody.

As a group, the congregations in question have done a reasonably good job of exploring the new material in the hymnal. Of the forty-four international hymns identified in the new hymnal, thirty-one, or 70 percent, were sung at least once between 1992 and 2003.[9] From the perspective of individual congregations, this statistic varies widely—one church used as few as five of the hymns in question while another used twenty-two—but within the conference as a whole, it would appear the majority of these hymns are at least being explored.

Conversely, only a select few of these hymns recur with any real frequency. Only six were sung more than ten times over the ten-year period in question, while fully one-third were sung only once. The most frequently sung international hymn, "Tú has venido a la orilla"/"Lord, you have come to the lakeshore" (*HWB* 229), was sung thirty-one times over this period; while "God loves all his many people" (*HWB* 397), the second most frequently occurring hymn, was sung twenty times. To better understand the significance of these numbers, however, it is helpful to compare these statistics with those of several non-international hymns. For example, "Heart with loving heart united" (*HWB* 420) was sung fifty-seven times over the same ten-year period. The "Mennonite Anthem," or former "606" (from the 1969 *Mennonite Hymnal*; now *HWB* 118), was sung fifty-one times, and two of the new additions to the hymnal, "Will you let me be your servant" (*HWB* 307) and "We are people of God's peace" (*HWB* 407), were sung forty-nine and thirty-seven times respectively. In fact, virtually all of the non-international hymns examined in this survey were sung more frequently than any of the most popular international hymns; only "Take thou my hand, O Father" (*HWB* 581) was sung less often, at eleven repetitions.

The most popular international hymns in *Hymnal: A Worship Book* are clearly those from African countries. Nine of thirteen African hymns included in this hymnal were sung, accounting for over 42 percent of all the international hymns sung between 1992 and 2003. Particularly popular were "God loves all his many people" (*HWB* 397), "Thuma mina" (*HWB* 434), and "Bwana Awabariki"/"May God grant you a blessing" (*HWB* 422), followed by "Asithi: Amen"/"Sing amen" (*HWB* 64), "Blessed are the persecuted" (*HWB* 230), and "In your sickness" (*HWB* 585). Latin American hymns also proved popular, accounting for 32 percent of international hymns sung during the period in question. Unlike the African hymns however, only two were sung with any real frequency: "Tú has venido a la orilla"/ "Lord, you have come to the lakeshore" (*HWB* 229), as mentioned, was the most frequently sung of all the international hymns, while "Cantemos al Señor"/ "Let's sing unto the Lord" (*HWB* 55) was also popular, occurring seventeen times over the period. Five additional hymns from this region were sung, though no more than five times each.

Hymns from other regions were decidedly less popular. Asian hymns, for example, accounted for only 13 percent of the total. Of the eleven Asian hymns included in the hymnal, only "Here, O Lord, your servants gather"(*HWB* 7) and "Heart and mind, possessions, Lord"(*HWB* 392) were sung with any real regularity at twelve and nine times respectively.[10] Eight of the nine Eastern European or Orthodox hymns were sung, representing 12 percent of all international hymns, but again, none with considerable frequency: "This is the day"(*HWB* 58), the most common, was sung only five times over the decade. But by far the most under-utilized group of hymns were those which originated among Native North Americans. Only one of these three hymns was sung, "Ehane he'ama"/"Father God, you are holy" (*HWB* 78), accounting for less than half of a percent of all the international hymns sung by these six churches between 1992-2003.[11]

Turning to an examination of changes in congregational usage of these hymns in the years following the introduction of *Hymnal: A Worship Book*, I discovered there has been some fluctuation concerning both the quantity and the variety of international hymns that have been incorporated into worship, whereas congregational preferences for particular hymns or cultural styles have remained largely consistent. Although numbers for each congregation varied greatly, all examined churches demonstrated a similar trend concerning the incorporation of international hymns following introduction of the new hymnal. In all cases, the first several years with the new hymnal were characterized by rapidly increasing usage of the international hymns, followed by a slight and gradual decline to the present state of use. Usage appears to have peaked in the final years of the millennium: 1998 and 1999 featured not only the highest incidence of international hymns in Sunday morning worship but also the greatest variety.

In general, those congregations with a specific program for introducing the new hymnal and its contents appear to have had the most success in incorporating international hymns into their services; that is, they have continued to sing a greater variety of the hymns on a more regular basis. By contrast, churches that did not deliberately promote the new hymnal were likely to experience a more dramatic decline in international hymn usage after the initial increase. These churches tended to become increasingly reliant upon a small selection of the newly familiar rather than continue to explore the unknown. Two interesting examples drawn from the survey will suffice to illustrate this point. St. Jacob's Mennonite Church appears to have been very conscientious in introducing *Hymnal: A Worship Book* to the congregation. Not only was an entire service devoted to its arrival, but throughout the first year, it was the source of virtually all special music in an attempt to introduce the congregation to many more new selections than would be possible in congregational hymn-singing alone. As a result, this congregation demonstrated a proportionally higher use of a wider variety of hymns than most other congregations surveyed. Tavistock Mennonite Church, on the other hand, did not appear to deliberately introduce the new hymnal. Bulletins over the first several years of use demonstrate a heavy reliance on hymns retained from the previous hymnal with little incorporation of international or other new hymns. In 1999, however, a "Singing School" was instituted as part of the adult Sunday school program using the new hymnal as a primary resource. The resulting change in congregational singing during Sunday morning worship was dramatic. Whereas previous years had averaged only three international hymns per year, seventeen were sung in 1999, an increased rate which continued through 2003.[12]

Having outlined how particular hymns, musical styles, and international regions are represented in the hymn-singing of Southern Ontario Mennonites, it is now possible to examine more closely how these hymns are being incorporated into weekly Sunday morning worship. Overall, there appears to be a tendency towards associating international hymns with internationally-oriented services, although the trend is not as evident as might be expected. Generally, when there is an international focus or element within a service, it is common to include one or more international hymns. This is particularly true in large urban or multicultural congregations and is particularly evident when a specific culture or region is identified. For example, when the New Life Church, an Hispanic-Mennonite congregation, visited Vineland United Mennonite Church, the morning's singing consisted entirely of Spanish hymns; when a Japanese speaker visited St. Jacob's Mennonite Church, a selection of Japanese hymns was included. When the international focus of a service is more general, however, as in the case of World Fellowship Sunday, World Communion Sunday, or missions Sundays, it is less likely that international hymns will be included. Rather, hymns that speak more generally to issues of Christian unity, the universal church, or the call to missions are more common.

When the focus of a service is a specific region or culture, the international hymns chosen tend to be unique to the service in question and are not generally reflective of particularly popular international hymns within a given congregation. That is, hymns for these services are selected primarily on the basis of their cultural origins and not for any textual or thematic reasons, nor on the basis of congregational familiarity. As a result, hymns for services such as these account for a large portion of those international hymns that were sung only once or twice over the period in question. Particularly popular international hymns, on the other hand, are more likely to be used within so-called "regular" services and to be treated in the manner of non-international hymns in that they are selected on the basis of thematic content or other inherent qualities, rather than their international style or origin.

As intriguing as it may be to examine the settings in which these hymns are sung, however, it is equally revealing to consider those settings in which they are not. Most notably, they are almost never incorporated into what more liturgical denominations might call the "High Holy Sundays," or those services which are deemed to be particularly formal or traditional such as those during the seasons of Advent and Lent, and at Christmas and Easter. This may be reflective of the fact that few of the international hymns in *Hymnal: A Worship Book* are seasonally specific: the few that were sung in these services are among those which do speak to a specific event in the Christian calendar. However, a close examination of the data suggests further that international hymns are more likely to appear in more informal or celebratory services such as during the summer months (May through September), at the start of the academic year, and in those services either planned by or giving special focus to children or youth (i.e. Vacation Bible School Sundays, Mennonite Youth Fellowship services, etc.). Taken together, these tendencies suggest that the international hymns of *Hymnal: A Worship Book* are still considered part of a special repertoire. Although clearly occupying an important place in the worship of many congregations, their usage suggests these hymns are still seen as distinct, as somehow set apart from the wider body of traditional or authentic Mennonite hymnody.

The publication of *Hymnal: A Worship Book* in 1992 coincided with a period of increasing global awareness among Mennonites not only within Southern Ontario but also across Canada. Like other denominations, Mennonites experienced a profound demographic shift throughout the twentieth century. Whereas in 1900, 98 percent of Mennonites lived in Europe or North America, in the year 2000, fully 60 percent of the global Mennonite population was living in countries in Asia, Africa, and Latin America.[13] The trend towards globalization is also evident within churches and conferences here in North America. According to the Diversity Project Report issued in 2002 by Mennonite Church Canada, there are now over forty congregations associated with MC Canada that represent cultures and ethnic backgrounds not traditionally common to this denomination. Weekly, these forty congregations minister to over 2,000 people in eleven different languages.[14] Furthermore, ethnic and cultural diversity within individual churches at the congregational level is also increasingly common, particularly in large urban settings.

The diversity of hymns to be found within the new hymnal, therefore, is reflective of larger trends within the denomination itself. However, I would suggest that in practice, the degree of congregational acceptance of these hymns is more reflective of the on-going challenges faced by non-dominant ethnic voices within Canadian Mennonite conferences and churches, both within Southern Ontario and beyond. While enthusiasm is frequently expressed by individuals, churches, and conferences concerning the unique gifts and perspectives that these diverse cultures bring to Mennonite experiences of church and worship, there are also on-going challenges and concerns inherent in bridging cultural, linguistic, and ethnic divides. Foremost among the concerns raised at both national and international levels are questions of representation, participation, and authority; specifically, how do we integrate "non-dominant ethnic voices" into a common Mennonite identity in meaningful and authentic ways?[15] While embracing the gifts these many cultures have to offer, traditional ethnic Mennonites, it appears, are still hesitant to recognize that Gutierrez is now a Mennonite name, that Kim Chi is a Mennonite food, and that "Ehane he'ama" is a Mennonite hymn.

The presence of many international hymns within *Hymnal: A Worship Book* has already contributed immensely to a broader understanding of Mennonite identity. If these hymns may still be considered part of a distinct repertoire, if the data presented here suggest they have been under-utilized within Mennonite churches of Southern Ontario, they are, nevertheless, an integral part of the worship of many congregations and in this they have ensured that Mennonites today are significantly more cognizant of their international brothers and sisters than they were ten or twenty years ago. However, if as Mennonites we believe that our singing not only reflects but also actively shapes our collective identity, it is imperative that we continue to strive for greater diversity in our congregational hymn singing, for in so doing, we will continue to craft a new global identity that honours the increasingly multicultural mosaic that is the Mennonite church today.

Notes

[1] *Hymnal: A Worship Book* (Elgin, IL: Brethren Press; Newton, KS: Faith and Life Press; Scottdale, PA: Mennonite Publishing House, 1992), iii.

[2] All church bulletins were obtained from the holdings of the Mennonite Archives of Ontario housed at the Conrad Grebel University College Library in Waterloo, Ontario. I am grateful to the staff of these organizations for their assistance in this research.

[3] Four of these six churches introduced the new hymnal immediately following its publication in 1992; one introduced it in 1996, and another not until 1999. However, no less than four calendar years were analysed for each congregation.

[4] Weddings, funerals, and other services with a similarly personal rather than corporate orientation were not included in the survey.

[5] A complete listing of the examined hymns can be found in Appendix 1. Several of the surveyed congregations also included international hymns in their worship drawn from sources other than *Hymnal: A Worship Book*. However, while the question of whether and how the new hymnal is being supplemented is also important, the intention of this paper is primarily to examine how the hymnal itself is being used. Therefore, these international hymns were not included in this survey.

[6] The application of any definition is always somewhat arbitrary and subject to the whims of interpretation. In compiling this list I have most certainly included or omitted hymns that, in another's hands, would have been treated differently. Not included in this survey are a number of hymns which could be rightly considered outside of a traditional Mennonite hymn repertory, including African American spirituals and gospel songs, hymns derived from Western folk tunes, and non-English hymns from various Euro-American nations whose stylistic or linguistic traits may evoke an international flavour. Examples include "Je louerai l'Eternel"/"Praise, I will praise you, Lord" (76), "Oyenos, mi Dios" (358), and "You shall go out with joy" (427). Hymns such as these were primarily excluded due to the fact that they originated in Western countries (France and the United States respectively) and that stylistically, they tended to closely resemble traditional Western-influenced hymnody.

[7] *HWB* is used throughout this paper to refer to hymns in *Hymnal: A Worship Book*.

[8] The four retained hymns surveyed included "For God so loved us"/"Gott ist die Liebe" (*HWB* 167), "Heart with loving heart united" (*HWB* 420), "Take

Thou my hand, O Father" (*HWB* 581), and the old "606," "Praise God from whom" (*HWB* 118). The four new hymns surveyed included "We are people of God's peace" (*HWB* 407), "Will you let me be your servant" (*HWB* 307), "Je louerai l'Eternel"/"Praise, I will praise you, Lord" (*HWB* 76), and "You shall go out with joy" (*HWB* 427).

[9] For the frequency with which each hymn occurred over the period in question, see Appendix 1.

[10] Interestingly, these two hymns were among the few international hymns included in the previous hymnal, *The Mennonite Hymnal* (Newton, KS: Faith and Life Press; Scottdale, PA: Herald Press, 1969), and were the only international hymns in that collection to be sung by any of the surveyed congregations in the years immediately preceding the release of *Hymnal: A Worship Book*.

[11] Without further research into the hymn selection process at each of these churches, it is impossible to determine what factors may have contributed to this particular pattern of hymn usage. One may only speculate why these Mennonites appear to have developed such an affinity for African hymns on one hand, while ostensibly finding Native North American hymns to be challenging, if not outright inaccessible on the other hand. What societal, cultural, musical, theological or political factors have influenced, or continue to influence, the asymmetrical ways in which Mennonites have heard and assimilated these hymnodies?

[12] Like other congregations in the survey, Tavistock experienced some decline in the years following the Sunday School program; however, the number of international hymns in use continued to remain elevated well above the numbers of previous years. By 2002, for example, the final full year analysed, nine international hymns were sung.

[13] Wilbert Shenk, *By Faith They Went Out* (Elkhart, IN: Institute of Mennonite Studies, 2000), 94; *Mennonite and Brethren in Christ Directory 2000*. While this demographic shift among Mennonites is particularly striking, it is in no way unique. Perhaps one of the most underestimated developments of the preceding century is the globalization of the Christian movement. Throughout the twentieth century, Christianity rapidly evolved from a predominantly Euro-American phenomenon into a global movement, deeply rooted in all continents. According to missiologist David Barrett, nearly 80 percent of Christians were living in Europe or North America in 1900, while in the year 2000, almost 60 percent were living in the southern hemisphere. From David B. Barrett and Todd M. Johnson, "Annual Statistical Data on Global Mission: 2002," *International Bulletin of Missionary Research* (Jan. 2002), 23.

[14] Samson Lo, "Mix of Cultures Presents a Challenge," *Canadian Mennonite* (June 2003) 7:12, 19.

[15] See, among others, John A. Lapp and Ed van Straten, "Mennonite World Conference 1925-2000: From Euro-American Conference to Worldwide Communion," *Mennonite Quarterly Review* 77 (January 2003):35-45; "Concerns from Multicultural Churches," *Canadian Mennonite* (August 2002) 6:15, 21; "Exploring Multicultural Involvement," *Canadian Mennonite* (July 2002) 6:13, 26; Samson Lo, "Mix of Cultures Presents a Challenge," *Canadian Mennonite* (June 2003) 7:12, 19; Karin Fehderau, "Non-traditional Voices Share Concerns and Joys," *Canadian Mennonite* (August 2002) 6:15, 20; "Workshop Explores Cultural Diversity," *Canadian Mennonite* (December 2002) 6:23, 33.

Apendix 1

International Hymn Usage, 1993-2003

Hymnal: A Worship Book	Title	Region of Origin	Number of times sung (1993-2003)
229	Tú has venido a la orilla	Latin America	31
397	God loves all his many people	Africa	20
55	Cantemos al Señor	Latin America	17
434	Thuma mina	Africa	16
422	Bwana awabariki	Africa	13
7	Here, O Lord, your servants gather	Asia	12
392	Heart and mind, possessions, Lord	Asia	9
64	Asithi: Amen	Africa	7
230	Blessed are the persecuted	Africa	7
585	In your sickness	Africa	7
293	God sends us the Spirit	Africa	6
58	This is the day	E. Europe/Orthodox	5
400	Santo, santo, santo	Latin America	5
136	From the depths of sin	E. Europe/Orthodox	4
144	Kyrie eleison	E. Europe/Orthodox	4
231	Oh, blessed are the poor in spirit	E. Europe/Orthodox	4
537	En medio de la vida	Latin America	4
270	Who are these	E. Europe/Orthodox	3
10	Jesus, we want to meet	Africa	2
62	Who is so great a God	E. Europe/Orthodox	2
202	The virgin Mary had a baby boy	Latin America	2

Hymnal: a Worship Book	Title	Region of Origin	Number of times sung (1993-2003)
267	Christ has arisen	Africa	2
78	Ehane he'ama	North America	1
160	God created heaven and earth	Asia	1
354	Fount of love, our Savior God	Asia	1
399	Now go forward	Asia	1
435	May the Lord, mighty God	Asia	1
460	Una espiga	Latin America	1
461	In the quiet consecration	E. Europe/ Orthodox	1
550	Living and dying with Jesus	E. Europe/ Orthodox	1
647	Por la mañana	Latin America	1
9	Jesus A, Nahetotaetanome	North America	0
35	Many and great, O God	North America	0
52	Praise the Lord	Asia	0
207	Niño lindo	Latin America	0
260	When I survey the wondrous cross	Africa	0
316	In this world abound scrolls	Asia	0
330	I believe in God	Africa	0
380	Let us pray	E. Europe/ Orthodox	0
468	O Bread of life, for sinners broken	Asia	0
513	To go to heaven	Africa	0
531	Ah, what shame I have to bear	Asia	0
562	Nada te turbe	Latin America	0
583	Ndikhokele, O Jehova	Africa	0

A Few Ways to be a Mennonite: Contemporary Christian Music in a Community of Hymns

Stephanie J. Krehbiel

In the summer of 1999, National Public Radio's *Morning Edition* reported on the annual conference of the Mennonite Church USA, held that year in St. Louis, Missouri.[1] In this story, thousands of Mennonites were heard singing several bars of a four-part hymn in a resonant hall. The reporter then interjected, "Now this is no choir, mind you, this is how Mennonites praise their God."[2]

The reporter's assessment of "how Mennonites praise their God" was one with which many Mennonites would likely agree. Mennonite worship can be stark and lacking in ritual in comparison with that of other Christian denominations. For this reason, congregational singing frequently provides the most affective moments in a worship service. Given the centrality of congregational singing in Mennonite religious practice, there has always been a great deal of discussion—and controversy—over what should be sung. In recent years, Christian churches throughout the United States have contended with the influence of contemporary Christian music on their worship and Mennonites, having almost entirely lost their historically separatist lifestyle, face this challenge alongside their Christian peers.

The congregations of the Salem and Salem-Zion Mennonite Churches in the rural area east of Freeman, South Dakota are the focus of this paper. Freeman, a town of approximately 1,300 in the southeastern part of the state, is like many small, agricultural communities today—struggling for survival amidst an economic landscape hostile to the interests of small-scale farming. Music plays a key role in this struggle, providing both entertainment and spiritual sustenance for the hard-working and financially strained members of Freeman's rural churches.

During my fieldwork in the community in the summer of 2002, the church members I spoke with were particularly eager to discuss the impact of contemporary Christian music on their congregations.[3] While this music has never been whole-heartedly embraced by either Salem or Salem-Zion, it has made an entrance in the community sufficient to activate both controversy and serious introspection about the purpose of music in worship. I argue in this paper that the introduction of contemporary Christian music into the Freeman churches has forced people to confront the impact of the outside world on their small community — not only the secular influences traditionally avoided by Mennonites, but also the influence of evangelical Christianity. The community's various responses to these influences indicate that even in a town of 1,300, there is more than one way to be a Mennonite.

One could easily write about what this music should be called; one could also take the term "contemporary Christian music" as a starting point for discussion of what kind of music belongs in that category. I won't pursue either of these avenues in this paper; other writers have admirably tackled the task of defining and categorizing this music.[4] Because people in Freeman tend to use the phrase "praise music," I use it interchangeably with "contemporary Christian music." Other variants that I have heard include "chorus music," "contemporary worship music," and "praise and worship music." Generally, this music uses non-liturgical instruments such as guitars, drums, bass, and electronic keyboard. There tends to be less written harmony than in hymns, although those comfortable with the genre add harmonies of their own.

At the Salem-Zion church, or "North" church, as it is known in the community, Pastor Abe Duerksen selects the majority of the hymns for worship services.[5] When asked his views on what music needs to accomplish in a worship setting, he mentioned contemporary Christian music, and explained why he generally shies away from it:

> The praise music that I have been familiar with . . . tends to draw attention to the singer rather than to the one to whom you are supposed to be singing in a worship setting. And I, as a pastor, sense that in my way of evaluating worship, [this] is not the direction I should be leading my people and pointing my people, and that singing as well as scripture or prayer or preaching, ought to be pointing us to God and to our creator, and music can be a part of that. . . . It should focus and direct our thoughts, our attention, our aspirations, our praise toward—toward our God, toward Christ. And the expression of God. Praise music, generically, is weak in doing that. I won't say it never does that. But it's more focused on "my feelings," and "I want," and "I like," and "I"—you find that personal pronoun in a lot of chorus music, or praise music, very frequently. And, again, an acculturation of Christianity is what it is, in my opinion.

A Few Ways to be a Mennonite

Abe, who has served at Salem-Zion for eleven years, made sure I knew he wasn't a musician. "If you're looking for somebody who knows a lot about music, you're interviewing the wrong person," he said. He hasn't had much musical training, and selects hymns based completely on their texts and the relevance of those texts to the theme of the service. (While in Freeman, I heard numerous compliments on his gift for hymn-selection, the most striking coming from a teenage girl who spoke of how powerful the hymn had been after a sermon in which Abe spoke about caring for his wife, who has early-onset Alzheimer disease.) When the subject of contemporary Christian music came up in our conversation about the latest Mennonite hymnal, Abe explained the shortcomings that he saw, based on the textual message he believes this music delivers.

Abe's perspective on this music was familiar to me, not only from other Freeman consultants, but also from Mennonites I've spoken with at other churches. My search for another point of view led me to Joleen Miller, the recently hired assistant pastor at Salem, or the "South" church. Joleen, whose primary responsibilities rest with youth ministry, has been actively engaged in contemporary worship since her college years, when she majored in Christian ministry with an emphasis in youth ministry. Joleen has been doing her best to bring contemporary Christian music to the South church, and her efforts, while welcomed by some, also meet with considerable resistance. I asked her how she would explain her choices to a person who didn't understand her approach to worship, and in response, she said this:

> Sometimes you're just overwhelmed with love for your dad . . . and you want to tell him you love him. . . . [F]or me, that's somewhat the same in worship. God might not have done specifically this huge thing in my life right at this moment—but sometimes you're just overwhelmed and you just want to tell him you love him and that you worship him and that, you know, he's worthy. . . . I think for me, contemporary worship allows me to do that more so with God. You can just kind of, just be yourself, and open yourself up to God . . . that's more of a personal thing, at least it is for me.

Abe and Joleen are simple to dichotomize. I might easily construct this argument: Abe, being male, middle-aged, and experienced in ministry, represents a voice of power. His desire to de-emphasize the individual comes deep from within the voice of Mennonite history, a history in which communal ideals have been a tool in the maintenance of patriarchy. Joleen, being young, female, and new to her job, is disempowered and disadvantaged, bearing the legacy of those individuals, women especially, who have been silenced, unable to express themselves in the sphere of worship. She is a lone voice fighting for her right to approach God on her own terms, rather than through the filter of a community in which she has little power.

And just as easily, I might argue this: Joleen, through her promotion of a music and worship style that is a popular and influential part of American Christianity, is asking people to turn their backs on a rich history of communal life in service to God, a history that has enabled them to resist the consumerist call of American culture. She wants them to make their own emotions their guide in worship, in defiance of their heritage. Abe, on the other hand, enables his church to ignore that same powerful call. He represents an Anabaptist ideal, that of the faithful adhering to their beliefs in face of overwhelming pressure to place their loyalties elsewhere.

I don't believe either of these models can do justice to the situation as it really is. For one thing, as individuals, neither Abe nor Joleen fits into these reductionist arguments, and neither deserves the blame implicit in them. Also, I doubt that any of my Freeman consultants would find that these arguments illustrate the truth as they see it. They might believe, as I do, that in these separate scenarios are fragments of truth, not about Abe and Joleen necessarily, but about their community and its power struggles.

In these churches, there is a larger conflict behind the different opinions about what kinds of music should be sung in church. In Freeman and elsewhere, I have frequently seen Mennonites attempt to resolve friction over congregational singing by suggesting that congregants learn to be tolerant of each other. Those seeking an end to the conflicts imply that the purpose of all worship music is essentially the same, and that the disputes that arise are a result of petty preferences that can be resolved by appealing to people's higher natures. Yet the same conflicts resurface. While inflexibility and intolerance are clearly present and partly responsible for struggles in the world of Mennonite church music, the preference for one kind of music over another is often an important manifestation of a theological and/or spiritual outlook. Congregational singing is, after all, a means through which to transfer values. What looks outwardly like a conflict over trivialities is often a more fundamental disagreement over what is spiritually important. Among my consultants in the Salem and Salem-Zion churches, a major issue at the forefront of the contemporary worship debate is this: who should receive the most emphasis in our worship, the individual or the community?

This brings us back to Abe and Joleen. There are many explanations for their differences, but a likely one, I believe, can be found by examining a common Anabaptist approach to spirituality. To be an Anabaptist, historically, is to be a member of a community. Individual interests are nearly always subsumed by those of the group, at least in theory, and personal modesty is paramount. The Amish call this *Gelassenheit,* or surrender. Donald Kraybill describes the concept in *The Riddle of Amish Culture*:

> Although Gelassenheit seems repressive to Moderns, it is a redemptive paradox for the Amish. They believe that the followers of Christ and the martyrs of old were called to lose their lives in order to save them. . . . The Amish believe that people who deny self and submit to divine precepts bring honor and glory to God. Members who yield to their neighbors are ultimately revering God. The person who forgoes personal advancement for the sake of family and community makes a redemptive sacrifice that transforms the church into the body of Christ. Gelassenheit is a social process that recycles individual energy for community purposes. . . . This deep conviction to yield self-interest for the sake of the community provides a powerful resource of cultural capital.[6]

Although Kraybill is focused on a community that practices a more radical version of these principles than do mainstream Mennonites, his description captures some of the reasoning behind Abe's sentiments. Few Mennonites use the word *Gelassenheit,* but in many ways they stand on the same spiritual feet as the Amish. The community paves a Mennonite's road to God. Serving the community is equivalent to serving God. And contemporary Christian music, as Abe pointed out, is often oriented toward the individual's experience. He was not my only consultant to express distaste, or at the very least, distrust, in the "I" and "me" language of this music; several people I spoke with made similar comments. Another Salem member, for instance, said of praise music, "I guess . . . the biggest . . . issue that I have is that it's supposed to be about me, as I'm singing it, it's not about God. You know, what I'm feeling, what I'm doing, you know, give me this, or I feel this."

To many people in Freeman, contemporary worship music represents Christianity at its most American—its most individualistic, commercial, and status quo. Abe referred to this when he called it an "acculturation of Christianity." Similarly, a Salem-Zion member commented, "Yeah, it [contemporary Christian music] is more entertaining. But I think it's also more me-centered. We're so terribly, you know, self-centered nowadays, in this country. And I think those songs reflect that." A worship style that refers to or reminds people of the dominant economic and cultural forces in American culture is very problematic to Mennonite worshippers who self-consciously locate their faith in a place beyond these forces.

However, those who enjoy contemporary worship music point to its capacity to nourish the individual faith experience in a way that hymn singing, according to them, does not. The same quality in this music that some worshippers object to—the recurring personal pronouns, the references to one's own faith—is for others the quality that draws them in and makes their worship experience real. In a Mennonite context, where community values are put at an especially high premium, some argue that there is a need for more individual nurture, especially of young people.

Joleen is probably the strongest advocate for contemporary music and worship at Salem, perhaps in the entire Salem/Salem-Zion community. With the help of a well-respected public school music teacher and keyboardist, Joleen has begun a "praise band" of teenagers at Salem that plays approximately once a month. On these Sundays, the band plays during the normal prelude time, and then does several songs with the congregation during the service. Joleen does not dislike hymns, but admits that a steady diet of them, without contemporary praise songs mixed in, makes God feel frustratingly distant to her.

One reason she gave for the community's resistance to contemporary worship was a fear of change and a lack of exposure to new ideas, explaining:

> I think they're scared to do anything different. I think it's something that they've always known. It's how it's always been ... church is serious, this is how you do things, this is how it is. And for most people in the church, they've never been anywhere else, I mean, they haven't gone away and moved somewhere and then come back, to have those different experiences.

In addition, Joleen suggested that people do not appreciate contemporary music because they are afraid to express emotions. In this view, she is not alone; hymn-lovers and proponents of contemporary Christian music alike agree that Mennonites have "issues" with emotions. Joleen's colleague John Stucky, the lead pastor at Salem, agreed: "We're very afraid of emotions in this church . . . we don't know how to deal with our emotions. And we don't know how to articulate emotions, we don't know how to express emotions." Many culturally Mennonite households enforce the idea that emotional display is self-indulgent, weak, or unseemly. Consequently, tearful displays are not popular in most churches, nor are unbridled expressions of joy. The aversion to bringing excess attention to one's self keeps nearly everyone well behaved and quiet in the pews. Because of this, the overtly emotional modus operandi of contemporary worship is, for many Mennonites, jarring and uncomfortable.

It would be quite wrong, however, to suggest that Mennonites do not feel anything strongly during their worship, or during the singing of hymns. It's a testimony to the power of their experiences that almost no one I spoke with in Freeman, despite their generally restrained approach to emotional display, was able to speak to me dispassionately about how they felt while singing in church, uncomfortable though they often were with my (admittedly sometimes artless) questions. In a conversation with David Hartzler, a Salem-Zion member who spent years farming in Brazil and returned to the Freeman community, we drifted to the subject of the singing at Salem-Zion, and he nearly brought himself to tears. "I think our singing is ... I just kind of like it. When Mark does the organ ... he konks out on a verse [i.e., he stops playing to let the congregation sing a cappella], and you have that—beautiful sound . . . ." David couldn't go on for a moment, so powerful was his immediate affective response at the thought of his congregation singing alone and in four parts.

Resistance to contemporary Christian music can often be traced to a dislike of the culture from which it comes (or the culture from which people perceive it coming). This culture, the aggressively evangelical contemporary Christian music industry, has come to exist almost as a denomination of its own, a community that borrows from established denominations but is not bound by them, and is unapologetically trend-conscious. William Romanowski writes, "The most salient feature in the evolution of the CCM [contemporary Christian music] industry was the continual coalescing of evangelical commitments and beliefs with other social and cultural trends in America, especially those that animated the mainstream entertainment industry."[7] This mode of "evolution" is one of the aspects of contemporary Christian music that seemed most objectionable to some of my consultants. A number of them remarked on the extraordinarily short shelf life of contemporary worship songs, contrasting them with hymns that had endured for centuries as evidence of their lack of intrinsic worth. Contemporary worship music's link to popular entertainment, particularly for Freeman community members with a strong investment and education in music, is part of why many people believe it doesn't belong in church. Clara Schrag, the choir director at Salem-Zion, said, "I will not use 'Jesus jingles,' as people call them ... I'm very fussy about that." She continued:

> We've got to do the best, I mean, the best quality music in our worship services ... that's where I'm coming from. And, and one thing that really strikes me is the music director in Henderson, Nebraska [a Mennonite enclave], he's been the music director there most of his life, and he also is a tenor soloist. Often the brides will ask him to sing at their weddings in the Henderson church. And they'll come to him with—the *Young and the Restless* theme, you know what I'm talking about, soap opera things ... and he tells them he will not sing it at their wedding. He says that's kind of like [asking] your mother to get you a gunny sack for a bridal dress. You know, I think that's a real good image. I

will sing it at your reception, but I will not sing it at your wedding ceremony. I think that's a very good analogy. You want to do the best in church.

To my knowledge, soap opera themes are not being considered for services in Freeman, but Clara made it clear that she sees a connection between this example and other worship music that borrows from mainstream, commercial sources.

An evangelical argument, of course, might be that mainstream entertainment styles and marketing schemes constitute not a cheapening of the worship experience but rather a means to an end, the end being the "salvation" of as many people as possible. Romanowski writes of the contemporary Christian music industry, "The success of evangelism was calculated by the number of souls that were saved; 'souls' were consumers, as measured by record sales, airplay, and concert tickets."[8] Joleen, although she isn't trying to sell records, recognizes that contemporary music may have some recruiting potential. She said, "People need to know the truth [i.e., the Christian message]. I mean, there's a lot of people, even in Freeman, probably, who don't go to church, or who aren't, you know, aren't a part of any congregation or anything like that, but how are we reaching out to them?" She adds that contemporary music can attract worshippers, "especially for the unchurched . . . there [are] big churches in bigger cities . . . who do use more of the contemporary worship to help draw people in, because . . . music is something that those people can relate to."

Such overtly evangelical language is uncommon in the Freeman churches. Indeed, it is not common among Mennonites in general. Despite their denomination's sophisticated and ambitious mission network, it is still rare to hear a Mennonite talk about "saving souls." Yet Joleen is not alone in her concern over finding new members. Many North and South church members worry about the survival of their congregations, noting that the Freeman Mennonite community loses many young people who are either unwilling or unable to make it in the troubled agricultural system there. Therefore, as long as contemporary Christian music is promoted as a means of bringing growth and vitality to churches, it will be both a bane and a temptation for the Freeman Mennonites, keeping their debates over theology and identity as relevant as ever.

Notes

[1] The Mennonite Church USA existed only in concept at this time, as the General Conference Mennonite Church and the Mennonite Church denominations did not finalize their merger until 2002, but the two groups were already holding annual conferences together.

[2] *Morning Edition*, National Public Radio, July 28, 1999.

[3] During my field research, I formally interviewed eleven members of Salem-Zion Mennonite Church and seven members of Salem Mennonite Church. Four of my consultants were teenagers, three were in their twenties, and the remainder were middle aged; two or three were above retirement age (I did not ask my consultants their ages, so these are approximations). All who were of working age were engaged in agricultural professions, and several were in music leadership positions in their churches. My conclusions are also influenced by a number of informal conversations I had with members of these communities. I emphasize that this research is not quantitative or survey-based; my information comes from qualitative ethnographic methods.

[4] Brian Wren discusses worship music definitions in Chapter 4 of his book *Praying Twice: The Music and Words of Congregational Song* (Louisville: Westminster John Knox Press, 2000). His perspective is clearly that of a more hymn-preferring church musician, but he is even-handed and offers some insight into how someone with decades of church music experience tackles the issue of what to call different kinds of music.

[5] The names of all consultants have been changed in order to protect their privacy.

[6] Donald B. Kraybill, *The Riddle of Amish Culture* (Baltimore: John Hopkins University Press, 1989), 32.

[7] William D. Romanowski, "Roll Over Beethoven, Tell Martin Luther the News: Evangelicals and Rock Music," *Journal of American Culture* 15, no.3 (Fall 1992): 80.

[8] Ibid., 81.

"Pleasure Enough": Four-Part A Cappella Singing as a Survival Strategy for a Mennonite-in-Exile

Laura H. Weaver

"Stop that damn Fisk organ," I think each Sunday as I hear that beautiful organ in a Presbyterian church. I can hardly hear the congregational singing—and when I do hear it, people are not singing in harmony. Although I enjoy organ concerts and the excellent intergenerational choir trained in the English cathedral tradition, when I'm in church I want to be surrounded by sopranos, altos, tenors, and basses, preferably singing a cappella. I'm ecstatic on the few occasions that I hear someone singing in harmony—Andy Hubbard, singing tenor as he stands behind me in the congregation, or Ron Attinger, singing bass as he walks up the aisle to help serve communion.

My musician friends elsewhere tell me that I'm lucky to hear that organ and that choir Sunday after Sunday. "I'd love to play that organ," an organist friend e-mailed me. Intellectually, I know that my musician friends are correct. But I'm a Mennonite who, because of graduate school and job locations, has unintentionally lived in exile from a predominantly Mennonite community ever since 1966. So I go home from church and listen to cassettes and CDs, like the "Table Singers" and the "Hochstetler Family" from Pennsylvania, and the original "Mennonite Hour" radio program from Virginia. Recently, I impulsively told a friend, "If I don't hear four-part a cappella singing, I shrivel up." I'm surprised that I said that openly to someone, but I've certainly been feeling that more and more. At seventy-three, I find that my hungers persist: for food and drink, for sex, and for four-part a cappella singing. I don't have the scientific background to explain what physical needs this singing satisfies. I just know that I need it to live with passion. It's not about theology, about creed. At least I don't think it is. Singing triggers feelings of physical pleasure, and I know that pleasure from singing is multi-dimensional; I need it all—laughter and tears.

Four-Part A Cappella Singing as a Survival Strategy

Another reason that I treasure this singing is, I'm sure, a feeling of community, as reported often in Marlene Kropf and Kenneth Nafziger's book, *Singing: A Mennonite Voice*.[1] This is a connection that even in exile, I can maintain. More of that later.

No wonder I link my need of singing with other hungers; no wonder I'm famished. From my birth through my teens I grew up with four-part a cappella singing in the Old Order (horse and buggy) Mennonite Church and then in the Lancaster Conference in Pennsylvania. This type of singing nourished me not only in Sunday morning church services but also in Sunday evening services and at social gatherings. On Sunday afternoons at my Old Order Mennonite grandparents' home we gathered around the kitchen table and sang hymns in both English and German (for example, "Gott ist die Liebe"). Later, in the Lancaster Conference, we young people sang at "cottage meetings" in the homes of sick or elderly people, and sometimes the Sunday evening church service was devoted entirely to hymn singing. And once a year—in July—occurred the glorious Atglen singing—an outdoor singing held at Atglen, Pennsylvania, in Kennel's Woods, a sloping piece of land owned by Joseph Kennel. Boards were placed across stones, boulders, and tree stumps; some people sat on those pieces of wood, and others sat on the ground or in automobiles parked nearby. The singing, led by song leaders, continued for a few hours. At these singings, held from 1933 until around 1963, people came from various states and also from Canada. The highest attendance was 7,000. All those singing occasions during my Old Order and Lancaster Conference period were so important that when in 2001, as preparation for a talk in Evansville, Indiana, I paged through the *Church and Sunday School Hymnal* (1902), I recognized most of the 500-some hymns included in it.

In my next Mennonite community, Harrisonburg, Virginia, the music continued. At Eastern Mennonite College, where I was first a student and then a teacher, we sang a cappella in chapel and at the beginnings of some classes. For example, I remember Professor G. Irvin Lehman's leading us in "I owe the Lord a morning song" in Old Testament history class. I also heard this singing in special programs by the Vesper Chorus and the Collegiate Chorus and in the annual performance of Alfred Gaul's oratorio, *The Holy City*, sung a cappella!

When I moved to Ohio to teach at Bluffton College, music continued to sustain me. There, in the setting of what was then the General Conference, some things changed. I learned to like organ accompaniment, and I became familiar with another Mennonite hymnal—with hymns like "So nimm denn meine Hände," "Grosser Gott, wir loben dich," and the former "606,"

"Praise God from whom," sometimes called the Mennonite anthem. But these were minor changes; congregational singing was still as important as food, drink, and sex.

From the time I left Bluffton in 1966 to go to the University of Kansas to work on a Ph.D. until the present, I have lived outside a predominantly Mennonite community. However, I have always identified myself as a Mennonite; I share the speaker's observation at the end of Julia Kasdorf's poem, "Mennonites": ". . . we cannot leave the beliefs/or what else would we be?"[2] And, although I realize that many different kinds of music are being sung and played in Mennonite churches these days, a core feature of my Mennonite identity is a cappella singing. After my move to Lawrence, Kansas, I no longer sang and heard this music regularly, but I did so occasionally; when I returned to Pennsylvania to visit relatives, I went to Lancaster Conference churches, later to the Akron Mennonite Church, and, in recent years, to Community Mennonite Church in Lancaster and University Mennonite Church in State College. I also often visited friends in Harrisonburg, Virginia; Goshen, Indiana; Bluffton, Ohio; North Newton, Kansas; and Champaign-Urbana, Illinois. Many of those church services, while using instrumental music, also include a cappella singing. Also, some Mennonite academic conferences, on writing at Goshen and on ritual at Hillsdale, Michigan, included a time for singing. Sometimes in Pennsylvania I even visited more conservative Mennonite churches where, despite my discomfort with the theology, I enjoyed the singing.

I heard this singing on unexpected special occasions, too. On September 13, 2002 (after my emergency flight from Evansville to State College), my sister, nieces and nephews, and I stood around my mother's bedside and sang hymns from memory for over an hour, during which time she died peacefully. At the graveside we sang again—a large group this time—from memory while relatives shoveled soil into the grave. I no longer had long hair rolled on a bun and my head covered as did the women around me. But we all knew the songs from memory, and we all wept as we sang. Shortly after my mother's death and funeral I walked in late at University Mennonite Church in State College. There, in a more liberal setting, the congregation was also singing, in four-part a cappella, the line "Earth has no sorrows that Heav'n cannot heal," from the hymn "Come, ye disconsolate." The singing led me to healing tears.

All of those singing occasions occurred naturally. But that hasn't been enough for me. I'm always searching for opportunities to hear this singing. I keep the Eastern Mennonite University Chamber Singers CD on my CD player (especially to listen to the unaccompanied pieces), and I remove it

Four-Part A Cappella Singing as a Survival Strategy

only when I put on other CDs. Some of the hymns, like the former "606" and "What is this place," I play again and again. Similarly, I keep a "Mennonite Hour" cassette on my cassette player. Another favorite cassette, despite its including accompaniment, is the Kansas Mennonite Men's Chorus, which I acquired only recently. When I heard it in the home of Lois and Keith Miller, other Mennonites in exile in Evansville, I became so excited that they loaned me their copy. Even when the singing is not a cappella, the familiarity of the hymns seduces me.

Through the years I've not only listened to recordings but also found live music. One time in the 1970s a Quaker friend and I drove from Springfield, Missouri, to Kansas to hear the Kansas Mennonite Men's Chorus. Also, during a Communal Studies Conference in Iowa, in 1996, I chose to go to the German Sunday morning service at an Amana church—a service that recalled my childhood experience in the Old Order Mennonite church.[3] We sat on hard benches with one board nailed across the back, and men and women sat on opposite sides of the room. We sang from a small black book resembling the Old Order Mennonite one, and the singing itself—a cappella in German—transported me to New Holland, Pennsylvania, during 1931-1939. I wept as I sang.

Fortunately, today in Evansville I'm not completely bereft of four-part a cappella singing. I attend concerts given by the Evansville Chamber Singers, who sing a cappella. Although there is no Mennonite church in the area, a few Mennonites meet once a month for a potluck, and sometimes we sing. (We could never agree enough to form a church, but we can sing together.) More importantly, I am a member of the Patchwork Central community, not a sewing group as the name might suggest but an inner-city ministry, where I experience singing and fellowship with an ecumenical worshipping community. Since 1988, Mennonite Voluntary Service (MVS) workers have been participating in Patchwork's programs. These young people have introduced the Patchwork community to four-part a cappella singing and the Mennonite hymnal. Included now in the Patchwork songbook are a number of Mennonite hymns, like "Will you let me be your servant." Although Patchwork has a band, sometimes Bill Hemminger (not a Mennonite but a trained musician intensely interested in this music) also leads us in four-part a cappella singing. We even have a small group (including a few Evansville Philharmonic Chorus members) called The Mennonite Connection that sings occasionally.

That MVS influence affected even my seventieth birthday party at Patchwork—a big event attended by fifty very diverse people: Christians from the Patchwork worshipping community and other friends from the

University of Evansville and elsewhere, including agnostics and atheists. Someone from Patchwork had distributed copies of "606," one of my favourite songs, and at this gathering, where we drank toasts of wine and beer, the group stood in a circle around me and sang that hymn.

Singing has not only nourished me in the past and present but also constitutes the dominant feature of my funeral plans. Often when I go to funerals, I respond much as I do to the Fisk organ. Solos in church and piped-in music at funeral homes make me want to cry out, "Let's sing!" I wish for the congregational singing at the funerals I attended as a child and a young person in Pennsylvania. Consequently, in my plans I have included a long list of hymns—more than can possibly be used—from which the minister can choose. I have asked that at least some of the hymns be sung a cappella and that a song leader be used. Although I haven't said so in my plans, in summing up my life I think of the lines in the song, "I have had singing" (which I first heard in a concert by the Evansville Chamber Singers). The text consists of eighty-five-year-old horseman Fred Mitchell's reminiscences: "The singing. There was so much singing then, and this was my pleasure too. We all sang, Oh, the chapels were full of singing, always boys in the fields. . . . Here I lie. I have had pleasure enough, I have had singing. I have had singing."[4] That's true for me, too. In Pennsylvania, Virginia, Ohio, Kansas, and Indiana, I have had pleasure enough; I have had singing.

When I began to think about this essay in November 2003, I thought I'd emphasize only my appetite for a cappella singing. Perhaps not only appetite but also nostalgia drives my quest to hear it. At age seventy-three, recently retired, I'm still active, writing, publishing, and participating in new projects with visual artists. However, when I'm sorting boxes and files containing academic and personal material covering seventy-three years, I naturally review the past. As I began writing this essay, I serendipitously read an explanatory endnote in David Weaver-Zercher's book *The Amish in the American Imagination,* referring to Fred Davis's *Yearning for Yesterday: A Sociology of Nostalgia.*[5] When I went to Davis's book and read about this "painful yearning to return home" and nostalgia's importance at a time of transition, its creation of a bond with an earlier self, and its "ability to filter out the unpleasant,"[6] an epiphany occurred! Now I know why I especially need to hear this singing now. Like one of Davis's informants, who rearranged items in her "memory box," literally a large cardboard box, and "with each . . . rearrangement . . . designed a slightly different past for herself,"[7] I can now overlook the plain clothes in my past and instead delight in the singing. When I hear this singing (either in person or on CDs and cassettes), I can feel connected to the Mennonite community; I can return home.

That community is re-created each time I hear and participate in such singing, and specifically certain familiar hymns. My nostalgic focus on a cappella singing is, I realize now, really an intensification of what has occurred ever since 1966. This music, a bridge over which I have traversed changes in my life (entrance into graduate school, new jobs, an amicable divorce), provided a stable, unbreakable community. And this connection can occur without complete creedal agreement with the text of the hymns. I can identify with Marshall King's experience reported in *Mennonot* (a magazine for Mennos "on the margin") and quoted by Kropf and Nafziger. King wrote about a gathering of Eastern Mennonite University graduates on Labor Day weekend in 1995 at Harpers Ferry, West Virginia, just before three of the group were going overseas for three years with Mennonite Central Committee: "On Sunday morning, we sat in a large circle and pulled out the blue hymnals. For almost two hours, we sang and shared and laughed and cried. That room held people at different places in their faith journey and a healthy share of Mennonots. But for two hours, we were one, a community of friends singing the songs of our youth and our future. We sang 606 by heart, the same way our children will."[8] Although that was written by a young man "two days before [his] . . . 27th birthday" about a group that I assume consisted of other twenty-something people, and I'm now seventy-three, that could be my experience: singing as a Mennonot and then writing, as he said he was, "sitting at a computer with a beer."[9]

King's image is appealing to me: sitting in a circle and singing. Such an experience would satisfy my appetite and meet my apparent need to feel Mennonite or at least Mennonot. It's more appealing than the sound of a Fisk organ or a trained choir. The image sounds and looks like home. And, marvelously, that home, that community, can be created anywhere; all we need is a group of people and some blue hymnals. And if we don't have hymnals, memory will do. We can sing from *it*—even in exile. That will be "pleasure enough."

Notes

[1] Marlene Kropf and Kenneth Nafziger, *Singing: A Mennonite Voice* (Scottdale, PA: Herald Press, 2001).

² Julia Kasdorf, "Mennonites," *Sleeping Preacher* (Pittsburgh: University of Pittsburgh Press, 1992), 34.

³ The Amana Church Society is the post-communal church of the Community of True Inspiration, which began in Germany in 1714 and existed in a communal form in the United States from 1842-1932. Today both a German and an English language service are still held in Amana on Sunday mornings. With some minor changes, the order of worship is as it was 100 years ago, including a cappella singing.

⁴ Fred Mitchell (text) and Steven Sametz (music), "I Have Had Singing," *Chanticleer Choral Series* (Chapel Hill, NC: Hinshaw Music, Inc., 1993), 2-4. Text based on Ronald Blythe,*Akenfield: Portrait of an English Village* (New York: Pantheon Books, 1969), 49-53.

⁵ David Weaver-Zercher, *The Amish in the American Imagination* (Baltimore: Johns Hopkins University Press, 2001), 210.

⁶ Fred Davis, *Yearning for Yesterday: A Sociology of Nostalgia* (New York: Free Press, 1979), 1, 54, 35, 37.

⁷ Ibid., 48.

⁸ Marshall King, "Defenses and Dreams of a Generation Xer," *Mennonot* 9 (Spring 1997): 5; quoted in Marlene Kropf and Kenneth Nafziger, *Singing: A Mennonite Voice* (Scottdale, PA: Herald Press, 2001), 163.

⁹ King, "Defenses and Dreams of a Generation Xer," 2.

Contributors

E. Douglas Bomberger is professor of musicology and chair of Fine and Performing Arts at Elizabethtown College. A graduate of Goshen College and the University of Maryland, he previously taught at the University of Hawaii, Ithaca College, and Goshen College.

Di Brandt has published numerous award-winning poetry books, including *questions i asked my mother*, *Agnes in the sky*, and *Jersualem, beloved*. *Now You Care*, her most recent collection (Coach House, 2003) was shortlisted for the Griffin Prize and the Trillium Award. Di Brandt was recently appointed Canada Research Chair in Creative Writing at Brandon University, Manitoba.

Victor Davies' compositions range from piano concertos to children's songs. Melodic, rhythmic, and accessible, his music is performed world-wide in theatres and concert halls, and on radio, television, cinema and CD. Performers include Canada's major orchestras, the London Symphony Orchestra (UK), the Royal Winnipeg Ballet, Wayne Marshall, Ofra Harnoy, Bramwell Tovey, Henriette Schellenberg, and Tracy Dahl.

Cheryl Denise grew up in Elmira, Ontario. Currently she and her husband, Mike Miller, are a part of Shepherds Field intentional community in Philippi, West Virginia. She is the author of the poetry book, *I Saw God Dancing*, published by Cascadia Publishing House and Herald Press.

Jonathan Dueck is Visiting Assistant Professor of Ethnomusicology in the School of Music at the University of Maryland. He is most interested in music and identity, and his research includes Mennonite music in urban Canada, shape-note music in the American South, and church music in sub-Saharan Chad.

Maureen Epp has taught music history and appreciation at the University of Toronto, Wilfrid Laurier University, and Conrad Grebel University College (University of Waterloo). Her published research include articles on fifteenth-century popular song, and she is currently editing a book on interdisciplinary approaches to performance issues in Medieval and Renaissance music.

Allison Fairbairn became fascinated with the music and culture of Mennonites while attending Rosthern Junior College (Rosthern, SK). She attended Canadian Mennonite Bible College (Winnipeg), and holds undergraduate degrees from the University of Saskatchewan. She is currently working on an MA in ethnomusicology at the University of Alberta, researching the influence of feminism and religion in the music of Tori Amos.

Katie J. Graber is currently a PhD student in ethnomusicology at the University of Wisconsin-Madison. Her master's thesis focussed on music at Madison Mennonite Church and how a group orients itself around a musical tradition. She is interested in how identity and music inform one another in American history and in musical-cultural contexts around the world.

Jeff Gundy is Professor of English at Bluffton University, where he was Faculty Scholar in 2004-05. His most recent books are *Deerflies* (poems, 2004) and *Walker in the Fog: On Mennonite Writing* (prose, 2005).

Stephen Jacoby is Professor of Music at Bluffton University and Director of Music at First Mennonite Church, both in Bluffton, Ohio. At the university he teaches organ, music history, music in worship, and conducts choral ensembles. He holds MA (organ pedagogy) and PhD (music history) degrees from Ohio State University.

Anna Janecek has degrees in church music and conducting from Canadian Mennonite Bible College and Conrad Grebel University College at the University of Waterloo, and an MA in musicology from the University of Toronto. She currently lives in Waterloo, Ontario, with her husband and daughter.

Contributors

Mark Jantzen is Assistant Professor of History at Bethel College (North Newton, Kansas), where he teaches courses in European and Mennonite history. He holds degrees from Bethel College, Associated Mennonite Biblical Seminaries, and the University of Notre Dame. He is married to Alice Hartman Jantzen and they have three children.

Doreen H. Klassen teaches anthropology and folklore at Sir Wilfred Grenfell College (Memorial University, Newfoundland). Publications on Mennonite music include *Singing Mennonite: Low German Songs among the Mennonites* and *International Songbook* (1990; edited for Mennonite World Conference). Recent research examines gesture in Zimbabwean women's storytelling, the politics of wall mural production in Winnipeg, Manitoba, and laundry practices in western Newfoundland.

Judith Klassen is a doctoral student in Ethnomusicology at Memorial University of Newfoundland, exploring Mennonite family music in Mexico and Manitoba. Her research is balanced by performance opportunities with the Newfoundland Symphony Orchestra and folk festivals around the province. Judith holds degrees in viola performance (University of Manitoba, Canadian Mennonite Bible College) and a Masters in ethnomusicology (York University).

Stephanie J. Krehbiel earned master's degrees in flute performance and ethnomusicology from Michigan State University. Currently living in Lawrence, Kansas, she is a free-lance writer studying the relationship between spiritual practice and activism in the American yoga community.

Leonard N. Neufeldt, born and raised in Yarrow, BC, has been a faculty member at the University of Washington, University of Texas (Odessa), Princeton University, and Purdue University. His publications include numerous books and articles on New England cultural and literary history, a two-volume history of Yarrow, and five volumes of poetry.

Mary K. Oyer spent the first few decades of her career teaching music history, cello, choir, and the related arts (music and visual arts) at Goshen College. During her 40s she moved to hymnody, researching and compiling for the *Mennonite Hymnal* (1969). Her emphasis expanded to include the music of other denominations and cultures, African (Kenya) and Far Eastern (Taiwan) in particular.

Contributors

Carol Ann Weaver, eclectic composer/pianist/professor at Conrad Grebel University College (University of Waterloo), creates fusions of roots and art music heard in Canada, USA, South Africa, Europe and Korea. Her CDs reflect collaborations with African jazz musicians, singer-songwriters Cate Friesen and Rebecca Campbell, writers Di Brandt, Julia Kasdorf, Jeff Gundy, Ann Hostetler, and others.

Laura H. Weaver is professor emerita of English at the University of Evansville (IN). She holds degrees from Eastern Mennonite University, University of Pennsylvania, and University of Kansas. Her publications focus on ethnicity, gender, and ageism. Excerpts from recent essays on her "plain" and "fancy" selves have been included in joint exhibits with visual artists in Indiana, Missouri, and California.

About Pandora Press

Pandora Press is a small, independently owned press dedicated to making available modestly priced books that deal with Anabaptist, Mennonite, and Believers Church topics, both historical and theological. We welcome comments from our readers.

Visit our full-service online Bookstore:
www.pandorapress.com

Harry Huebner, *Echoes of the Word: Theological Ethics as Rhetorical Practice* Anabaptist and Mennonite Studies Series (Kitchener: Pandora Press, 2005). Softcover, 274 pp. Includes bibliography and index. ISSN 1494-4081 ISBN 1-894710-56-8

John F. Haught, *Purpose, Evolution and the Meaning of Life,* Proceedings of the Fourth Annual Goshen Conference on Religion and Science, ed. Carl S. Helrich (Kitchener" Pandora Press, 2005). Softcover, 130 pp. Includes index. ISBN 1-894710-55-X

Gerald W. Schlabach, gen. ed., *Called Together to be Peacemakers: Report of the International Dialogue between the Catholic Church and Mennonite World Conference 1998-2003* The Bridgefolk Series (Kitchener: Pandora Press, 2005). Softcover, 77 pp. ISSN 1711-9480 ISBN 1-894710-57-6

Rodney James Sawatsky, *History and Ideology: American Mennonite Identity Definition through History* (Kitchener: Pandora Press, 2005). Softcover, 216 pp. Includes bibliography and index. ISBN 1-894710-53-3 ISSN 1494-4081

Harvey Neufeldt, Ruth Derksen Siemens and Robert Martens, eds., *First Nations and First Settlers in the Fraser Valley (1890-1960)* (Kitchener: Pandora Press, 2005). Softcover, 287 pp. Incudes bibliography and index. ISBN 1-894710-54-1

David Waltner-Toews, *The Complete Tante Tina: Mennonite Blues and Recipes* (Kitchener: Pandora Press, 2004) Softcover, 129 pp. ISBN 1-894710-52-5

John Howard Yoder, *Anabaptism and Reformation in Switzerland: An Historical and Theological Analysis of the Dialogues Between Anabaptists and Reformers* Anabaptist and Mennonite Studies Series (Kitchener: Pandora Press, 2004) Softcover, 509 pp., includes bibliography and indices. ISBN 1-894710-44-4 ISSN 1494-4081

Antje Jackelén, *The Dialogue Between Religion and Science: Challenges and Future Directions* (Kitchener: Pandora Press, 2004) Softcover, 143 pp., includes index. ISBN 1-894710-45-2

Ivan J. Kauffman, ed., *Just Policing: Mennonite-Catholic Theological Colloquium 2001-2002* The Bridgefolk Series (Kitchener: Pandora Press, 2004). Softcover, 127 pp., ISBN 1-894710-48-7.

Gerald W. Schlabach, ed., *On Baptism: Mennonite-Catholic Theological Colloquium 2001-2002* The Bridgefolk Series (Kitchener: Pandora Press, 2004). Softcover, 147 pp., ISBN 1-894710-47-9 ISSN 1711-9480.

Harvey L. Dyck, John R. Staples and John B. Toews, comp., trans. and ed. *Nestor Makhno and the Eichenfeld Massacre: A Civil War Tragedy in a Ukrainian Mennonite Village* (Kitchener: Pandora Press, 2004). Softcover, 115pp. ISBN 1-894710-46-0.

Jeffrey Wayne Taylor, *The Formation of the Primitive Baptist Movement* Studies in the Believers Church Tradition (Kitchener: Pandora Press, 2004). Softcover, 225 pp., includes bibliography and index. ISBN 1-894710-42-8 ISSN 1480-7432.

James C. Juhnke and Carol M. Hunter, *The Missing Peace: The Search for Nonviolent Alternatives in United States History* Second Expanded Edition (Kitchener: Pandora Press, 2004; co-published with Herald Press.) Softcover, 339 pp., includes index. ISBN 1-894710-46-3

Louise Hawkley and James C. Juhnke, eds., *Nonviolent America: History through the Eyes of Peace* Wedel Series 5 (North Newton: Bethel College, 2004, co-published with Pandora Press) Softcover, 269 pp., includes index. ISBN 1-889239-02-X

Karl Koop, *Anabaptist-Mennonite Confessions of Faith: the Development of a Tradition* (Kitchener: Pandora Press, 2004; co-published with Herald Press) Softcover, 178 pp., includes index. ISBN 1-894710-32-0

Lucille Marr, *The Transforming Power of a Century: Mennonite Central Committee and its Evolution in Ontario* (Kitchener: Pandora Press, 2003). Softcover, 390 pp., includes bibliography and index, ISBN 1-894710-41-x.

Erica Janzen, *Six Sugar Beets, Five Bitter Years* (Kitchener: Pandora Press, 2003). Softcover, 186 pp., ISBN 1-894710-37-1.

T. D. Regehr, *Faith Life and Witness in the Northwest, 1903-2003: Centenninal History of the Northwest Mennonite Conference* (Kitchener: Pandora Press, 2003). Softcover, 524 pp., includes index, ISBN 1-894710-39-8.

John A. Lapp and C. Arnold Snyder, gen.eds., *A Global Mennonite History. Volume One: Africa* (Kitchener: Pandora Press, 2003). Softcover, 320 pp., includes indexes, ISBN 1-894710-38-x.

George F. R. Ellis, *A Universe of Ethics Morality and Hope: Proceedings from the Second Annual Goshen Conference on Religion and Science* (Kitchener: Pandora Press, 2003; co-published with Herald Press.) Softcover, 148 pp. ISBN 1-894710-36-3

Donald Martin, *Old Order Mennonites of Ontario: Gelassenheit, Discipleship, Brotherhood* (Kitchener: Pandora Press, 2003; co-published with Herald Press.) Softcover, 381 pp., includes index. ISBN 1-894710-33-9

Mary A. Schiedel, *Pioneers in Ministry: Women Pastors in Ontario Mennonite Churches, 1973-2003* (Kitchener: Pandora Press, 2003) Softcover, 204 pp., ISBN 1-894710-35-5

Harry Loewen, ed., *Shepherds, Servants and Prophets* (Kitchener: Pandora Press, 2003; co-published with Herald Press) Softcover, 446 pp., ISBN 1-894710-35-5

Robert A. Riall, trans., Galen A. Peters, ed., *The Earliest Hymns of the Ausbund: Some Beautiful Christian Songs Composed and Sung in the Prison at Passau, Published 1564* (Kitchener: Pandora Press, 2003; co-published with Herald Press) Softcover, 468 pp., includes bibliography and index. ISBN 1-894710-34-7.

John A. Harder, *From Kleefeld With Love* (Kitchener: Pandora Press, 2003; co-published with Herald Press) Softcover, 198 pp. ISBN 1-894710-28-2

John F. Peters, *The Plain People: A Glimpse at Life Among the Old Order Mennonites of Ontario* (Kitchener: Pandora Press, 2003; co-published with Herald Press) Softcover, 54 pp. ISBN 1-894710-26-6

Robert S. Kreider, *My Early Years: An Autobiography* (Kitchener: Pandora Press, 2002; co-published with Herald Press) Softcover, 600 pp., index ISBN 1-894710-23-1

Helen Martens, *Hutterite Songs* (Kitchener: Pandora Press, 2002; co-published with Herald Press) Softcover, xxii, 328 pp. ISBN 1-894710-24-X

C. Arnold Snyder and Galen A. Peters, eds., *Reading the Anabaptist Bible: Reflections for Every Day of the Year* introduction by Arthur Paul Boers (Kitchener: Pandora Press, 2002; co-published with Herald Press.) Softcover, 415 pp. ISBN 1-894710-25-8

C. Arnold Snyder, ed., *Commoners and Community: Essays in Honour of Werner O. Packull* (Kitchener: Pandora Press, 2002; co-published with Herald Press.) Softcover, 324 pp. ISBN 1-894710-27-4

James O. Lehman, *Mennonite Tent Revivals: Howard Hammer and Myron Augsburger, 1952-1962* (Kitchener: Pandora Press, 2002; co-published with Herald Press) Softcover, xxiv, 318 pp. ISBN 1-894710-22-3

Lawrence Klippenstein and Jacob Dick, *Mennonite Alternative Service in Russia* (Kitchener: Pandora Press, 2002; co-published with Herald Press) Softcover, viii, 163 pp. ISBN 1-894710-21-5

Nancey Murphy, *Religion and Science* (Kitchener: Pandora Press, 2002; co-published with Herald Press) Softcover, 126 pp. ISBN 1-894710-20-7

Biblical Concordance of the Swiss Brethren, 1540. Trans. Gilbert Fast and Galen Peters; bib. intro. Joe Springer; ed. C. Arnold Snyder (Kitchener: Pandora Press, 2001; co-published with Herald Press) Softcover, lv, 227pp. ISBN 1-894710-16-9

Orland Gingerich, *The Amish of Canada* (Kitchener: Pandora Press, 2001; co-published with Herald Press.) Softcover, 244 pp., includes index. ISBN 1-894710-19-3

M. Darrol Bryant, *Religion in a New Key* (Kitchener: Pandora Press, 2001) Softcover, 136 pp., includes bib. refs. ISBN 1-894710- 18-5

Trans. Walter Klaassen, Frank Friesen, Werner O. Packull, ed. C. Arnold Snyder, *Sources of South German/Austrian Anabaptism* (Kitchener: Pandora Press, 2001; co-published with Herald Press.) Softcover, 430 pp. includes indexes. ISBN 1-894710-15-0

Pedro A. Sandín Fremaint y Pablo A. Jimémez, *Palabras Duras: Homilías* (Kitchener: Pandora Press, 2001). Softcover, 121 pp., ISBN 1-894710-17-7

Ruth Elizabeth Mooney, *Manual Para Crear Materiales de Educación Cristiana* (Kitchener: Pandora Press, 2001). Softcover, 206 pp., ISBN 1-894710-12-6

Esther and Malcolm Wenger, poetry by Ann Wenger, *Healing the Wounds* (Kitchener: Pandora Press, 2001; co-pub. with Herald Press). Softcover, 210 pp. ISBN 1-894710-09-6.

Otto H. Selles and Geraldine Selles-Ysselstein, *New Songs* (Kitchener: Pandora Press, 2001). Poetry and relief prints, 90pp. ISBN 1-894719-14-2

Pedro A. Sandín Fremaint, *Cuentos y Encuentros: Hacia una Educación Transformadora* (Kitchener: Pandora Press, 2001). Softcover 163 pp ISBN 1-894710-08-8.

A. James Reimer, *Mennonites and Classical Theology: Dogmatic Foundations for Christian Ethics* (Kitchener: Pandora Press, 2001; co-published with Herald Press) Softcover, 650pp. ISBN 0-9685543-7-7

Walter Klaassen, *Anabaptism: Neither Catholic nor Protestant*, 3rd ed (Kitchener: Pandora Press, 2001; co-pub. Herald Press) Softcover, 122pp. ISBN 1-894710-01-0

Dale Schrag & James Juhnke, eds., *Anabaptist Visions for the new Millennium: A search for identity* (Kitchener: Pandora Press, 2000; co-published with Herald Press) Softcover, 242 pp. ISBN 1-894710-00-2

Harry Loewen, ed., *Road to Freedom: Mennonites Escape the Land of Suffering* (Kitchener: Pandora Press, 2000; co-published with Herald Press) Hardcover, large format, 302pp. ISBN 0-9685543-5-0

Alan Kreider and Stuart Murray, eds., *Coming Home: Stories of Anabaptists in Britain and Ireland* (Kitchener: Pandora Press, 2000; co-published with Herald Press) Softcover, 220pp. ISBN 0-9685543-6-9

Edna Schroeder Thiessen and Angela Showalter, *A Life Displaced: A Mennonite Woman's Flight from War-Torn Poland* (Kitchener: Pandora Press, 2000; co-published with Herald Press) Softcover, xii, 218pp. ISBN 0-9685543-2-6

Stuart Murray, *Biblical Interpretation in the Anabaptist Tradition,* Studies in the Believers Tradition (Kitchener: Pandora Press, 2000; co-published with Herald Press) Softcover, 310pp. ISBN 0-9685543-3-4 ISSN 1480-7432.

Loren L. Johns, ed. *Apocalypticism and Millennialism,* Studies in the Believers Church Tradition (Kitchener: Pandora Press, 2000; co-published with Herald Press) Softcover, 419pp; Scripture and name indeces ISBN 0-9683462-9-4 ISSN 1480-7432

Later Writings by Pilgram Marpeck and his Circle. Volume 1: The Exposé, A Dialogue and Marpeck's Response to Caspar Schwenckfeld. Trans. Walter Klaassen, Werner Packull, and John Rempel (Kitchener: Pandora Press, 1999; co-published with Herald Press) Softcover, 157pp. ISBN 0-9683462-6-X

John Driver, *Radical Faith. An Alternative History of the Christian Church,* edited by Carrie Snyder. Kitchener: Pandora Press, 1999; co-published with Herald Press) Softcover, 334pp. ISBN 0-9683462-8-6

C. Arnold Snyder, *From Anabaptist Seed. The Historical Core of Anabaptist-Related Identity* (Kitchener: Pandora Press, 1999; co-published with Herald Press) Softcover, 53pp.; discussion questions. ISBN 0-9685543-0-X
Also available in Spanish translation: *De Semilla Anabautista*, from Pandora Press only.

John D. Thiesen, *Mennonite and Nazi? Attitudes Among Mennonite Colonists in Latin America, 1933-1945* (Kitchener: Pandora Press, 1999; co-published with Herald Press) Softcover, 330pp., 2 maps, 24 b/w illustrations, bibliography, index. ISBN 0-9683462-5-1

Lifting the Veil, a translation of *Aus meinem Leben: Erinnerungen von J.H. Janzen*. Ed. by Leonard Friesen; trans. by Walter Klaassen (Kitchener: Pandora Press, 1998; co-pub. with Herald Press). Softcover, 128pp.; 4pp. of illustrations. ISBN 0-9683462-1-9

Leonard Gross, *The Golden Years of the Hutterites*, rev. ed. (Kitchener: Pandora Press, 1998; co-pub. with Herald Press). Softcover, 280pp., index. ISBN 0-9683462-3-5

William H. Brackney, ed., *The Believers Church: A Voluntary Church*, Studies in the Believers Church Tradition (Kitchener: Pandora Press, 1998; co-published with Herald Press). Softcover, viii, 237pp., index. ISBN 0-9683462-0-0 ISSN 1480-7432.

An Annotated Hutterite Bibliography, compiled by Maria H. Krisztinkovich, ed. by Peter C. Erb (Kitchener: Pandora Press, 1998). (Ca. 2,700 entries) 312pp., softcover, electronic, or both. ISBN (paper) 0-9698762-8-9/(disk) 0-9698762-9-7

Jacobus ten Doornkaat Koolman, *Dirk Philips. Friend and Colleague of Menno Simons*, trans. W. E. Keeney, ed. C. A. Snyder (Kitchener: Pandora Press, 1998; co-published with Herald Press). Softcover, xviii, 236pp., index. ISBN: 0-9698762-3-8

Sarah Dyck, ed./tr., *The Silence Echoes: Memoirs of Trauma & Tears* (Kitchener: Pandora Press, 1997; co-published with Herald Press). Softcover, xii, 236pp., 2 maps. ISBN: 0-9698762-7-0

Wes Harrison, *Andreas Ehrenpreis and Hutterite Faith and Practice* (Kitchener: Pandora Press, 1997; co-published with Herald Press). Softcover, xxiv, 274pp., 2 maps, index. ISBN 0-9698762-6-2

C. Arnold Snyder, *Anabaptist History and Theology: Revised Student Edition* (Kitchener: Pandora Press, 1997; co-pub. Herald Press). Softcover, xiv, 466pp., 7 maps, 28 illustrations, index, bibliography. ISBN 0-9698762-5-4

Nancey Murphy, *Reconciling Theology and Science: A Radical Reformation Perspective* (Kitchener, Ont.: Pandora Press, 1997; co-pub. Herald Press). Softcover, x, 103pp., index. ISBN 0-9698762-4-6

C. Arnold Snyder and Linda A. Huebert Hecht, eds, *Profiles of Anabaptist Women: Sixteenth Century Reforming Pioneers* (Waterloo, Ont.: Wilfrid Laurier University Press, 1996). Softcover, xxii, 442pp. ISBN: 0-88920-277-X

The Limits of Perfection: A Conversation with J. Lawrence Burkholder 2nd ed., with a new epilogue by J. Lawrence Burkholder, Rodney Sawatsky and Scott Holland, eds. (Kitchener: Pandora Press, 1996). Softcover, x, 154pp. ISBN 0-9698762-2-X

C. Arnold Snyder, *Anabaptist History and Theology: An Introduction* (Kitchener: Pandora Press, 1995). ISBN 0-9698762-0-3 Softcover, x, 434pp., 6 maps, 29 illustrations, index, bibliography.

Pandora Press
33 Kent Avenue Kitchener, ON N2G 3R2
Tel.: (519) 578-2381 / Fax: (519) 578-1826
E-mail: info@pandorapress.com
Web site: www.pandorapress.com